THE CORE AND THE PERIPHERY

THE CORE AND THE PERIPHERY

Data-Driven Perspectives on Syntax Inspired by Ivan A. Sag

Edited by
Philip Hofmeister and Elisabeth Norcliffe

CSLI
PUBLICATIONS
STANFORD

Printed in the United States
17 16 15 14 13   1 2 3 4 5

Library of Congress Cataloging-in-Publication Data

The core and the periphery : data-driven perspectives on syntax inspired by Ivan A. Sag / Edited by Philip Hofmeister and Elisabeth Norcliffe.

pages cm. – (CSLI Lecture Notes ; 210)
Includes bibliographical references and index.
ISBN 978-1-57586-721-2 (pbk. : alk. paper) –
ISBN 978-1-57586-720-5 (cloth : alk. paper) –
ISBN 978-1-57586-722-9 (electronic)

1. Grammar, Comparative and general–Syntax. 2. Phrase structure grammar. 3. Cognition–Data processing. 4. Psycholinguistics–Data processing. I. Sag, Ivan A., 1949-2013 honouree. II. Hofmeister, Philip, editor of compilation. III. Norcliffe, Elisabeth, editor of compilation.

P291.C634 2013
415–dc23

2013019589

CIP

∞ The acid-free paper used in this book meets the minimum requirements of the American National Standard for Information Sciences—Permanence of Paper for Printed Library Materials, ANSI Z39.48-1984.

CSLI was founded in 1983 by researchers from Stanford University, SRI International, and Xerox PARC to further the research and development of integrated theories of language, information, and computation. CSLI headquarters and CSLI Publications are located on the campus of Stanford University.

CSLI Publications reports new developments in the study of language, information, and computation. Please visit our web site at
http://cslipublications.stanford.edu/
for comments on this and other titles, as well as for changes and corrections by the author and publisher.

Contents

Introduction

Equally problematic is the bifurcation drawn between 'core' phenomena and the 'periphery' of language. The core phenomena are meant to be 'pure instantiations of Universal Grammar', while the periphery consists of 'marked exceptions (irregular verbs, etc.)' (see Chomsky & Lasnik 1993). The move away from constructions has thus led to the study of 'Core Grammar' and to the systematic exclusion of other phenomena. Though the core/periphery distinction is seldom discussed in the MP literature, its pervasive effect on analytic practice is self-evident.

But how are we to know which phenomena belong to the core and which to the periphery? The literature offers no principled criteria for distinguishing the two, despite the obvious danger that without such criteria, the distinction seems both arbitrary and subjective. The bifurcation hence places the field at serious risk of developing a theory of language that is either vacuous or else rife with analyses that are either insufficiently general or otherwise empirically flawed. There is the further danger that grammatical theories developed on the basis of 'core' phenomena may be falsified only by examining data from the periphery – data that falls outside the domain of active inquiry.

– Ivan A. Sag. 2010. English Filler-Gap Constructions. *Language*, 86.3: 486-545

THIS quote from one of Ivan Sag's most recent papers encapsulates an approach to linguistics that pervades this book: linguistic phenomena are often nuanced, gradient, and not easily categorized. Sometimes, data are a little messy. In syntactic research, utterances are not always straightforwardly classifiable as either 'acceptable' vs. 'unacceptable' or 'relevant' vs. 'irrelevant', as some classic linguistics texts would suggest. The job of the syntactician is, for better or worse, to deal with the mess, and make some sense of it.

At the core, on this view, are the many syntactic structures that unequivocally fall into one category or another. These are the syntactic data that any theory worth its salt can account for. These are the data that a professional linguist can recite and construct with relative ease. These are the cases where no prior context is necessary to find a minimal pair starkly contrastive, or a particular formulation natural and useable. These are the data for which there is unanimity across large groups of people speaking the same language.

Outside these core examples, though, exists a periphery of data. They are peripheral in the sense that they do not come quickly to mind. They require a certain amount of contextual support to either imagine or to seem natural. They sometimes have something just a little 'off' with them, but not enough to make them crashingly bad. After hearing such mildly aberrant constructions enough times, they can suddenly sound entirely natural.

As Ivan notes, what objective reason is there to say that these peripheral data should not be relevant for linguistic theory, especially if the line between them and the core examples is blurry? Put slightly differently, what a particular linguist can imagine sitting in a cozy office may not represent the full diversity of language or the conditions in which some syntactic configuration may naturally occur. In this sense, there is an unspoken humility in the above quote: the relevant phenomena are more than what a single person can imagine. Fortunately, as many of the chapters of this book emphasize, taking on messy, complex, and large datasets has its rewards. The end result of an inclusive view on data is often a more satisfying picture of many interrelated language dynamics.

This is the secondary but related theme of this book. Linked to his perspective on data, Ivan's oeuvre has running through it a motif that explanations of grammatical phenomena are not merely understandable in terms of structural generalizations, but also semantic, pragmatic, prosodic, historical, and psychological generalizations. Grammar, on this view, is not merely about hierarchical relationships or linear order principles, but a complex interplay amongst principles at various levels of linguistic representation. The formalisms that Ivan has championed over the years — Generalized Phrase Structure Grammar (GPSG), Head-driven Phrase Structure Grammar (HPSG), and Sign-based Construction Grammar (SBCG) — embody this ethos to a T. These formalisms capitalize upon rich interactions between semantic, syntactic, discourse, and phonological properties to explain distributional data. Indeed, the flexibility of these systems and their ability to express generalizations at various levels of linguistic representation give them the necessary power (and comparatively unique ability) to deal with more than just the core, but the periphery, too.

These two complementary themes are interwoven throughout this book. In accord with Ivan's perspective on the relationship between syntactic theorizing and data, the papers in this volume reflect the view that the data one uses should come not just from the core arsenal of linguistic examples, but also from the periphery. Indeed, there really is no such distinction in the papers considered here. Data is data. The papers here also reflect the wide range of data that Ivan has considered in his own investigations: intuitions, corpus data, cross-linguistic data, and experimental results. By considering such data, the papers in this volume arrive at more sophisticated and nuanced understandings of linguistic phenomena than they could have otherwise. In analyzing these phenomena, many of the papers here showcase the true power and elegance of the formalisms that Ivan has refined and promoted. They reflect Ivan's abiding interest in everything language-related—his belief that the best explanations of linguistic data recognize that language is not just order, hierarchies, denotations, articulation, or identity, but the interaction of all of these.

IN 2007, Ivan was elected to the American Academy of Arts and Sciences in the same class as former Vice President Al Gore, former Supreme Court Justice Sandra Day O'Connor, Google CEO Eric Schmidt, New York mayor Michael Bloomberg, and director Spike Lee. In 2005, he was awarded the Victoria Fromkin Prize for distinguished contributions to the field of linguistics by the Linguistic Society of America. Four years earlier, he received the title of Professor Honoris Causa from the University of Bucharest, Romania.

The path Ivan followed to reach this position of eminence was not exactly straightforward or easy.[1] For starters, he has never been *just* interested in syntax. This is perhaps most obviously evident in the strong connections between (morpho-)syntactic features and semantic/pragmatic features in HPSG and related formalisms, mentioned above. But the passion for understanding language, what makes Ivan a linguist's linguist, what makes him a challenging conversant in any discussion about language, pre-dates these formalisms.

His graduate career began at the University of Pennsylvania where Ivan pursued a career as an Indo-Europeanist by studying Sanskrit. Despite completing all the necessary coursework for his degree, he didn't complete his PhD there. Instead, he transferred to MIT where he could delve deep into theoretical linguistics. As this volume highlights, his 1976 dissertation there, supervised by Noam Chomsky, plays a vital role in discussions of ellipsis and anaphora to this day.

[1]For some of the more harrowing aspects of his journey, have a look at his personal retelling, 'The Element of Surprise', given to his former high school alma mater: http://lingo.stanford.edu/sag/mburg-speech.pdf

Ivan could have occupied and made a name for himself by concentrating on the themes in his dissertation for the next forty years. Indeed, Ivan has returned to these topics from time to time, but it would be against some fundamentals of his nature to be content studying only one thing. In the time since his dissertation, he has also studied and written on a huge number of topics including coordination, referential indices, quantificational scope, clitics, free word order and linearization principles, interrogatives, auxiliaries, island effects, processing constraints, and idioms, to name a scant few. In many cases, these works have turned out to be landmarks in the field. At Stanford Linguistics department colloquia, he was known to be able to ask questions that you only wished you could have thought of at talks ranging over topics from syntax to sociolinguistics to psycholinguistics.

Ivan has also always been quick to share his knowledge and enthusiasm for language and linguistics. He has supervised at least 66 MA and Ph.D. students according to his website, though there's more than a possibility that he's being understated on who he has actually advised. As superficial evidence of his pedagogical abilities, he won the Dean's Teaching Award in 1982 at Stanford, and was Director of the Symbolic Systems Program from 2005 to 2009. But beyond these hard facts about who he has supervised and taught, the truth of the matter is that Ivan inspired, advised, and looked after many other linguists. This goes far beyond his home university. As just one example, besides directing the Institute in 1987 at Stanford and acting as Associate Director for several others, he has been a fixture at the Linguistic Society of America's Summer Institutes, teaching courses, organizing social activities, and housing for multiple generations of linguists.

Over the past two years, while Elisabeth and I have overseen this book and spoken to others about Ivan—from the United States to Germany to the United Kingdom to South Korea—I have repeatedly heard how Ivan inspired them to tackle difficult problems in linguistics, how Ivan has sacrificed his time to consider issues that did not directly relate to his own research programme, and how Ivan made them feel part of a larger linguistics community. In fact, working on this project, I've started to wonder whether there's anyone Ivan *doesn't* know in the linguistics community. For my own part, I can say that syntax became a pre-occupation of mine because Ivan made it clear how it was not an isolated system (as I felt studying Minimalist syntax a decade ago) but part of a richer, dynamic system that included interactions with cognitive limitations. Frankly, I also have been simply energized by talking with the man. It makes me feel that what I am doing is worth doing.

As friends and colleagues of Ivan know, he has never been *just* interested in linguistics, either. His path to a PhD and an academic career at Stanford since 1979 has included stints of musical obsession that involved organizing musical shows for the likes of Muddy Waters and Howlin' Wolf and forming a handful of rock bands of his own—*The Motley Crew*, *The Red, White, and Blues Band*, and most recently *Dead Tongues*. His bands (with Ivan playing funky, organ-grinding, in-your-face keyboards and blues guitar, or providing vocals) have been at the social heart of many Institutes, playing rock music at Linguistic Institutes at Stanford (1987, 2007), Arizona (1989), Santa Cruz (1991), Michigan State (2003; Dead Tongues/Abbott Brothers) and Harvard-MIT (2005). I can only say this from the perspective of someone who's been in the field for roughly 12 years, but if being a linguist is just a little cool, that's got something to do with Ivan.

I could spend pages more here telling you about how innovative and influential Ivan's work has been, how his knowledge of language was a key part of the development of GPSG in the 1980s, which developed into HPSG, and most recently, SBCG. I could tell you about some hairdos and facial hair that no one could rock but Ivan. I could tell you about his impact on natural language processing. I could tell you about how he's a real mensch. I *could* do this, but the other contributions to this book do a much better job.

BY our count, Ivan Sag has written, co-written, edited, or co-edited scholarly works with more than seventy-five different people in the past forty years, not including conference presentations and unpublished work. A quick perusal of this list (see the end of this preface for an alphabetized list) identifies a veritable who's who in academic linguistics, not to mention many well-established and influential researchers in natural language processing. It cannot go unmentioned, either, that Ivan has been a driving force to the annual international HPSG conferences that have occurred every year since 1993. These conferences have brought together hundreds of researchers and helped spread the influence of HPSG across the world.

It was in light of this awe-inspiring collaborative nature that we ventured to assemble a collection of papers from a (proper) subset of Ivan's co-conspirators. No doubt this book could've reached biblical proportions, literally speaking, had we invited all those researchers who had built upon Ivan's ideas in some way or another. But it seemed most fitting to illustrate the impact of Ivan's mind by sampling from the most immediate and affected sources.

In the opening chapters of this volume, we see the fruit of some of Ivan's earliest and most influential work. As noted by **Jason Merchant**, the generalizations and data discussed in Ivan's MIT dissertation impacted generations of researchers and feed directly into the research conducted by **Philip Miller & Geoff Pullum**. Their research hinges on a theoretical distinction between types of anaphora originally proposed by Ivan (and his colleague Jorge Hankamer), viz. that some anaphora could not be used felicitously without a linguistic antecedent. As Miller & Pullum illustrate, discourse constraints on the use of these anaphors strongly restrict their felicity. These observations follow from casting a wide net, using corpus-based research methods to identify the circumstances under which the critical anaphora occur.

Similarly, **Dan Flickinger & Tom Wasow** develop an account of so-called *do-be* constructions in English. The genesis of this work relates back to the LinGO project at CSLI, which has played a strong role in the broader non-transformational spirit of West Coast syntax and natural language processing research, as recounted by **Annie Zaenen & Lauri Karttunen**. By attempting to build a broad coverage parser, i.e. one that adequately handles rich and nuanced datasets, Flickinger and Wasow struck upon the intracacies of the *do-be* construction. As they note at the outset of their paper, it was only via inspection of many relevant examples that they could arrive at satisfying generalizations about the construction. Indeed, as they graciously admit, some of their original intuitions and hypotheses about this construction proved to be wrong once they, too, widened the net. Their conclusions rely on the fact that the intricacies of a construction like the *do-be* construction, and its overlap with other constructions, are only evident via inspection of many instances of this syntactic construction in various discourse contexts.

The chapter by **Stephen Wechsler** highlights one of the most attractive features of HPSG: the ability to express rich interactions between syntactic and semantic features. As **Elizabeth Coppock** reviews in her prelude, the HPSG system ties together the syntactic agreement system with features of referential indices. Wechsler capitalizes upon this ability to express interactions between syntax and semantics (and the theory of index agreement due to Ivan and his colleague Carl Pollard) in order to account for apparent number agreement mismatches.

In developing an account of sentential negation, **Bender & Lascarides** delve deeply into data from starkly different languages: English, on the one hand, and Turkish and Inuktitut, on the other. The Minimal Recursion Semantics framework that they utilize represents another formalism that has Ivan at its historical center. **Dan Flickinger** explains how this formalism complements the LinGO project at CSLI because of its ability to underspecify scopal properties, thereby reducing ambiguity. The full capabilities of this system, however, are not entirely evident from investigations of English alone, but shine through when cross-linguistic data is brought to bear on the issue.

Anne Abeillé, Danièle Godard, and Jean-Marie Marandin develop an account of declarative questions in French, arguing that they represent proposals that the addressee must ratify. The arguments for this account, as with many of the papers collected here, stem from both intuitive judgments and corpus work. **Jonathan Ginzburg**, who co-authored a seminal volume on interrogatives with Ivan, emphasizes that the broader context of this work concerns how the meaning of interrogatives relates to propositions and how linguists should ontologically categorize various utterances. In this chapter by Abeillé, Godard, and Marandin, we further see that questions about grammar (in this case, the grammar of questions) involves a complex interplay between syntactic, semantic, and pragmatic forces.

In **Rui Chaves'** chapter, the full expressive power of the syntactic formalisms Ivan has championed is evident. **Paul Kay** sets the stage for this chapter by detailing the origins of the latest and perhaps most dynamic syntactic framework Ivan has shepherded: Sign-based Construction Grammar. Chaves uses this framework to sketch an account of how part of speech labels can be replaced with distributional generalizations made on the basis of both morphosyntactic and semantic properties. The motivation for such a move stems from the lack of formal definitions for part of speech labels, as well as crosslinguistic variation with respect to how lexical categories align with semantic representations. Building such an account further allows Chaves to refine an account of apparent non-constituent coordination phenomena.

Some of the later chapters in this volume reflect Ivan's more recent forays into experimental linguistics. A casual observer might ask what triggered Ivan's seemingly sudden leap into this array of research, but the answer is that he is fundamentally behaving as he always has by pursuing the most complete picture of the data. Experimental data simply provide another means for characterizing and identifying grammatical differences, sometimes in a more nuanced way than traditional intuitive judgments allow for. As **Laura Staum Casasanto** observes, Ivan's empirical investigations with acceptability judgments have opened up the possibility for explanations of phenomena in terms of interactions of grammatical and processing machinery. In this vein,

Philip Hofmeister and Elisabeth Norcliffe address the question of whether resumptive pronouns facilitate dependency processing, despite the evidence that resumptives elicit lower acceptability ratings than gaps in a variety of syntactic contexts. This study highlights that only via controlled psycholinguistic experiments do some surprising facts come to light, e.g. that grammatical and processing-based biases may be orthogonally-related to one another.

Continuing this theme, **Joanna Nykiel** investigates fine-grained differences in sluicing constructions. As she illustrates, the semantic and syntactic complexity of the correlate interacts with the syntactic and semantic complexity of the *wh*-remnant, something which would be hard to glean from intuition alone. This work builds off of collaborative work between Ivan and **Philip Hofmeister** on the relationship between the complexity of *wh*-elements and how corresponding retrieval sites are processed.

Mirroring Ivan's collaborative spirit, many people contributed to this volume in ways not directly visible from the table of contents. Besides those who have introduced the main chapters, a variety of reviewers also helped to make the book what it is: Ash Asudeh, Robin Cooper, Dan Flickinger, Florian Jaeger, Jonathan Ginzburg, Bob Levine, Chris Potts, and Steve Wechsler. Additional thanks go to Emma Pease for help in typesetting this volume and Dikran Karagueuzian for his faith in our abilities to pull this off. Special thanks go to Peter Sells, Penny Eckert, Doug Arnold, Louisa Sadler, and Lis Norcliffe for helping me in composing this introduction. Many thanks are owed to all of them for sharpening the contributions to this volume and making the jobs of the editors much easier.

—Philip Hofmeister

Ivan Sag's Collaborators on Books, Journal Articles, and Chapters in Edited Volumes

Anne Abeillé
Inbal Arnon
Timothy Baldwin
Michael Barlow
K. John Barwise
John Beavers
Emily Bender
James Blevins
Hans C. Boas
Francis Bond
Gosse Bouma
Rui Chaves
James Collins
Ann Copestake
Henriette DeSwart
Daniel Flickinger
Janet D. Fodor
Marilyn Friedman
Gerald Gazdar
Mark Gawron
Jonathan Ginzburg
Danièle Godard
Jeff Goldberg
Jeff Good
Margaret Griffin
Gregory Guy
Jorge Hankamer
Donald Hindle
Philip Hofmeister
Masayo Iida
Florian Jaeger
Aravind Joshi
Ron Kaplan
Lauri Karttunen
Walter Kasper
Paul Kay
Jong-Bok Kim
Jonathan King
Ewan Klein
Fabre Lambeau
John Lamping
Mark Liberman
Egon Loebner
Bob Levine
Robert Malouf
Christopher Manning
Gary Marcus
Philip Miller
Geoff Nunberg
John Nerbonne
Joanna Nykiel
Anne Paulson
Carl Pollard
Daria Popova
Ellen Prince
Derek Proudian
Geoffrey K. Pullum
Matthew Purver
Susanne Riehemann
Stuart Shieber
Neal Snider
Laura Staum Casasanto
Anna Szabolcsi
Henry Thompson
Harry Tily
Hans Uszkoreit
Leonoor van der Beek
Aline Villavicencio
Athena Voloumanos
Thomas Wasow
Bonnie Webber
Steven Weisler
Ping Xue
Annie Zaenen

≈ 3 ≈

Revisiting Conditions on Predicate Anaphora

JASON MERCHANT

Ivan Sag's contributions to the study of ellipsis cannot be understated. These contributions began with his 1976 dissertation (Sag 1976a); this dissertation is a monumental work, one that combined new and important empirical observations with a brilliant new theory. In terms of its influence, its only peer in linguistics is Ross (1967); it remains a touchstone for all subsequent work on ellipsis and one which repays each rereading with new insights and directions. It is not merely of historical interest: there are puzzles and observations and analytical suggestions in Sag's dissertation which remain as central to work on ellipsis today as they were when Sag wrote about them.

It is sometimes thought that Sag's dissertation is about verb phrase ellipsis, or, as he suggested it be called and as Miller and Pullum take up, POST-AUXILIARY ELLIPSIS (PAE) in English. But, in fact, the chapter devoted to PAE (or VP Deletion) is shorter that the one devoted to gapping, and both are required reading for researchers on these topics to this day. Sag prefigured entire areas of research whose importance would not be recognized for decades, including the variable distribution of active/passive mismatches between the antecedent and the elided VP, quantifier and pronominal binding effects, and even the variable power of ellipsis to repair island effects. After noting Ross's 1969 discovery that sluicing appears to repair islands, he shows that Chomsky's 1972 analysis of this fact cannot be correct: Chomsky posited

The Core and the Periphery.
Philip Hofmeister and Elisabeth Norcliffe (eds.).

that "clauses containing violations of [island] constraints be marked with '#', which (if left undeleted) doom a sentence to ungrammaticality at the level of surface structure" (Sag 1976, 314). To show why such a solution does not work, Sag provides the following pair of examples (p. 314), with his stigmata:

(1) ?Betsy liked Peter, but Larry, she claimed she didn't Ø. [Ø= like]

(2) *Betsy liked the guy who told her about Peter, but Larry, she didn't Ø. [Ø= like the guy who told her about]

Sag's ability to recognize the kinds of examples relevant to establishing a particular syntactic point is legendary, and this pair provides a perfect example of this astonishing capability.

Sag also published a number of papers on ellipsis in the decade that followed, including Sag 1976b and Sag 1979, and, with Jorge Hankamer, Hankamer and Sag 1976 and Sag and Hankamer 1984. These latter papers address an apparent empirical distinction between what the authors dubbed 'surface' and 'deep' anaphora; in Hankamer and Sag 1976 (and in Sag 1976a), 'surface' anaphora is claimed to require a linguistic antecedent, while 'deep' anaphora can be resolved purely 'pragmatically'. This dichotomy, one of the most cited in the subsequent literature on ellipsis and anaphora, was significantly revised in Sag and Hankamer 1984. In that latter paper, whose importance has been underappreciated, the 'surface' vs. 'deep' distinction is jettisoned in favor of 'ellipsis' vs. 'model-theoretic anaphora'. And it is precisely this dichotomy that Miller and Pullum take up in their paper in this volume. They show, on the basis of a careful empirical investigation, that PAE and the predicate anaphors *do it*, *do this*, and *do that* are subject to a number of overlapping discourse conditions, in particular that focus on the subject or on the auxiliary are subject to differing well-formedness conditions (following in the spirit of López and Winkler 2000 and Winkler 2005) and that the interactions of these can explain the patterns of endophoric and exophoric uses of PAE and of *do it/this/that*.

While Miller and Pullum concentrate on these two kinds of predicate anaphora, further work will show whether exophoric uses of clausal ellipsis as in sluicing fall under a similar generalization, or whether the kind of open proposition that provides the understood material in a sluice is different from the kind of open proposition that is under discussion by Miller and Pullum for PAE. (This may, in turn, reduce to a version of the question of whether it is linguistically necessary to posit a type difference between predicates and open propositions, a contentious area.) It may well be that exophoric sluicing patterns with exophoric subject focus PAE with extraction out of the putative VP:

(3) [Context: A has taken her daughter and son to a kiosk that has two kinds of candy, and told the children they may each choose one piece. The son quickly chooses a piece, but the daughter eyes the candy for longer.] A: #I wonder which one.

(4) [Same context]: A: #I wonder which one *she* will.

As Miller and Pullum point out with respect to their (36), this kind of PAE requires a salient open proposition, and 'in general, non-linguistic context cannot make an open proposition salient enough'.

It seems reasonable to hope that this paper will also stimulate work on other kinds of ellipses, including nominal ellipses of various sorts, gapping, pseudogapping, and null complement anaphora. A number of these phenomena have been claimed to be 'surface' anaphoric, but little detailed corpus work of the kind undertaken by Miller and Pullum has been done, so it remains to be seen whether the larger data set shows the properties that Miller and Pullum identify for PAE and *do it/this/that.* Once the result of such detailed empirical investigation is known, we can then ask whether the fruitful line of analysis proposed by Miller and Pullum will or should extend to these further phenomena.

Although Sag in the intervening decades has made fundamental contributions to every other area of syntax as well, he has not entirely left his roots in ellipsis behind: in Ginzburg and Sag 2000 and Beavers and Sag 2004, he explores a wider range of elliptical constructions and offers, once again, insightful and different analyses, ones that eschew entirely the level of logical form that he used as a centerpiece of his 1976 dissertation. Few researchers can hope to have accomplished as much as Ivan in the area of ellipsis and to have contributed so much in this area; almost none can claim to have done so merely as one of dozens of areas of research.

References

Beavers, John and Ivan A. Sag. 2004. Ellipsis and apparent non-constituent coordination. In S. Müller, ed., *Proceedings of the 11th International Conference on Head-driven Phrase Structure Grammar*, pages 48–69. Stanford, CA: CSLI Publications.

Chomsky, Noam. 1972. *Spheres of Influence in the Age of Imperialism.* Nottingham: Bertrand Russell Peace Foundation.

Ginzburg, Jonathan and Ivan A. Sag. 2000. *Interrogative Investigations.* Stanford, CA: CSLI publications.

Hankamer, Jorge and Ivan A. Sag. 1976. Deep and surface anaphora. *Linguistic Inquiry* 7:391–426.

López, Luis and Susanne Winkler. 2000. Focus and topic in VP-anaphora constructions. *Linguistics* 38(4):623–664.

Ross, John R. 1967. *Constraints on Variables in Syntax*. Ph.D. thesis, MIT.

Ross, John R. 1969. Guess who? In R. Binnick, A. Davison, G. Green, and J. Morgan, eds., *Papers from the 5th Regional Meeting of the Chicago Linguistics Society*, pages 252–286. Chicago Linguistics Society, Chicago.

Sag, Ivan A. 1976a. *Deletion and Logical Form*. Ph.D. thesis, MIT, Cambridge, MA.

Sag, Ivan A. 1976b. A note on verb phrase deletion. *Linguistic Inquiry* 7(4):664–671.

Sag, Ivan A. 1979. The nonunity of anaphora. *Linguistic Inquiry* 10:152–164.

Sag, Ivan A. and Jorge Hankamer. 1984. Towards a theory of anaphoric processing. *Linguistics and Philosophy* 7:325–345.

Winkler, Susanne. 2005. *Ellipsis and focus in generative grammar*. Berlin: Mouton de Gruyter.

1

Exophoric VP Ellipsis

PHILIP MILLER AND GEOFFREY K. PULLUM

1 Introduction

The question addressed in this paper emerged 35 years ago out of a classic paper by Jorge Hankamer and Ivan Sag (1976) and a response to it (Schachter 1977; see also Schachter 1978).[1] Hankamer & Sag drew a distinction between DEEP ANAPHORA and SURFACE ANAPHORA. A central claim of their paper was that deep anaphoric devices can be used either endophorically (i.e. anaphorically if linked to an earlier antecedent or cataphorically if the antecedent follows) or exophorically (with no linguistic antecedent). Exophoric uses are interpreted either through ostension or via inference from the nonlinguistic context. Surface anaphoric devices, on the other hand, were claimed to require endophoric linkage to an antecedent identical in form (with the exception of minor inflectional variation) to the material that is ellipted or pronominalized away.

In subsequent work, these hypotheses were modified. Sag (1976) showed that it was logical form (albeit a fairly surface-similar level

[1]We are pleased to dedicate this paper to our good friend Ivan Sag, whose insightful work on ellipsis and many other topics has influenced and enlightened us for more than three decades. An earlier version was presented (by Pullum, to an audience including Sag) at the 2012 LSA meeting in Portland and (by Miller) at the 2nd conference on Topics in the Typology of Elliptical Constructions in Paris. We thank Chris Barker, Francis Cornish, Jonathan Ginzburg, Liliane Haegeman, Dan Hardt, Philip Hofmeister, Polly Jacobson, Anne Jugnet, Laura Kertz, Jason Merchant, Hannah Rohde, Jeff Runner, Tom Wasow, Bonnie Webber, and an anonymous reviewer for their very useful constructive comments on earlier drafts. They are of course not responsible for the opinions expressed or the errors that remain.

The Core and the Periphery.
Philip Hofmeister and Elisabeth Norcliffe (eds.).

of logical form) that was crucial for surface anaphors, not syntactic surface structure; Sag and Hankamer (1984) proposed that it is not the external nonlinguistic context itself that contributes to the interpretation of deep anaphors, but instead elements of the discourse model built up by the hearer as a discourse proceeds. They therefore proposed to call the 'deep' kind of anaphora MODEL-INTERPRETIVE anaphora and the surface kind simply ELLIPSIS.

We concentrate here on what is very often called 'VP Ellipsis', though that is a very poorly chosen term (as Hankamer [1978, 66n] points out), because it is neither necessary or sufficient that it should involve ellipsis of a VP.[2] Here we follow Sag's terminological suggestion (1976, 53) that it should be called POST-AUXILIARY ELLIPSIS (PAE). The defining characteristic is not that a VP is omitted but that a constituent or constituent sequence immediately following an auxiliary is missing.[3] Example (1a) is an instance of PAE that does have a missing VP; and (1b) and (1c) are instances that do not (in (1c) the ellipted sequence does not even form a constituent according to classical constituency tests; for example, it cannot be clefted). In (1d), we see an ellipted VP that is not an instance of PAE—it illustrates Null Complement Anaphora (NCA), a construction of the deep-anaphoric or model-interpretive type (Hankamer and Sag 1976 discuss the properties distinguishing NCA and PAE).

(1) a. We don't want to cancel the parade, but we could [$_{\mathrm{VP}}$ ~~cancel the parade~~]. [PAE]
  b. You think I'm dumb, but I'm not [$_{\mathrm{AdjP}}$ ~~dumb~~], you know. [PAE]
  c. He said there would be results quite soon, and indeed there were [$_{\mathrm{NP}}$ ~~results~~] [$_{\mathrm{AdvP}}$ ~~quite soon~~]. [PAE]
  d. I couldn't reach him, though I tried [$_{\mathrm{VP}}$ ~~to reach him~~] several times. [NCA]

Further examples of PAE are given in (2). The underlined part is the antecedent and the counterfactual location of the missing material represented as '___' is (like the struck-out parts in (1)) merely an expository device, not a suggested syntactic or semantic analysis.

[2] It may not be necessary to assume any ellipsis at all. Schachter (1978) argues that the auxiliaries simply function as 'propredicates' in these constructions. Jacobson (2003: 74–76), similarly, argues that 'missing material is supplied in roughly the same way as for the case of free pronouns.'

[3] We assume (with e.g. Gazdar et al. 1985) that infinitival *to* is a defective non-finite auxiliary verb. This analysis is not endorsed by Huddleston et al. (2002), but is robustly and convincingly defended by Levine (2012).

(2) a. Be back at six if you can ___. [tautosentential anaphoric PAE]
b. I rebooted the server. I had to ___. [discourse-anaphoric PAE]
c. If we must ___, we'll break in. [tautosentential cataphoric PAE]
d. A: Did you remember to get the milk?
B: Yes I did ___. [discourse-anaphoric PAE]

Hankamer & Sag claim that PAE is an instance of surface anaphora, and that in consequence it can never be exophoric ('deictic' or 'pragmatically controlled' in their terms). They contrast it with anaphoric VP substitutes like *do it*, *do this*, or *do that*, and the Null Complement Anaphora construction of (1d), all of which they claim instantiate deep anaphora, and thus can freely be exophoric. These constructions also allow an ANTECEDENT-TRIGGER that is not identical to the necessary antecedent.

By 'antecedent' here we mean the actual segment of text that if substituted for the anaphor or ellipsis site would achieve the same reference. We take the term 'antecedent-trigger' from Cornish (1999), who uses it to designate the segment of text allowing one to construct the antecedent (he uses 'antecedent' to refer to the discourse-model representation making interpretation of the anaphor or ellipsis possible). For instance, in (8b) below, *survival* is an antecedent trigger, not an antecedent. The antecedent would be *survive*, which does not actually appear in the text. In cases where the antecedent-trigger and antecedent are identical, we will usually use the shorter term 'antecedent'.

Hankamer & Sag present many striking contrasts; for example (with the prefix '#' signaling, throughout this paper, discourse infelicity in the given context):

(3) [Context: Sag raises a cleaver and prepares to hack off his left hand.]
a. Hankamer: #Don't worry, he never actually does ___. [PAE]
b. Hankamer: Don't worry, he never actually does it. [*do it*]

Schachter (1977) responded to Hankamer & Sag with a series of counterexamples (not very different from a number of examples that were actually noted in footnotes to their paper, e.g. p. 409, fn. 19), arguing that PAE can be freely exophoric, though a certain pragmatic difficulty often attends the recovery of a PAE interpretation from the context. The reply by Hankamer (1978) claims that all of Schachter's examples are independently explicable in a way that does not challenge the general claim of impossibility for exophoric PAE.

In our view, what is needed in a resolution of this debate is not just an answer to the boolean question of whether or not PAE can freely be exophoric, but also an explanatory account embracing two counterposed facts:

(4) a. The Hankamer–Sag ban seems too general in that it disbars exophoric PAE by a hard syntactico-semantic constraint: We need an explanation of why Schachter was able to exhibit any examples that seemed even remotely acceptable.

b. Schachter's claim that PAE can freely be exophoric seems too general in that it allows exophoric PAE anywhere and everywhere: We need an explanation of why exophoric instances of PAE are so rare and restricted.

Hankamer's response to Schachter concentrated on two key points:

(5) a. The range of exceptional cases of deictic uses of PAE is very limited and semantically conventionalized — much more restricted than the range of readings available for the corresponding clause where the post-auxiliary material is expressed.

b. The fact that in cases where PAE is unacceptable you *can* pick up the same antecedent with *do it/this/that* shows that the antecedent is indeed recoverable from context.

So Hankamer's answer to (4a) is that there is no general phenomenon of exophoric PAE at all. The anomalous apparent exophoric PAE utterances are few in number and virtually lexicalized: they represent a few scattered idioms, based on the syntactic form of anaphoric PAE sentences, that would need to be included in a comprehensive phrasebook for English, such as those in (6).

(6) a. Shall we? [Courteous invitation to dance.]

b. May I? [Polite request for permission to invade a person's space, e.g. by taking away an unoccupied chair or performing some action that involves touching them.]

Pullum (2000) argued that Hankamer's position could be supported on purely quantitative grounds: the number of plausible cases of exophoric PAE that had been gathered or even invented (and it was mostly the latter) was minuscule compared to the number of potential ones. Hankamer & Sag themselves drew attention to (7a, b); Schachter suggested contexts for (7c – j); and Pullum additionally suggested contexts for exophoric uses of (7k – p).

(7)
a. Don't!
b. You didn't!
c. Does she or doesn't she?
d. You mustn't!
e. I shouldn't.
f. Shall we?
g. You shouldn't have!
h. May I?
i. Please do.
j. If you can, I can.
k. You wouldn't!
l. Don't you dare!
m. Must you?
n. Shall I?
o. Should I?
p. Dare we?

These very few intuitively plausible cases need to be set against the entire range of grammatical combinations of auxiliary verb sequence with subject pronoun, with or without negation and/or inversion. The number of such combinations is in the thousands; 1,500 would be a conservative figure. Most of them have never been attested in exophoric use. This amounts to an informal kind of Bayesian argument: if Schachter were right, it would be extremely improbable that the evidence would look this way, and the improbable nature of the observed corpus supports Hankamer's thesis. Moreover, many of the cases in (7) do show some signs of having a special meaning or restricted context of use when they are exophoric, as Hankamer claimed.

We have nothing to say against the idea that some exophoric PAE uses may be fixed formulae with unpredictable restrictions of sense. It is entirely compatible with our position that there might be such quasi-idiomatic formulae. However, it is a little suspicious that (to our knowledge) not a single one of them has ever been recorded in a standard dictionary. Moreover, we show later (see §3.2 and §3.3) that Hankamer was wrong about some specific examples, and more generally we argue that it is by no means a requirement that exophoric cases of PAE should have special idiomatic meanings.

Various studies in the literature since 1978 (e.g. Webber 1979; Dalrymple et al. 1991; Hardt 1993; Kehler 2000; Jacobson 2003, 2008, 2009; Kertz 2010) have questioned the idea that PAE was a case of surface anaphora as Hankamer & Sag defined it. They exhibited examples where there was no syntactically identical antecedent in the discourse, but rather a distinct antecedent-trigger from which the relevant antecedent could be inferred, as in (8a), with a switch from active to passive and the attested example (8b), where the antecedent is a derived nominal.

(8) a. Actually I have implemented it [= *a computer system*] with a manager, but it doesn't have to be [~~implemented with a manager~~]. (Kehler 2000, 549, example (24))

b. Mubarak's survival is impossible to predict and, even if he does [~~survive~~], his plan to make his son his heir apparent is now in serious jeopardy. [COCA: CBS Evening News]

This line of work defended the idea that all anaphors were semantically resolved and hence were all deep anaphors in the sense of Hankamer & Sag. The studies in question tacitly assume that exophoric PAE is possible and cite examples of the same sort as those given by Schachter (see, for instance, Chao 1987, 83ff.; Hardt 1993, 34, see (108)–(110); Johnson 2001, see (120); Jacobson 2003, 79, see (31), (32); Jacobson 2008, 55, see (41); Jacobson 2009, 86, see (4)).

The only authors we are aware of who develop an actual analysis are Jacobson (2003, 2008, 2009) and Merchant (2004, 718–723). Both defend the position that exophoric PAE exists and offer some account of how PAE works semantically. Merchant, furthermore, provides new attested data.

The general idea that exophoric PAE does exist is thus now accepted by many linguists. However, no convincing explanation has been provided for why such a small minority of examples appear to be acceptable, or for the putative fact that exophoric occurrences are so rare.

Merchant has some analytical proposals; we return to his account in §3.5, where we will explain why we think it is unconvincing.

Our claim is that the debate between Hankamer & Sag on one side and Schachter on the other was fundamentally misframed, because both maintained the implicit assumption that anaphoric uses of PAE and *do it/this/that* are freely interchangeable except for the following two specific constraints on the latter:

(9) Constraints on *do it/this/that* assumed by Hankamer and Schachter alike:[4]

(i) *Do it*, *do this*, and *do that* contain main verb *do*, so they cannot substitute for stative predicates,[5] whereas there are no semantic constraints on PAE.

[4] We will mostly be grouping *do it*, *do this*, and *do that* together as *do it/this/that*, ignoring the various differences between them. As reported in Miller (2011), the difference between the three forms seems very largely parallel to the difference between *it*, *this* and *that*, as discussed for instance in Gundel et al. (1993).

[5] The exact formulation of this constraint has been under considerable debate, some papers having argued that an agentive or actional predicate is required; see e.g. Houser (2010) for a synopsis.

(ii) Because they are deep anaphors, *do it/this/that* allow their antecedent-trigger to be very different from the required antecedent, but this is not the case with PAE.

Thus, they are making the assumption that PAE and *do it/this/that* should be freely interchangeable in cases where the antecedent-trigger and antecedent are identical and the antecedent is agentive.

Recent corpus investigation (partially summarized in Miller 2011) has shown, however, that this assumption is radically unsound. There are in fact strong discourse constraints on the choice between verbal anaphors — just as there are for the choice between nominal anaphors, as discussed e.g. in centering theory (Grosz et al. 1995), accessibility theory (Ariel 1990), and givenness theory (Gundel et al. 1993). Our claim is that Hankamer was wrong about exophoric PAE in that it can indeed be freely deployed in exophoric uses in all the situations where it satisfies the general discourse conditions on its use that apply in anaphoric contexts, too.

It is not even quite correct to say that exophoric PAE is rare. At the very least, it is misleading to say that. Many circumstances prevent the exophoric use of PAE, but it seems to occur as often as the demands of the non-linguistic context happen to motivate it — it is free to occur exophorically within the range of the circumstances that allow it to occur at all.

However, we claim that Schachter was wrong, too. He failed to note that there are quite dramatic discourse constraints on exophoric PAE. It isn't true that speakers can use PAE exophorically anywhere they think they can get away with it. Stringent discourse conditions have to be satisfied, and only in the fairly infrequent situations where nonlinguistic context is capable of satisfying them is there, ceteris paribus, a chance for an exophoric PAE use to be felicitous.

Schachter's error was to overlook the special discourse preconditions and Hankamer's error was to diagnose a general ban on exophoricity instead of just the effects of the special discourse preconditions.

2 Conditions on the anaphoric use of PAE

There are some syntactic contexts where PAE is the only possible choice, so that there is no alternation with *do it/this/that*: examples include interrogative tags and certain comparative and relative structures. There are also cases where *do it/this/that* can occur but PAE cannot: in American English anyway,[6] supportive *do* in PAE occurs

[6] Here we set aside the British English VP-substitutive *do* in *I don't know if she lives nearby; she may do.* This is claimed by Pullum and Wilson (1977), Baker

only in finite forms, whereas the transitive *do* of *do it/this/that* occurs freely in both finite and non-finite forms. The following discussion is limited to those cases where there are no morphosyntactic restrictions on the alternation between PAE and *do it/this/that*.

We distinguish two different types of PAE, which we will call Auxiliary-Choice and Subject-Choice. Miller (2011) argues, on the basis of a corpus investigation, that the two kinds of PAE have to satisfy distinct discourse requirements. We characterize the two kinds of PAE and state the discourse requirements in (10).

(10) a. Type 1: Auxiliary Choice
Formal characteristics: The subject of the antecedent is identical with the subject of the PAE construction and the auxiliary is (at least weakly) stressed, signaling a new choice of tense, aspect, modality, or (in the most overwhelmingly frequent case) polarity.
Discourse requirement: A choice between the members of a jointly exhaustive set of alternative situations must be highly salient in the discourse context, and the point of the utterance containing the PAE is strictly limited to selecting one member of that set.

b. Type 2: Subject Choice
Formal characteristics: The subject of the antecedent is distinct from the subject of the PAE construction, and stressed if it is a pronoun.
Discourse requirement: A particular property[7] must be highly salient in the discourse context, and the point of the utterance containing the PAE must be strictly limited to identifying something or someone possessing that property.

At root, the distinction between Auxiliary-Choice and Subject-Choice is the 'auxiliary focus' vs. 'argument focus' distinction of the important paper by Kertz (2008), also used by Miller (2011), but we want to avoid any suggestion that the technical notion of focus is the key here.[8]

(1984), and Miller (2002) to be a non-finite occurrence of supportive *do*.

[7]Miller (2011) uses the term 'open proposition', following the terminology of e.g. Ward (1988).

[8]There can be cases of dual focus, as in (i), though they are rare:

(i)A: I didn't think anyone wore bell-bottoms any more.
B: Well, it turns out that Hénry DÓES! / HÉNRY dóes!

The nucleus (marked by small capitals) can be either on the subject or on the auxiliary, depending on speaker intentions. We have not yet investigated the extension of the discourse conditions in (10) to these mixed cases.

Kertz makes the very significant point that the distinction is relevant for the acceptability of voice mismatches in PAE: auxiliary-focus PAE allows active/passive mismatches (see (8a) above) whereas subject-focus cases of PAE do not. In what follows we show that a lot more hangs on the distinction between the two kinds of PAE, and that when the properties of the two kinds of anaphoric construction are understood, the facts about exophoric use can be explained.

2.1 Anaphoric Auxiliary-Choice PAE

In order to clarify the empirical content of the discourse requirement on Auxiliary-Choice PAE we need to state what kinds of contexts can make the choice between the members of a jointly exhaustive set of alternative situations highly salient (the following list is not intended to be exhaustive, but it covers the main cases, extending the results of Miller 2011).

2.1.1 Assertions

Asserting p makes the p vs. $\neg p$ alternative salient in the sense of placing it on the table for the addressee to accept or reject. This sets up the conditions for using Auxiliary-Choice PAE. This context accounts for a large number of typical anaphoric uses of PAE, namely contradiction or confirmation of a previous assertion, which amounts to choosing one of the members of the set. In these contexts, on the other hand, *do it* and *do this* are infelicitous.

(11) A: He shops in women's.
B: No, he doesn't. [COCA]
Compare #*No, he doesn't do it/this/that.*

(12) A: Her friend grew up in Florida. And in the Northeast, and at the end of the book [she] returns to Vietnam.
B: She does. I mean, the story is really touching. [COCA]
Compare #*She does it/this/that.*

Note that, as mentioned in (10a), PAE is only felicitous if the point of the utterance is to choose one of the members of the set of alternatives. If the speaker's intention goes beyond that, PAE becomes infelicitous and *do it/this/that* become acceptable:[9]

[9] As noted by Miller (2011), *do it* is frequently accompanied by a non-contrastive adjunct (60% of the cases in his corpus) whereas this is never the case with PAE.

(13) A: He shops in women's.
B: He never does it alone. / He does it all the time. / He does it because that's the only place he can find things his size.
#He never does alone. / #He does all the time. / #He does because that's the only place he can find things his size.

In (13), B's utterances do not simply contradict or confirm A's previous assertion. The focus is not on whether the previous assertion is true or false (p vs. $\neg p$), but rather on the contents expressed by the adjunct (*never ... alone*, *all the time*, *because that's the only place he can find things his size*). Thus, the second part of the constraint expressed in (10a) is not satisfied and PAE is not felicitous. On the other hand, *do it/this/that* are felicitous in such contexts, the choice between them being made on the basis of considerations of accessibility/givenness under conditions closely resembling those governing the choice between simple *it/this/that*.

Given this, it should be noted that *do that* (and to a lesser extent *do it* and *do this*) can be used to suggest that the point of the utterance goes beyond a simple choice between the members of the set of alternatives, without explicitly indicating what is at stake. For example, in (11), if B simply uttered *He does that* as an answer (without an additional adjunct as in (13)), it might be taken to suggest that the person referred to as 'he' has some other activity contrasting with shopping in women's that she intends to discuss. Or, she might be suggesting, with appropriate intonation, an implicit evaluative comment of the '*Can you believe it?!*' type. Thus, in these and subsequent examples in this paper, any cross-hatch before *do that* (or before *do it/this/that*) should be interpreted as indicating *either* infelicity *or* the presence of a clearly different contextual effect from simple choice between alternatives effected by PAE.

As opposed to actually asserting p, having p as background information in the context causes PAE to become infelicitous and makes *do it/this/that* possible, as in (14a) (adapted from an attested COCA example) where p = 'Jake named a dragon after you' is in a relative clause. If we turn the relative clause into an asserted main clause as in (14b), PAE becomes felicitous and *do it/this/that* become less felicitous.

(14) a. A: The dragon Jake named after you is a real beauty.
B: He didn't do that.
Compare #*He didn't.*

b. A: Jake named a dragon after you.
B: He didn't.
Compare #*He didn't do it/this/that.*

c. Susan is furious over Jake's naming a dragon after you.
(i) He didn't.
(ii) He didn't do that.

There are cases, though, where what might seem to be an unasserted proposition p does allow the use of PAE, as in (14c). The question here hinges on the criteria chosen for defining an assertion. Following a suggestion by Francis Cornish (pers. comm.), we can use Erteschik-Shir's 'lie test' (Erteschik-Shir 2007, 39, 164), as a criterion: if it is felicitous to contradict a phrase or clause in a previous utterance by saying *that's a lie, she/he/... didn't* then that phrase or clause is asserted in that utterance. If the contradiction is infelicitous, on the other hand, then the phrase or clause corresponds to backgrounded and not asserted information. Under normal circumstances, an utterance of a declarative main clause is always interpreted as an assertion in this sense.

This is why *do it/this/that* are infelicitous as an answer in (14b) (except in the cases mentioned above where the point is to go beyond simple choice among the alternatives). On the other hand, the proposition p = 'Jake named a dragon after you' is expressed as a gerund-participial clause in (14c). Depending on the context of utterance, it might or might not be felicitous to contradict it, e.g. by saying *That's a lie, he did no such thing.* This explains why (14c) allows both PAE and *do it/this/that.*

Turning back to (14a), it is clear that trying to continue it with *that's a lie ...* would be completely infelicitous. Such an example cannot be interpreted as asserting that Jake named a dragon after you, and this explains that PAE is infelicitous.[10]

[10] As Anne Jugnet (pers. comm.) points out to us, the fact that a p is presupposed (in the classical technical sense) does not automatically make PAE infelicitous. For instance, in (14c) the gerund is presupposed and similarly for the complements of factive predicates as in:

(i)A: *I'm sorry that I can't solve this problem.*
B: *Yes, you can/I'm sure you can do it.*

Thus we conclude that a proposition can be both presupposed and asserted in the relevant sense.

2.1.2 Questions

Asking a polar question with p as content makes the p vs. $\neg p$ choice salient and an answer using PAE chooses one member of the set. This context accounts for a large number of uses of anaphoric PAE such as (15).

(15) A: Senator Brown, does this bill end too-big-to-fail?
B: Yeah, it does. [COCA]
Compare #*Yeah, it does it/this/that.*

Note that in this configuration *do it* and *do this* are again infelicitous, and *do that* triggers the specific contextual effects mentioned above (for instance, *do that* becomes as felicitous as PAE if B's answer continues as follows: *Yeah, it does that. But it also leads to some serious problems for the federal budget in the near future.*).

2.1.3 Permission

A request for permission to make p true (16a), or advice about whether or not to make p true, or directly evoking the possibility or necessity of p (16b), where p is an event under control of the speaker (and possibly other participants including the addressee), makes the p vs. $\neg p$ choice salient and thus makes PAE felicitous. Note that here too, *do it/this/that* would be infelicitous.

(16) a. 'Can I go now?' he asked. 'Of course you can.' [COCA]
Compare #*Of course you can do it/this/that.*
b. A: Before I leave FAO Swartz, there's just one thing I really, really have to do. May I?
B: Of course. [COCA]
Compare #*May I do it/this/that?*

2.1.4 Directives

Uttering a directive with the propositional content p makes the choice between compliance and non-compliance salient. Anaphoric cases of this type are illustrated in (17). Note again that the variants with *do it/this/that* are less felicitous.

(17) A: Come here.
B: No, I won't. [COCA]
Compare #*No, I won't do it/this/that.*

(18) A: Let's load it up for you.
B: Please do. [COCA]
Compare #*Please do it/this/that.*

(19) A: Go ahead.
B: May I? [COCA]
Compare #*May I do it/this/that?*

2.2 Anaphoric Subject-Choice PAE

Anaphoric cases of Subject-Choice PAE are felicitous if the property denoted by the antecedent of the ellipted material is salient in the discourse context. This is illustrated by (20a, b), the relevant properties being the property of cheering and the property of saying something. Note again that *do it/this/that* are dispreferred in these contexts.

(20) a. The boys cheered. I did too. [Compare #*I did it / this / that too.*]
b. She didn't say anything, and I didn't either. [Compare #*I didn't do it/this/that either*]

3 Exophoric uses of PAE

First, a word on data. One of the discoveries that led to our writing this paper was that it is possible to find not just endophoric but also (though this sounds implausible) exophoric instances of PAE in large corpora. Most of the data discussed in this paper come from the extremely useful COCA corpus.[11] COCA examples are explicitly marked as such. They were obtained by systematic searches on patterns we thought were likely to yield examples of exophoric PAE, on the basis of the suggestions in the literature and the results on endophoric PAE reported in Miller (2011). Figuring out what the nonlinguistic context was had to be done by hand, as it were, through a sensitive reading of the context and the application of common sense. Further data in what follows are the result of doing controlled manipulations of COCA examples to pinpoint the relevance of certain factors and to make certain intuitively judged contrasts clear. We have used a few invented examples to illustrate cases that we think are acceptable but for which no attested examples could be found.

3.1 Exophoric Auxiliary-Choice PAE

3.1.1 Nonlinguistic context can't assert

Non-linguistic evidence provided by the context for the truth or falsity of p does not make the p vs. $\neg p$ alternative accessible in the same way as asserting p does. In other words, the mere fact that p is obviously

[11]The Corpus of Contemporary American English [COCA; available online at http://www.americancorpus.org] contained, at the time when this paper was written, 425 million words from 1990 to the present. Like all other scholars using it, we are greatly indebted to its creator, Mark Davies.

true does not place *p* on the table. This explains why it is that mere situational or behavioral indications of the truth of *p* do not make an exophoric PAE of the following type felicitous:

(21) [Context: You are doing Toyota jumps and showing other signs of glee]
#I'm glad you are!

It is thus in general impossible to find exophoric cases corresponding to the endophoric cases of §2.1.1. And this is what explains the anomaly in (3): the non-linguistic context of Sag raising a cleaver simply cannot raise to salience the choice between 'Sag regularly mutilates himself on stage during lectures' vs. 'Sag does not regularly mutilate himself on stage during lectures,' so the PAE in (3) is anomalous.

As pointed out to us by Philip Hofmeister, non-linguistic communicative acts (considered as such by the addressee on the basis of recognition of a communicative intent, see Grice (1957), who already discusses non-linguistic cases) can parallel linguistically expressed assertions. This explains the acceptability of the following interesting apparent counterexample proposed by an anonymous reviewer:

(22) [Context: Fred is filthy, and has passed out on the sidewalk. Tom and Bob recognize him. Tom looks at Bob and taps his left forearm twice, clearly suggesting the possibility that intravenous drug use is implicated.]
Bob: Does he? Does he really?

Clearly, in a case like this, Tom has a communicative intent (note 'looks at') and Bob recognizes it as such. The situation would have been exactly parallel if Tom had said *He's using intravenous drugs.* Note also that this non-linguistic communicative act passes Erteschick-Shir's lie test just as well as the spoken variant: both could have been followed by *You're lying, he'd never touch drugs.* The difference with (21) is that in that example the signs of happiness are not interpreted as having a communicative intent (the lie test fails), at least under normal circumstances. If there is any reason to believe that there is such a communicative intent — e.g. if the person making the signs is an expert mime playing the role of a deaf-mute — then (21) becomes more acceptable.

3.1.2 Nonlinguistic context can't ask questions

Similarly, the non-linguistic context cannot generally simulate a yes/no question speech act. Thus, once again, it is not surprising that we do not find exophoric variants corresponding to the endophoric cases in

§2.1.2.[12]

3.1.3 Permission

By contrast, a p vs. $\neg p$ alternative can definitely be made salient via a request for permission to do something in a situation where the course of action that the speaker is considering is obvious from the non-linguistic context and is under the speaker's control. In such cases there is a clear fork point in the future and PAE is felicitous, forcing the addressee to choose one branch of the alternative. This is illustrated by Schachter's *May I?* example given in (6b) above. We found 17 clear examples of this type in the spoken section of COCA, as opposed to 9 clear examples of anaphoric uses of the type (16b), as well as the following example of *Can we?*:

(23) The aisles at the Lakewood Wal-Mart are surprisingly packed at 11 p.m. 'Can we? Can we?' Vanessa tugs at her mother, pointing to a rack of 'Lady and the Tramp" DVDs. Diaz shrugs. OK. [COCA]

Though we have found no examples in COCA, it seems pretty clear that other phrases such as *Can I?*, *Could I?*, *Could we?*, etc. are all acceptable in similar contexts. One can also easily imagine various forms with indirect interrogatives, e.g. *Do you think I can?*, *Do you think we could?*, etc.

Similarly, if the speaker asks for advice on whether or not to do something, or proposes to do something, again in a situation where the course of action that the speaker is considering is obvious from the non linguistic context and is under the speaker's control, a p vs. $\neg p$ alternative is made salient and PAE is felicitous (note that the action may involve not only the speaker but also the addressee and/or other participants). This is illustrated by examples of the *Should I?* type proposed by Pullum (2000), illustrated in (24a) and in the constructed example (24b) with *Do I have to?* Proposals are illustrated by Schachter's *Shall we?* example, given above in (6a).

[12]Cornish (1999: 126) provides the following example from his own experience, and considers it (correctly, we think) to be exophoric. A departmental secretary was about to leave at the end of the working day. The photocopier was supposed to be turned off at night, as was well known. The secretary gave 'a quizzical look' toward the photocopier and then toward Cornish, who happened to be the last person in the office that evening. Cornish said: 'I will, don't worry!' Note that it is the quizzical look towards the photocopier, and the local policy, which made the alternatives ('turn it off' vs. 'not turn it off') salient in a way exactly parallel to the yes/no question in (15). This example is thus very similar to (22) in that it involves a non-linguistic communicative act. On the role of 'quizzical looks' and other factors that can boost the salience of abstract entities, see also Gundel et al. (2003).

(24) a. Once in my room, I took the pills out. 'Should I?' I asked myself. [COCA]

b. [Entering a construction site, A hands a helmet to B].
B: Do I have to?

One might object that (24a) represents an internal monologue, so the speaker would have a linguistic antecedent available in an earlier thought and it is therefore not a clear exophoric case. But note that the example seems to remain felicitous if one replaces *myself* by *him*, imagining that the speaker is holding the pills in her hand. In similar contexts, one can easily imagine utterances like *Should we?* or *Dare I?* or *Dare we?* or *Shall we?* — and again, some of the indirect interrogative variants (like *Do you think I should?* or *Do you think I have to?*) are clearly acceptable.

It should be emphasized again that in all of the cases discussed, PAE would have been just as felicitous if the course of action, for which the speaker requests permission or advice, or makes a proposal, had been conveyed by linguistic means, making the examples anaphoric. For instance, in (23), Vanessa might have said *I want to buy a DVD. Can we?* There is nothing special about these exophoric instances.

3.1.4 Directives

Another type of case where exophoric PAE is felicitous involves situations where it is obvious that the addressee(s) (or the adressee(s) and some other participants) has performed an action, or is performing it, or is about to do so, and the speaker utters an opinion about whether they should or should not have done so (or be doing so, or do so). This makes explicit that there were/are two options available, p or $\neg p$. Thus the speaker's very utterance forces the addressee to accomodate the p vs. $\neg p$ alternative and makes it salient. This situation covers the second major group of regularly occurring exophoric cases of PAE, which include Hankamer & Sag's *Don't!* and *You didn't!*, Schachter's examples *You mustn't!*, *You shouldn't have!*, *Please do!*, *How could you?*, and Pullum's examples *You wouldn't!*, *Don't you dare!*, and *Must you?*. These are illustrated in the following examples.[13]

(25) Mabel shoved a plate into Tate's hands before heading for the sisters' favorite table in the shop. 'You shouldn't have.' She meant

[13] Philip Hofmeister (pers. comm.) points out to us that imminent possibilities might be added as a possible context, as in a situation where two people are watching a race and the participant in whom they have a special interest becomes more likely to beat his opponents. One of them might say *He just might!* This is a variant of our directives context, where it is obvious that some other participant is about to perform an action.

it. The sisters had to pool their limited resources just to get by. [COCA]

(26) When the rain began on Thursday, I simply had the kids throw on slickers and use plastic grocery bags to cover backpacks. I rode with them to school, for solidarity, but when we pulled up, an upperclassman looked at them, then me, and said half-accusingly, 'How could you?' Our family experiment had suddenly gone from cool and hip to strange and compulsive. [COCA]

The speaker can also comment on his or her own actions or on the actions of a group in which he/she is included: *I musn't!*; *I shouldn't have!*; *How could I!*.

(27) She phones him very early the next morning. I'm so sorry, V., she says. You're not half bad at it, S., he says. Pulling people's strings. I know, she says, I shouldn't have. You made me feel, he says, like a piece of dirt. Yes, she says. I'm terribly sorry. [COCA]

Finally, though it is harder to find naturally occurring examples, the speaker can comment on the actions of a 3rd person participant if the situation is sufficiently clear, as in the following example.

(28) Vonnie's first words to her [= Giselle] were 'That fucking bastard. How could he?' Confused, Giselle turned to look behind her and then realized that Vonnie was referring to her eye. The shiner... [COCA]

To conclude the discussion of §3.1.3 and §3.1.4, it is crucial to note that in all of these cases replacing PAE by *do it/this/that* while keeping the context identical makes the examples infelicitous and in some cases uninterpretable:

(23′) #Can we do it/this/that?

(24a′) #Should I do it/this/that?

(24b′) #Do I have to do it/this/that?

(25′) #You shouldn't have done it/this/that.

(26′) #How could you do it/this/that?

This further confirms that the choice between PAE and *do it/this/that* is not free in discourse. When the appropriate discourse conditions are met, PAE does not simply become a possible alternative for the deep anaphors; rather, it is the preferred choice or even in some cases the only possible choice.

3.2 The role of explicitly stated alternatives

At this point, it is worth coming back to the cases discussed in §3.1.2, asking why a putative case of exophoric PAE of the type illustrated in (29) is systematically infelicitous (in the absence of some non-linguistic communicative act of the type in (22)).

(29) a. #Does he?
     b. #Did he?

Indeed, one might suggest that by asking the question the speaker forces the addressee to accommodate a p vs. $\neg p$ alternative, making it salient in a way similar to those illustrated in §3.1.3 and §3.1.4 above. The problem here is that nothing in the context makes the relevant proposition p accessible to the addressee in a way parallel to what we saw with cases of requesting permission or advice or giving directives. This then leads us to the question of why Schachter's Clairol ad example (30a), which provided the title for his 1977 paper, sounds far better than the simpler (30b), which we judge to be infelicitous.

(30) a. Does she or doesn't she?
     b. #Does she?

By explicitly setting up the alternative linguistically, the speaker makes explicit a partition of the possibilities and imposes exhaustivity. A search on this type of example shows that Hankamer (1978) was only partially right in claiming that the felicity of the example is due to taboo avoidance and that "The common meaning of the expression in question, of course, is 'Does she or doesn't she screw?'" (Hankamer 1978, 68), the Clairol ad being a deliberate evocation of this idiomatic meaning. But Hankamer is wrong. Consider the following attested example:

(31) Brock, 27, an advertising rep, adds, 'Downloading porn isn't as good as sex, but at least I don't have to stress about pleasing her or worry, Did she or didn't she? It's self-centered, but hey, I'm a guy. That's how we think sometimes.' [COCA, from *Cosmopolitan* magazine]

This example is clearly exophoric and involves avoidance of talk about sex, but the meaning is not that suggested as idiomatically fixed by Hankamer, but rather, clearly, 'Did she or didn't she achieve orgasm?' More interestingly, it appears that similar examples are possible without any reference to sexual matters. Consider the following examples:

(32) a. More to the point, the committee uncovered no evidence linking Palmeiro to steroids use before the hearing. The committee's report, in fact, provides information that could be seen as supporting Palmeiro's contention that he never intentionally – his word – used steroids. At the same time, the report raises questions that create doubt about his stance. In the end, the conclusion one draws from the evidence, having nothing to do with the date of the hearing but with the overall question – did he or didn't he? – will probably vary with the individual viewing the evidence. [COCA, from *The New York Times*]

b. #... having nothing to do with the date of the hearing but with the overall question – did he? – will probably vary with the individual viewing the evidence.

c. More to the point, the committee uncovered no evidence linking Palmeiro to steroids use before the hearing. In the end, the conclusion one draws from the evidence, having nothing to do with the date of the hearing but with the overall question – did he or didn't he? – will probably vary with the individual viewing the evidence.

Though (32a) is endophoric, strictly speaking, several points are worth noting. First, replacing the explicit alternative with simple *did he?* as in the constructed variant (32b) clearly makes PAE much less felicitous. This is largely due to the distance between the antecedent (*used steroids*) and the ellipsis site which makes the antecedent insufficiently salient.

Furthermore, it would be possible to remove two sentences in (32a), including the antecedent (*used steroids*), as in (32c), without making the example infelicitous because the segment *evidence linking Palmeiro to steroids* can serve as an antecedent-trigger allowing one to infer the necessary the antecedent (*use steroids*).

What all of this shows is that PAE is really not working under its usual anaphoric conditions in these cases (and clearly could not be analyzed as a surface anaphor in the (32c) variant). Rather, it is accessing the overall cognitive representation (what Sag and Hankamer (1984) call the discourse model, see also Cornish (1999)) that the addressee constructs on the basis of discourse and, in the general case, extralinguistic contextual information.

It is interesting to note in this context that we have found several cases where an explicit alternative of this general type (Aux + Pronoun + *or* + Auxn't + Pronoun*?*) is used as a title or section head in the press or in information broadcasts. For example:

(33) Arol Costello, CNN anchor: Will he or won't he? Convicted sniper John Allen Muhammad has been subpoenaed in the trial of alleged accomplice Lee Boyd Malvo, but it is not certain whether he will testify. [COCA: CNN LiveDaybreak]

Such examples are not really cataphoric to the body of the article. Rather, they are a rhetorical device aiming to capture attention by puzzling the reader or addressee. But it should be noted that once again the conditions have to be respected: replacing the explicit alternative by simple *Will he?* makes the title infelicitous, no matter how arrestingly puzzling it might be.

3.3 The relevance of taboo avoidance

Let us now return briefly to Hankamer's idea, mentioned in the previous subsection, that avoidance of taboo topics can exceptionally license exophoric PAE. An example like the following, with a clear case of exophoric PAE after *to*, suggests that there is something correct about this.

(34) I became aware of what she was doing slower than a sixteen-year-old should have. That she saw me looking changed nothing. On the beanbag, naked, she turned to me and said very simply: Do you want to? [COCA, from *Harper's Magazine*]

However, that does not license us to just dismiss such examples as idiomatic and irrelevant. In other cases, taboo avoidance will be achieved by *do it* rather than PAE. For example, in a context where A is a close friend of B and A knows that B went on a date with C and that B was hoping to have sex with C, B could start a conversation with A on the following day by saying (35a). On the other hand, (35b) would be infelicitous as there is no salient alternative in the context.

(35) a. We did it!
b. #We did!

It is not simply the case, then, that taboo avoidance makes PAE more likely. It makes anaphoric and elliptical constructions more likely in general. But the choice between PAE and *do it* is based on the same factors as usual in such contexts. Note, in particular, that in (34), we are in a case of the type discussed in §3.1.3, which we have shown makes exophoric PAE felicitous.

3.4 Exophoric Subject-Choice PAE

As mentioned above, anaphoric Subject-Choice PAE requires a property to be salient in the discourse context. In general, non-linguistic context cannot make a property salient enough.[14]

Suppose A is struggling silently to get the lid off a jar, and having no success. It would be unacceptable — indeed, bizarre — for B to say, *Oh,* I *can; give it to me.* To make it acceptable, somehow the specific property $\lambda x[x\ canopenthejar]$ has to become salient in the discourse. It is not simply that someone has to say something; (36) would be just as bizarre:

(36) [Context: A is struggling to get the lid off a jar.]
  A: They put these damn things on way too tight.
  B: #Oh, *I* can; give it to me.

What has to happen is that the specific property $\lambda x[x$ can open the jar$]$ has to become a salient recent part of the discourse, e.g. like this:

(37) [Context: A is struggling to get the lid off a jar.]
  A: I can't open this damn jar. (property: being able to open the jar)
  B: Oh, *I* can; give it to me.

Here B's utterance is entirely felicitous. It provides a clause with a new choice of subject and asserts that this new subject denotes someone with the salient property.

Schachter (1977) noted one (invented) exophoric case of this type: on seeing someone accomplish something daring one can say, *If you can, I can* (note also, *I will if you will*, cited in Jacobson 2008, 86). Here the saliency-enhancing device is in the linguistic material of the PAE utterance itself: what is said has the logical form *if* $f(x)$, $f(y)$, setting up an explicit alternation between subjects. That is not at all the same as uttering something like *I will*, which would be unacceptable. In its very form, by contrasting $f(x)$ with $f(y)$, it focuses on the choice of subjects and makes the property f salient and thus accessible.

In the jar-lid context discussed above, *B* could felicitously say something like *Well if you can't, I bet I can* even if *A* didn't speak.

Once again, contrary to what Hankamer suggests, there is no fixed expression here; numerous variants are possible. Consider this vignette:

[14] Independent evidence for the fact that non-linguistic context is usually incapable of making a property salient comes from Ward (1988), who claims that fronting requires a salient open proposition and argues that the reason fronting cannot be used discourse-initially is that non-linguistic context cannot satisfy that requirement.

(38) [Context: *A* and *B* have been eating cherries; a single cherry remains.]
A to *B*: If you don't, I will.

This seems felicitous. But it is the presence of the explicit alternation between subjects that is crucial to achieving felicity. Replacing *B*'s utterance by *I will* would be highly infelicitous.

Finally, it should be noted that in cases like (38), it appears to be possible to get full NP subjects in exophoric PAE. We believe full NPs are infelicitous in endophoric and exophoric Auxiliary-Choice PAE because the alternative situations p and $\neg p$ (which share the same subject) must be highly salient. When this is true, the referent of the subject will also be highly salient in the context, and that will tend to make reference to it by a pronoun the only felicitous possibility (see Gundel et al. 1993). However, there are contexts in which a non-pronominal subject NP can occur in an exophoric PAE utterance. Suppose a third party, Jane, had been enjoying the above-mentioned cherries but had left the room for a minute, and imagine this:

(38′) *A* to *B*: If you don't, Jane will.

Examples of the type in (38) suggest a variant on (37) which seems to improve simple Subject-Choice *I can*. Imagine a situation where a group of friends come to a stand at a fair where you are supposed to try to knock down an arrangement of cans by throwing a single baseball. In this case, the stereotypical context of a game based on throwing skills seems to make the property of knocking down all the cans more accessible, and it seems marginally possible, though still not very likely, that one of the group might start a conversation saying (39).

(39) I bet I can.

However, imagine that four members of the group have tried the game and none has yet succeeded. The repetition of attempts with an alternation of players appears to have an effect similar to that discussed in (38), and it would seem much more felicitous for a fifth member of the group to utter (39) at that point. The repeated attempts have raised the discourse profile of the property of knocking down all the cans.

3.5 Exophoric PAE as the ellipsis of *do it*

We would now like to compare our analysis of exophoric PAE to what is, to our knowledge, the most extensive discussion of the phenomenon in the literature since the 1970s, namely that of Merchant (2004, 718–23). Merchant (2004, 720) makes the following claim:

> In all cases [...] the elided VP is [$_{\text{VP}}$ *do it*]. The meaning of this VP is licensed by the discourse relevance of some action; it need not have a determinate propositional content, if by determinate we mean that the hearer can determine precisely what the speaker had in mind [...] What is linguistically relevant is that actions and participants in those actions can be raised to enough salience to resolve the anaphora involved in the VP expression *do it* (whatever *it* refers to here). Under these conditions, this VP may also be elided, yielding the above examples [i.e. his examples of exophoric PAE — PhM&GKP.]

Merchant (2004, 721) attempts to explain the frequent difference[15] in felicity between the unellipted version with *do it* and the PAE version by suggesting that 'with *do it*, a hearer must accommodate the presupposition associated with the pronoun *it*; in general, this is easily done, and this form of anaphora [...] can be (merely) pragmatically controlled, fairly uniformly across speakers. VP-ellipsis, on the other hand, requires satisfaction of a different presupposition (of e-givenness, on the theory assumed here [...]).'

The idea is thus that PAE must satisfy both the usual constraints on *do it* and a further presupposition of e-givenness, and is thus more constrained. Merchant (2004, 672) defines e-givenness as follows: 'an expression E is e-given iff there is an antecedent A which entails E and which is entailed by E, modulo ∃-type-shifting'.

These proposals raise several problems. First, the essence of the original objection to Schachter (1977) by Hankamer (1978) remains applicable to a certain extent: if the non-linguistic context can provide an appropriate antecedent for *do it*, then it is unclear why this antecedent cannot further serve as the 'A' in Merchant's definition of e-givenness and consequently license PAE in all cases. Second, and more crucially, it completely fails to account for one of the central facts which we have discussed above, namely that in some contexts PAE is far more felicitous than *do it*, both in endophoric and exophoric uses, whereas in others, where the antecedent apparently has the same degree of accessibility, the opposite is true.

Consider the following further examples. In (40a), we exhibit an attested example from the soap opera *As the World Turns*; (40b,c) are invented variants.

(40) a. [Context: Allie and Casey manage to lock Noah and Luke (who have been avoiding each other) together on a roof in a desperate attempt to get them to talk. When they realize that they have been trapped, the following conversation occurs.]

---

[15] It is important to note that he assumes that the variant with *do it* will always be the more felicitous of the two, if there is a difference.

Noah: Please tell me they didn't.
Luke: They did.
(Compare Noah saying: *#Please tell me they didn't do it.*)

b. [Context: similar to case (a) except that there are reasons to believe Alley and Casey might be homophobes.]
Noah: Please tell me they didn't do it because we're gay.
Luke: They did.
(Compare Noah saying *#Please tell me they didn't because we're gay.*)

c. [Context: similar to case (a) except that it's not to get them to talk, it's just a joke Allie and Casey often play on Noah and Luke.]
Noah: Please tell me they didn't do it again.
Luke: They did.
(Compare Noah saying: *#Please tell me they didn't again.*)

It is very hard to see how Merchant's analysis can account for the fact that PAE is so much worse in (40b,c) than in the original (40a). We contend that it is impossible to claim that there is a difference in accessibility of the antecedent between these different cases (if anything, one would expect that the antecedent is more accessible in (40c), where it is an habitual event, than in (40a, b)). Thus, there is no reason to expect that the antecedent is less e-given in one case than another. But it is even harder to see how Merchant's analysis can account for the fact that the variant with *do it* is so much worse than PAE in (40a), since *do it* is supposed to have one less condition on its occurrence than PAE and the very possibility of PAE depends on the prior possibility of *do it*, from which it derives by ellipsis.

On the other hand, the discourse constraints on PAE proposed above in (10) explain the judgments on (40a,b,c) easily. In (40a), the context is one similar to the type discussed in §3.1.4. It is obvious that the participants Allie and Casey have just performed an action (scheming to get Noah and Luke together on the roof and locking them on it). By uttering *they didn't*, Noah chooses one branch of the alternative p or $\neg p$, where p is the event in question, and forces Luke to accomodate the alternative. By uttering the imperative *Tell me they didn't*, Noah further invites Luke to violate Grice's maxim of quality by uttering an obvious untruth ('They didn't lock us on the roof'). This leads to implicatures of the type 'What they did is unbelievable.' In examples (40b,c) on the other hand, there is an adjunct (the non-contrastive *because we're gay* in (40b) and the contrastive *again* in (40c)), and the point of Noah's utterance is no longer strictly limited to choosing one branch of an alternative (see (10a)). Rather, in (40b) the focus of the question is the reason for Allie and Casey's action and in (40c) it is the repetition. As discussed above in §2.1.1, this makes the use of PAE infelicitous and that of *do it* felicitous.

The central flaw in Merchant's analysis is that it makes the choice between *do it* and PAE dependent on the accessibility of the antecedent (thus establishing a parallel with the choice of nominal anaphors as analyzed by e.g. Ariel 1990 and Gundel et al. 1993). Now it is true, as discussed in Miller 2011, that PAE requires a highly salient antecedent. But what should make us immediately suspicious of this idea is that according to theories of accessibility and givenness, *it* requires a highly salient antecedent ('in focus' in the terms of Gundel et al. 1993), as opposed to e.g. *this* and *that* (which require an 'activated' or 'familiar' antecedent in the terms of Gundel et al. 1993), so that there is no reason to expect *do it* to allow antecedents that are other than highly salient (as opposed to *do this* and *do that*), see Miller (2011). Though it may be the case that PAE requires an even higher degree of salience of its antecedent than *do it*, it is highly unlikely that accessibility or salience of the antecedent is the crucial factor in the choice between PAE and *do it*.

To conclude this section, we would like to argue against one further hypothesis about the choice between PAE and *do it/this/that* that might be suggested, namely that more complex anaphoric forms are dispreferred in general due to something like the Gricean maxim of Quantity and that consequently there would be a dispreference for the more complex *do it/this/that* when you could do without the last word. Once again the contrast in acceptability between (40a) and (40b,c), in which a more complex form is obligatory despite the antecedent being at least as accessible, suggests that this idea is untenable.[16]

4 Conclusion

It was an intriguing suggestion by Hankamer & Sag that anaphoric devices come to us partitioned into deep (model-interpretive) anaphora, interpreted via the semantic discourse model built up in the mind of the hearer, and ellipsis, interpreted via access to the syntactic logical form of a sentence. The data that were used to support the suggestion stimulated a great deal of further study and made it appear that exophora and endophora were strikingly distinct. What we have done

[16]This idea is made even less appealing by the evidence in Miller 2011 showing that among (i) PAE, (ii) *do it/this/that*, and (iii) *do so*, it is the third that has the most stringent accessibility requirement, despite its being more syntactically complex than PAE.

here is to relate exophora to endophora more closely,[17] explaining both the uncontroversial existence of exophoric Post-Auxiliary Ellipsis and the reasons for its apparent rarity.

The solution lies in seeing that anaphoric and elliptical devices develop highly specialized discourse functions and conditions. Exophoric uses of ellipsis are not banned by a general constraint from which exceptions can only be granted by idiomatization; but if they are to be resolved in meaning they have to meet the very same discourse conditions that they are required to meet when they are used anaphorically.

For nonlinguistic context to satisfy the conditions in the right way, while by no means impossible, is not easy. Hence the illusion of impossibility that misled Hankamer & Sag.

References

Ariel, Mira. 1990. *Accessing Noun Phrase Antecedents*. London: Routledge.

Baker, Carl L. 1984. Two observations on British English *do*. *Linguistic Inquiry* 15(1):155–157.

Chao, Wynn. 1987. *On Ellipsis*. Outstanding Dissertations in Linguistics. New York: Garland.

Cornish, Francis. 1999. *Anaphora, Discourse, and Understanding: Evidence from French and English*. Oxford: Oxford University Press.

Dalrymple, Mary, Stuart Shieber, and Fernando Pereira. 1991. Ellipsis and higher–order unification. *Linguistics and Philosophy* 14.4:399–452.

Erteschik-Shir, Nomi. 2007. *Information Structure: The Syntax–Discourse Interface*. Oxford: Oxford University Press.

Gazdar, Gerald, Ewan Klein, Geoffrey K. Pullum, and Ivan A. Sag. 1985. *Generalized Phrase Structure Grammar*. Oxford: Basil Blackwell.

Grice, H. P. 1957. Meaning. *The Philosophical Review* 66(3):377–388.

Grosz, Barbara, Aravind Joshi, and Scott Weinstein. 1995. Centering: A framework for modeling the local coherence of discourse. *Computational Linguistics* 21:203–225.

Gundel, Jeanette, Nancy Hedberg, and Ron Zacharski. 1993. Cognitive status and the form of referring expressions in discourse. *Language* 69(2):274—-307.

Gundel, Jeanette, Michael Hegarty, and Kaja Borthen. 2003. Information structure and pronominal reference to clausally introduced entities. *Journal of Logic, Language and Information* 12(3):281–299.

Hankamer, Jorge. 1978. On the nontransformational derivation of some null VP anaphors. *Linguistic Inquiry* 9:66–74.

[17]This goes in the direction of the general position defended by Cornish, following e.g. Bühler and Lyons, according to which there is no clearcut distinction between deixis and anaphora, the latter being dependent on the former (see Cornish 1999, chapter 2 for further discussion and references).

Hankamer, Jorge and Ivan A. Sag. 1976. Deep and surface anaphora. *Linguistic Inquiry* 7:391–426.

Hardt, Daniel. 1993. *Verb Phrase Ellipsis: Form, Meaning, and Processing*. Ph.D. thesis, University of Pennsylvania. Distributed as IRCS Report 93–23.

Houser, Michael John. 2010. *The Syntax and Semantics of Do So Anaphora*. Ph.D. thesis, University of California, Berkeley, Berkeley, CA.

Huddleston, Rodney, Geoffrey K. Pullum, et al. 2002. *The Cambridge Grammar of the English Language*. Cambridge: Cambridge University Press.

Jacobson, Pauline. 2003. Binding without pronouns (and pronouns without binding). In G.-J. M. Kruijff and R. T. Oehrle, eds., *Resource–Sensitivity, Binding and Anaphora*, pages 57–96. Dordrecht: Kluwer.

Jacobson, Pauline. 2008. Direct compositionality and variable–free semantics: The case of antecedent contained deletion. In K. Johnson, ed., *Topics in Ellipsis*, pages 30–68. Cambridge: Cambridge University Press.

Jacobson, Pauline. 2009. Do representations matter or do meanings matter: The case of antecedent containment. In E. Hinrichs and J. Nerbonne, eds., *Theory and Evidence in Semantics*, pages 81–107. Stanford, CA: CSLI Publications.

Johnson, Kyle. 2001. What VP ellipsis can do, and what it can't, but not why. In M. Baltin and C. Collins, eds., *The Handbook of Contemporary Syntactic Theory*, pages 439–479. Cambridge: Blackwell.

Kehler, Andrew. 2000. Coherence and the resolution of ellipsis. *Linguistics and Philosophy* 23:533–575.

Kertz, Laura. 2008. Focus structure and acceptability in verb phrase ellipsis. In N. Abner and J. Bishop, eds., *Proceedings of the 27th West Coast Conference on Formal Linguistics*. Cascadilla Proceedings Project.

Kertz, Laura. 2010. *Ellipsis Reconsidered*. Ph.D. thesis, University of California, San Diego, La Jolla, CA.

Levine, Robert D. 2012. Auxiliaries: *To*'s company. *Journal of Linguistics* 48(1):187–203.

Merchant, Jason. 2004. Fragments and ellipsis. *Linguistics and Philosophy* 27:661–738.

Miller, Philip. 2002. Les emplois non finis de *do* auxiliaire. In C. Delmas, ed., *Construire et reconstruire en linguistique anglaise: syntaxe et sémantique*, pages 185–198. Saint–Etienne: Publications de l'Université de Saint–Etienne.

Miller, Philip. 2011. The choice between verbal anaphors in discourse. In I. Hendrickx, S. L. Devi, A. Branco, and R. Mitkov, eds., *Anaphora Processing and Applications: 8th Discourse Anaphora and Anaphor Resolution Colloquium, DAARC 2011*, vol. 7099 of *Lecture Notes in Artificial Intelligence*, pages 82–95. Berlin: Springer.

Pullum, Geoffrey and Deirdre Wilson. 1977. Autonomous syntax and the analysis of auxiliaries. *Language* 53:741–788.

Pullum, Geoffrey K. 2000. Hankamer was! In S. Chung, J. McCloskey, and N. Sanders, eds., *Jorge Hankamer WebFest*, http://babel.ucsc.edu/Jorge/.

Sag, Ivan A. 1976. *Deletion and Logical Form*. Ph.D. thesis, MIT, Cambridge, MA.

Sag, Ivan A. and Jorge Hankamer. 1984. Towards a theory of anaphoric processing. *Linguistics and Philosophy* 7:325–345.

Schachter, Paul. 1977. Does she or doesn't she? *Linguistic Inquiry* 8:763–767.

Schachter, Paul. 1978. English propredicates. *Linguistic Analysis* 4:187–224.

Ward, Gregory. 1988. *The Semantics and Pragmatics of Preposing*. Outstanding Dissertations in Linguistics. New York: Garland.

Webber, Bonnie. 1979. *A Formal Approach to Discourse Anaphora*. Outstanding Dissertations in Linguistics. New York: Garland.

3

Unification and Computational Linguistics on the West Coast

Annie Zaenen and Lauri Karttunen

In the mid-1980s, the mood among linguists in the Bay Area was optimistic. Non-transformational approaches to syntax had gotten some traction and Stanford saw a concentration of researchers interested in developing these alternatives to the transformational approach to linguistics, which had revealed itself as psychologically implausible and increasingly bizarre from a theoretical perspective. Around this time, CSLI was created by Stanford, while SRI and PARC and got off the ground with a generous grant from the System Development Foundation (SDF). GPSG/HPSG, LFG, and PATR were all developed by researchers that shared the view that syntax and semantics could be modeled using rigorous discrete mathematical and logical methods. The ultimate aim, however, was a model of discourse. Not only linguists, but also philosophers, computational scientists and psychologists were involved. The overall project was Situated Language with Ivan acting as the manager of a subproject on Integrated Syntactic and Semantic Accounts of Discourse.

But to tackle discourse we needed first to get syntax out of the way. How hard could that be, given the conceptual and computational tools we had at our disposal? Ivan not only spearheaded the development of GPSG and later HPSG, he was also the driving force in explaining to the world at large the communality among all these efforts as based on common insights and techniques. The common thread was unification,

The Core and the Periphery.
Philip Hofmeister and Elisabeth Norcliffe (eds.).

a technique first promoted as usable for the analysis of natural languages by Martin Kay in the early 1980s. The main theoretical insight was that linguistic structures could be described through a system of simultaneously satisfied constraints, guaranteeing the monotonicity of the system, and dispensing with the syntactic transformations of the MIT tradition.

How hard could syntax be? Very hard it turned out. While we had heady discussions about how to deploy unification based formalisms, it was the work in the trenches that was brought home that message. There was always a new construction or a new twist or a new lexical meaning adding to the ambiguity of the grammar. After Jane Robinson at SRI, Dan Flickinger (HPSG) and Tracy King (LFG) took the lead in developing broad coverage grammars for various languages that are still being worked on. As a group we learned that the available theoretically motivated linguistic descriptions cover only a small part of what is needed for computational natural language understanding. The weight of specific lexical items and of specific constructions became apparent and theoretical and computational linguistics parted ways again.

Natural Language Processing became a useful, and potentially money making enterprise, by bringing in statistical methods to provide shortcuts where linguistic phenomena are not well understood as probabilistic phrase structure grammars derived from treebanks turned out to be adequate for information extraction tasks. The West Coast version of theoretical linguistics learned from the computational adventure that more careful empirical methods than those used in traditional introspection based syntax and semantics were necessary to make further progress as well as a rethinking of the boundaries between competence and processing.

HPSGers and LFGers both continue to use the computational tools developed in the eighties to provide precise descriptions of may previously unstudied linguistics phenomena in diverse languages. The next contribution by Dan Flickinger and Tom Wasow sketches the path taken by the HPSG branch.

2

A Corpus-driven Analysis of the Do-Be Construction

DAN FLICKINGER AND THOMAS WASOW

1 Introduction

In the early 1980s, Ivan was invited to start a natural language project at Hewlett Packard Labs, just up the hill from the Stanford campus. At the time, with several collaborators, he was developing the theory of Generalized Phrase Structure Grammar (see Gazdar et al. 1985), which seemed particularly well-suited for computational implementation. The linguists on the project (Ivan, Carl Pollard, Geoff Pullum, the two of us, and, later John Nerbonne) worked closely with a team of programmers (whose composition changed considerably over the years) to develop a system that could parse a broad range of English sentences and translate them into appropriate semantic representations. We found the problem of balancing computational efficiency with linguistic generality at once difficult and immensely productive. This interplay of computational and linguistic concerns led to so many modifications of our theoretical framework that, at one point, it was renamed Head-driven Phrase Structure Grammar (HPSG).

Ivan and Carl worked out the theory of HPSG in detail in two books (Pollard and Sag 1987, 1994) and a number of articles. Dan, along with Derek Proudian, led the team that kept improving the implementation's coverage and efficiency. Almost a decade after its start, the HP natural language project was closed down.

In the mid-1990s, Ivan started the LinGO lab at Stanford's Center for the Study of Language and Information (CSLI), initially with fund-

The Core and the Periphery.
Philip Hofmeister and Elisabeth Norcliffe (eds.).

ing from the German Verbmobil project. Dan was hired to oversee the development of a broad-coverage HPSG-based system for both parsing and generation of English. This system, known as the English Resource Grammar or ERG (see Flickinger 2000, 2011), is conceptually a direct descendant of the system built at HP Labs, but was built from scratch, incorporating many advances in theory and technology that have become available over the intervening decades. A number of students and postdoctoral researchers contributed to the development of the ERG over the years, notably (and alphabetically): Tim Baldwin, Emily Bender, Francis Bond, Ann Copestake, Rob Malouf, Stephan Oepen, and Susanne Riehemann.

In order to test the performance of the ERG, Dan periodically runs corpora through it. After years of development, the grammar now provides complete coverage of about 90% of the sentences in such corpora as the English Wikipedia and the Wall Street Journal, and is usually missing analyses for only one or two phrases within the sentences it cannot fully parse. Seeing what kind of sentences it fails to provide reasonable parses and semantic representations for provides both a metric of progress in the development of the system and pointers to where work is needed. Over the years, people affiliated with the LinGO project have met frequently (sometimes on a weekly basis, sometimes less regularly) to discuss how to deal with types of examples that the ERG was having trouble analyzing. This paper arose out of one of these meetings.

2 The *Do-Be* Construction

One relatively common type of sentence that the ERG was not successfully analyzing is exemplified in (1).[1]

(1) a. what you have to do is get ready
    b. all the government does is send out checks
    c. the thing I'm doing is trying to learn from my mistakes
    d. the best one can do is compare one risk to the next
    e. the least we should do is make it as much fun as possible

These are examples of what we will refer to as the do-be construction or DBC. The salient characteristics of DBC are the following:

[1]Except where noted, examples are taken from the Corpus of Contemporary American English (http://corpus.byu.edu/coca/). We have edited many of the examples, to remove material irrelevant to the point we are making. Since some of the removed material originally preceded or followed what we present, we give our corpus examples without initial capitalization or final punctuation. Invented examples are capitalized and have final punctuation.

A. One of seven specific words (*what, all, thing(s), best, least, most,* and *worst*) appears near the beginning of the subject.
B. The subject contains a subordinate clause (a relative clause or possibly an embedded question) with a gap in it.
C. Embedded in the clause within the subject is some form of the verb *do*.
D. The main verb of DBC is a copula.
E. The copula is followed by a verb phrase.
F. The verb heading the post-copula VP is interpreted as having the same subject as the occurrence of *do* mentioned in C above.
G. The form of the verb heading the post-copula VP depends on the form of *do*.
H. The copula expresses identity; that is, the post-copula VP and the subject have the same denotation.

We will elaborate on each of these properties in §4 below. Corpus searches revealed that not all of them are categorical constraints. In particular, we found some possible counterexamples to A and C. Some types of counterexamples are exceedingly infrequent and of arguable acceptability, so it seems reasonable to treat them as ungrammatical (perhaps performance errors). Others that are more common and less marginal might be instances of other, related constructions. We will deal with specific cases in our discussion of the properties.

The reader may wonder at this point why anyone not engaged in building a broad-coverage English language system should have any interest in a detailed examination of this particular type of sentence. We have three answers, one methodological, one theoretical, and one concerning the role of grammar in computational linguistics.

The first examples of DBC to attract our attention started with the word *what*. A bit of discussion led us to realize that the properties that made these *what* sentences hard to analyze were shared by examples starting with *all* or *the thing*. But it wasn't until we began examining corpus data that we realized that there were four other words that could be used in place of *thing*. This was just the first of many incorrect generalizations we arrived at about DBC on the basis of introspection about invented examples. For example, we believed at one time that the post-copula VP had to be in base form; but we were wrong. And introspection convinced us that the gap in the clause within the subject could not be the subject of that clause (that is, that the subject had to contain a non-subject relative clause), until we came across some counterexamples[2] in the data from the Corpus of Contemporary American

[2] See (8) below for two of them.

English (COCA). Corpus searches repeatedly revealed to us that the constraints on DBC are more intricate than we had earlier thought.

The lesson we draw from this is that, whenever possible, linguists should supplement their introspective and experimental data with naturally occurring usage data. We hasten to add that we are not arguing for exclusive reliance on corpora. Quite the contrary, it should be obvious that every type of linguistic data has its pros and cons. The best-supported theories are those that receive support from a variety of types of evidence.

The second conclusion we draw from our investigation of DBC is that the theory of grammar needs to have mechanisms for expressing the intricate complexes of constraints that define phenomena like DBC. In particular, mechanisms are needed for expressing properties that distinguish DBC from other sentence types, and the ways in which DBC are similar to other sentence types. Further, we identify several subtypes of DBC; a grammar of English must allow expression of the features that distinguish the subtypes, as well as their commonalities. In §6 below, we demonstrate how a constraint-based grammar incorporating a lexical inheritance hierarchy can both capture the generalizations and make the distinctions that we note.

The analysis we present is formalized within the system currently implemented in the ERG. It is possible that a still higher level of generality could be achieved in a theory incorporating a formal notion of construction in the sense of Fillmore, Kay and O'Connor (1988), as long as it also included a type hierarchy allowing the expression of both overlaps and distinctions among construction types, as a means of minimizing redundancy while maintaining descriptive adequacy. The theory of Sign-Based Construction Grammar (SBCG) developed by Ivan Sag and collaborators (Sag 2010; Boas and Sag 2012; Sag 2012) is just such a theory.

The third lesson we draw from our investigation of DBC is that grammar has a place in large-scale natural language processing systems. The intuitions that motivate A-H above are quite robust, and receive strong support from our corpus data. They exemplify the kind of interconnected morphological, syntactic, and semantic properties that languages have conventionalized. We doubt that a purely data-driven system, relying solely on co-occurrence statistics in corpora, could deal with the range of DBC examples our analysis handles, without simultaneously accepting many superficially similar strings that are not, in fact, well-formed English sentences. While we make no attempt to demonstrate that DBC requires a grammar, we hope our discussion puts the burden of proof on those who think grammar is unnecessary.

3 Our Data

We extracted examples of DBC from the Corpus of Contemporary American English (COCA), a 425-million word web-based database, with a suite of user-friendly search tools, compiled by Mark Davies. COCA is tagged for part of speech, but not parsed.

Our basic search pattern was: [vd*] [vb*] [v*], which, in the notation of COCA, means a sequence consisting of any form of the verb *do*, immediately followed by any form of the verb *be*, immediately followed by any form of any verb. This pattern produced 9914 hits. COCA displays the hits by the exact word string matching the search pattern, listing the number of hits for that string; we downloaded all strings with at least two hits. This gave us a collection of 7100 examples. These were culled and coded by Rebecca Greene.[3]

6471 of these 7100 examples (91%) are at least arguably instances of DBC – a surprisingly high success rate, given the simplicity of our search pattern. A few dozen of these are questionable, either in terms of well-formedness or in terms of their status as instances of DBC. These 6471 serve as the primary database for our discussion below. In addition, we conducted searches with *to* between [vb*] (the copula) and [v*] (the post-copula verb), with adverbs between each of the adjacent pairs of verbs in our pattern, and with two-word prepositional phrases between [vd*] (*do*) and [vb*]. These searches yielded a few thousand more hits, but we did not study them systematically. We do, however, make use of some examples taken from these additional searches below.[4]

[3]Specifically, she coded for: whether the subordinate clause in the subject is introduced by *that*, what form of *do* appears in that clause, and what the form of the main verb of the post-copula VP is. She also noted any properties of individual examples that she thought might be of interest.

[4]Two other searches, which we will not discuss in detail, involved looking at the frequency of DBC broken down by genre, and by history. The genre breakdown revealed that DBC is used predominantly in speech (though with *all* it is also used frequently in fiction), supporting our intuition that DBC is a relatively informal construction. The historical breakdown (based on the Corpus of Historical American English, http://corpus.byu.edu/coha/, a 400-million word corpus of sources from 1810 to 2009) showed that DBC first started appearing around 1820 or 1830, remained quite infrequent for a century, and then gained frequency for the following half century, before leveling off. This pattern is nearly identical across the three main subtypes of DBC, namely, those with *what*, those with *all*, and those with *thing*. This provides some support for our claim that the three types constitute a single construction.

4 Characteristics of the *Do-Be* Construction

4.1 Seven Words

In the vast majority of our DBC examples, the head of the subject is one of the three words *what, all*, or *thing(s)*. The clear exceptions to this generalization are of two types: cases in which other words appear in place of these three, and cases in which the word in question is not the syntactic head of the subject. Cases of the latter type are exemplified in (2).

(2) a. one of the first things John and Glenn do is take a look around the city
 b. a big part of what we do is give them the wind field on the entire storm

But in these and all other cases of this kind, what precedes the word in question serves to quantify or partition the noun phrase headed by that word. This is true even in cases like (2a), in which the singular form of the copula indicates that *one*, not *things*, is the syntactic head of the subject. Arguably, then, *what* and *thing* can be regarded as the semantic heads of the subject NPs in which they appear.[5]

As noted earlier, there are four other words that occur as the head of the subject: *best, least, most*, and *worst*. These are quite rare, accounting for only 131 of the examples in our database: 64 with *least*, 57 with *best*, 6 with *most*, and 4 with *worst*. These examples seem somewhat formulaic: the word in question is never preceded by anything but *the* and (occasionally) *very*, and the following relative clause almost always contains a modal, usually *can* or *could*. We will have little to say about examples with one of these four words as head of the subject, because we believe that they behave very much like those with *thing*.

The fact that it is just these seven words that have to appear in the head of the subject of DBC examples is no doubt in part due to the semantics and pragmatics of the construction. Following a reviewer suggestion, we checked COCA to see what nouns most frequently head objects of the verb *do*. We found that *thing* is by far the most frequent, with *business, research, work, job, harm*, and *damage* all occurring at least 400 times as the head noun of the object of some form of *do*. We then searched for strings where one of these nouns heads the subject of a sentence that otherwise looks like an instance of DBC. We found only two:

(3) a. the only business I did was to talk to the secretary of the Treasury

[5] Our data contain no such examples with *all*.

b. part of the work we do is to raise the public's awareness of women farmworkers' realities

It appears from the rarity of such examples that the very restricted set of nouns that appears as the head of the subject in DBC examples is in part conventionalized – a fact about English that must be learned. Notice that substituting some other word – even a near synonym or, in the case of *thing*, another semantically light noun, usually leads to unacceptability.[6]

(4) a. what/*whatever I do is give everyone a fair chance
b. now what/*how we do is follow the other approach
c. all/*everything a person tries to do is survive
d. all/*the sum total you've got to do is bury your partner
e. the first thing/*act he does is put his arm around Larry
f. one thing/*step we don't want to do is reduce the size of the force

4.2 The Subordinate Clause

We will treat the subordinate clause in the subject of DBC uniformly as a relative clause (RC). Faraci (1970) and others have argued that the examples starting with *what* are embedded questions, but Akmajian (1979) and others have argued that they are relative clauses. Without going into the arguments on the two sides of this debate (see den Dikken 2001 for a summary), we will adopt the RC analysis because the subordinate clauses in the other types of DBC (that is, those with *all, thing*, etc.) are clearly RCs.

Although relative clauses are normally optional modifiers, the RC in DBC is obligatory, as shown in (5), where the asterisk outside the

[6]The following six examples from our database are prima facie counterexamples to this claim:
(i) everything he's doing is trying to help somebody else
(ii) part of this procedure that we're doing is making sure that we don't go near those pressure barriers
(iii) the only compliance work he's doing is making sure my lunch is still hot when it gets here
(iv) part of the work that I do is going to different hospitals in Denver
(v) the only way we could do is hit them with the pipeline of money going to all these organizations
(vi) the third occupation that I want to do is be an aeronautical engineer
However, (i)-(iv) all contain post-copula phrases that could be analyzed as gerundive NPs, and hence not instances of DBC. (v) and (vi) strike us as unacceptable. All six of these examples come from spoken data, and hence could well be speech errors. Since their status as counterexamples is questionable and they constitute less than 0.1% of our database, we feel comfortable with our claim that DBC sentences require one of the seven words we cite.

parentheses means that the sentence is unacceptable without the parenthetical material.

(5) a. all *(you have to do) is follow the road
    b. the best *(you can do) is observe
    c. the first thing ?*(we do) is make up a new name
    d. what *(I think that I do) is write an adventure novel

The RC is usually finite, but with *thing* as the head, it may be infinitival:

(6) the smart thing to do was leave her there

Such cases are relatively rare; only 93 of our 1119 examples with *thing* have infinitival RCs. In these cases, the understood subject of *do* is contextually determined, unless the infinitival relative is a *for-to* clause:

(7) the best thing for you to do is learn how to be patient

When the RC is finite, the gap is almost always something other than the subject of the RC. Only five cases of RCs with a subject gap occur in our database (three of them beginning *all that was left to do*), though it is our impression that they are more common among examples in which the post-copula VP is infinitival (that is, begins with *to*).

(8) a. all that was left to do was get the teams lined up
    b. what needs to be done is simply achieve literacy

Among the finite RCs with non-subject gaps, the occurrence of a relativizer *that* is extremely rare: our database contains only 106 examples. When the subject is headed by *what*, it is categorically impossible to have *that* as a relativizer:

(9) what (*that) the Judiciary committee did was say, no

This is not surprising, since neither free relatives nor embedded questions ever take *that* as a relativizer or complementizer. But even if we exclude *what*-DBC cases, *that* occurs as a relativizer in less than 3% of our examples. By comparison, 43% of the non-subject RCs in the Switchboard corpus have *that* as a relativizer (see Wasow et al. 2011).

We believe that the rarity of *that* relativizers in DBC is related to the obligatoriness of the RC. Wasow et al. (2011) argue that the relativizer *that* occurs at a lower rate when the RC it introduces is more predictable (see also Jaeger 2006 for a more thorough corpus study). This observation can be explained in functional terms: a uniform rate of information transfer enhances communicative efficiency (Levy and Jaeger 2007; Jaeger 2010, 2011). Since the RC in the subject of DBC is obligatory, it is highly predictable, so including *that* would usually lead to a trough in information density. Thus, the low rate of *that* in these examples supports Wasow and Jaeger's earlier work, as well as the theory of uniform information density.

4.3 The Verb *do*

The examples that got us started on our investigation of DBC all contained forms of the verb *do*, and *do* appears in our search pattern for finding instances of the construction. The results of our searches using that pattern consequently all contained instances of the verb *do* within the RC in the subject. We initially tested for the obligatoriness of *do* in the construction by substituting other verbs in selected examples from our corpus searches and consulting our own intuitions about them. This led us to conclude that a form of *do* was indeed obligatory. It seemed to us that no other verb could be substituted – not even another semantically light verb or one identical to the verb following the copula.

(10) a. what we do/*make is create Frankensteins
   b. the first thing we do/?*try is make up a new name
   c. all they did/*took was take a daily walk
   d. the least you could do/*be is be a little grateful

However, a corpus search substituting other verbs in the search pattern revealed that the situation is not so straightforward. We conducted searches replacing *do* in the original pattern with *make, try, take*, and *be*. In all cases, the number of hits was vastly smaller than with *do* (by at least an order of magnitude), and most of them differed in many other ways from our DBC examples.

For instance, when the verb *make* was substituted in the search pattern, the subject in almost all of the examples was headed by a noun (like *mistake, adjustment*, or *decision*) that occurs often in collocation with *make*, and almost all of the post-copula VPs were headed by *-ing* forms or infinitives. Similarly, when the verb was *take*, the subjects were headed by nouns like *step, risk*, and *action*; and, again, the post-copula VPs were mostly headed by *-ing* forms or infinitives. Typical examples are given in (11).

(11) a. the biggest mistake she made was doing this in Columbus, Ohio, instead of Aruba
   b. the best decision I could make is to go back and finish my education
   c. The biggest risk I've ever taken is going on American Idol and trying to be myself
   d. the first step we must take is to improve our knowledge of the subject

Substituting *try* in the search pattern resulted in only a handful of hits similar to DBC, again with *-ing* forms or infinitives heading the post-copula VP.

Substituting *be* for *do* in our search pattern yielded more hits, but the vast majority of these are cases where the main copula is predicative (e.g. *what the alternative might be is known only to the eye of faith*), the post-copula phrase is arguably adjectival (*all I wanted to be is loved*), or examples we feel comfortable treating as ungrammatical speech or transcription errors (e.g. **what we are is are looking at a new electorate*).

The examples with post-copula VPs headed by *-ing* forms or infinitives, while still far rarer when the subject lacks an occurrence of *do*, are too numerous to ignore. Although we do not have a definitive analysis of such cases, we think it is no coincidence that these are the only two forms that may head a VP functioning as the subject of a clause:

(12) a. Going on American Idol made me famous.
b. To improve our knowledge of the subject would help us understand the problem.
c. *Went on American Idol made me famous.
d. *Improve our knowledge of the subject would help us understand the problem.

Arguably, then, VPs headed by these two verb forms may be treated like noun phrases in certain contexts, including the position following a copula expressing identity. If so, these apparent counterexamples to the claim that *do* is obligatory in the subject of the DBC might be instances of another related construction. We leave this as an open question for now.

Our searches for instances of DBC with other verbs substituting for *do* turned up a very small number of additional potential counterexamples:

(13) a. all it takes is run my finger down the page
b. what I think the process should be is withdraw, as you pointed out, one piece of it
c. what you don't want to be is be part of that conducting line from the line down to the ground
d. what we think the right process should be is let the Congress set the priority

Given the rarity and (in our opinion) marginality of these examples, we will tentatively stick with our claim that some form of *do* is obligatory in DBC. In our concluding section, we return to the issue of the status of strong statistical generalizations that are not categorical.

The *do* in the subject of DBC sentences is not the auxiliary *do*, as evidenced by examples like the following:

(14) a. the only thing that the yellow bulb didn't *(do) was keep the bugs away
b. what it does do is give him more energy

The obligatory occurrence of *do* may be deeply embedded within the relative clause.

(15) a. all she had ever meant to do was make her mother proud of her
b. one thing I never have trouble getting her to do is eat
c. what I'm really working to try to do is get people past the pro- and anti-war arguments

Although *do* is rarely embedded more than one or two levels down in our corpus data, it is not hard to construct acceptable sentences in which it is more deeply embedded:

(16) What I instructed you to tell Pat to ask Sandy to try to be sure to do was get to the meeting on time.

We conclude that *do* may be arbitrarily deeply embedded in the RC. However, the intervening clauses and verb phrases must be complements. It is not acceptable for *do* to be buried somewhere in an adjunct:

(17) *What I will sleep until you do is wake me up.

In most cases, *do* is the last word of the subject, but modifiers are possible between *do* and the copula that serves as the main verb of DBC.

(18) a. what I suggest we do instead is put on our wigs
b. all he wanted to do in July was make the team
c. the most interesting thing we do in bed is eat cereal

The material intervening between *do* and *be* can be arbitrarily long, as is easily seen by adding more modifiers in (18c) – e.g. *The most interesting thing we do in bed on summer mornings when we have enough time and don't have to worry about cleaning up is eat cereal.*

The obligatory *do* in the subject RC can be in any of its inflectional forms: present, past, base, infinitive, present participle, past participle, or passive participle.

(19) a. what this bill **does** is allow you to sue your employer
b. all I **did** was sit around

c. the least we should **do** is make it as much fun as possible
d. the last thing she wants to **do** is get up early and make the call
e. all this is **doing** is helping parents raise their kids
f. what he has **done** is set his case in writing
g. what has to be **done** is to ask the health industry to sacrifice

4.4 The Copula

The copula in DBC is usually finite, but it may be preceded by auxiliary verbs that impose another form on it.

(20) a. the best thing to do would be bring in the bloodhounds
b. what Pat Buchanan has done has been complain about George Bush

Again, no synonym or near synonym can be substituted.

(21) a. what I do is/*equals set out the seven steps for thinking it through
b. the thing you always have to do is/*constitutes prove to people you belong there

We confirmed this through a corpus search in which we replaced the copula in the search pattern by an arbitrary verb.

The crucial property of the DBC copula is that it expresses identity. This is what Akmajian (1979) and others have called the specificational interpretation of the copula, and still others have called equative. This is to be distinguished from the predicational use of *be*. Sentences that look superficially very similar can differ with respect to which of these interpretations of the copula makes sense, as in (22).

(22) a. what we really need to be doing is building up the regular army
b. What we really need to be doing is being discussed in the Pentagon.

Some examples are ambiguous between the two interpretations:

(23) The thing we have been doing is keeping the police chief awake at night.

The properties of DBC we have enumerated hold only of sentences with this identity interpretation of the copula. For example, in (23), *thing* can be replaced by *dance* and *doing* can be replaced by *planning*, but only if *keeping the police chief awake at night* is predicated of the subject NP, not if it is equated with it.

4.5 The Post-Copula VP

Almost all of the examples in our database have non-finite VPs following the copula; that is, the head verb is in base, infinitive, present participle, or past participle form. We did, however, find eleven examples in which the verb is finite, two of which are given in (24).

(24) a. the first thing I did was went to the public library
b. what it does is takes the candidate off the ballot

Although such examples are exceedingly rare and arguably less than fully acceptable, we see no compelling reason to rule them out, so we treat them as grammatical.

If the form of *do* in the subject is a present participle, then the verb heading the post-copula VP must be a present participle (and conversely). If *do* is any other form, the head of the VP may be in base form, infinitive form, or the same form as *do*. This is illustrated in (25).

(25) a. all he's doing is talking about sport
b. *All he's doing is (to) talk about sport.
c. what Microsoft does is make the computing experience easier
d. What Microsoft does is makes/to make/*made/*making the computing experience easier.
e. the first thing he did was take the players' names off the backs of the jerseys
f. The first thing he did was took/to take/*takes/*taken/*taking the players' names off the backs of the jerseys.
g. what they have done is take it on an interim basis
h. What they have done is taken/to take/*took/*taking it on an interim basis.

The understood subject of the post-copula VP is the same as the subject of *do*. This is evident from the interpretation of DBC examples, and is also demonstrated by bound anaphors, when they are in the VP.

(26) a. the first thing people did was bless themselves
b. what Steve and Marlene have to do is eliminate themselves
c. all they do is tell each other how great they are
d. all we could do is make our way down through the cedar trees

Despite the intuition that the verb *do* is in some sense standing in for the post-copula VP, that VP may express a stative predicate, as exemplified by the line from an old Bob Dylan song, *All I really want to do is, baby, be friends with you.* (27) gives more examples from COCA.

(27) a. what I think we would all like to be able to do is know that the energy choices we're making as a nation are good for the environment
b. the smarter thing to do is realize that blueberries have a nice taste
c. all it has to do is be attached
d. all you will do is be sick until you go home
e. the best Smits can do is be tall, and at 7'4" he's got that covered

Interestingly, the post-copula VP may contain negative polarity items (NPIs) if *do* in the subject is in an environment where NPIs are licensed, as (28) shows.

(28) a. what we don't do is add any taxes
b. the only thing he won't do is serve you dinner on anything resembling disposable paper.
c. what he can't do is invade his neighbors anymore
d. another thing she does not have to do is decide any cases of real significance
e. what they were unable to do was provide any connection

In similar-looking sentences with a predicative interpretation of the post-copula VP, no such licensing is possible:

(29) *What we aren't doing is upsetting to anyone.

Similar contrasts have been known for many years. The examples in (30) are from den Dikken (2005), who cites Ross (1972), Akmajian (1970), and Halvorsen (1978) in this connection.

(30) a. What I have never noticed is any sign of dissatisfaction.
b. *What I never noticed was noticed by any of us.

We assume that NPI licensing is determined by the semantics (see Ladusaw 1979, *inter alia*), so that the facts in (28) will not need any special stipulations, if the semantics of DBC is correctly analyzed.

4.6 Inversion

Another interesting property of DBC that we discovered when we examined our corpus data is that many of DBC examples cannot naturally be converted into yes-no questions through inversion of the copula. For example, inverting the examples in (1) yields (31).

(31) a. ?*Is what you have to do get ready?
b. *Is all the government does send out checks?

c. ?*Is the thing I'm doing trying to learn from my mistakes?
d. *Is the best one can do compare one risk to the next?
e. *Is the least we should do make it as much fun as possible?

In our corpus data, we found two examples in which speakers tried to invert DBC sentences but produced ungrammatical results – in one case by doubling *is*, and in the other by using *is* where the copula should have been *be*.

(32) a. *is what you do is take the other guy's best issue
b. *wouldn't all they need to do is shut off your power

The analysis we have implemented in the ERG does not allow the copula in DBC to be inverted. It seems plausible, however, that what makes examples like (31) sound so bad is a processing fact, not a grammatical one[7]. This assumption receives some support from the fact that inversion becomes more acceptable if the post-copula VP is introduced by *to*, as in *Wouldn't all they need to do be to shut off your power?*.

5 Ross's Proposal

Ross (2000, 2008), following earlier suggestions[8], proposes that pseudoclefts be derived via a deletion rule from sentences which underlyingly have a full clause following the copula. For example, under such an analysis, (33a) would be derived from (33b) via deletion of the second occurrence of *we need to*.

(33) a. what we need to do is invest in our future
b. What we need to do is we need to invest in our future.

Ross makes no attempt to state the relevant deletion rule precisely, nor does he say what its domain of applicability is. Thus, we can only conjecture whether he would advocate a similar treatment of the other subtypes of DBC. Still, this approach has several appealing features.

Perhaps the most attractive property of the deletion analysis is that the type of structure it posits as the source of pseudoclefts does in fact occur with some frequency, at least in speech. Moreover, the subject-sharing between *do* and the post-copula VP automatically follows from

[7]Of course, saying that (31) and (32) are due to processing problems would not constitute an analysis. As Mary Dalrymple (p.c.) has pointed out to us, any processing account would have to explain why sentences with predicational uses of the copula sound so much better when inverted:
(i) ?*Is what the White House is doing trying to go on offense?
(ii) Is what the White House is doing causing Congress to worry?

[8]Akmajian (1970) cites an unpublished 1968 paper by Bach and Peters as the source of the idea.

this analysis, as does the possibility of licensing negative polarity items in the VP with negation (or another licenser) in the subject RC.

The form dependencies between VP and *do* are a bit trickier to handle under Ross's analysis. Ross assumes that the verbal morphology is added to verbs via a transformation (affix-hopping of some sort), which may apply either before or after the deletion transformation. But this would not cover the biconditional dependency with present participles. That is, it would not be able to rule out (34a) without similarly ruling out (34b).

(34) a. *What we were doing was keep his organs alive.
b. what he had done was find a way to alter the cellular process

Moreover, it is by no means clear how the deletion rule would be restricted to examples with one of our seven words in the subject and *do* in the subject RC, when the post-copula constituent is a VP. That is, the deletion rule would have to be constrained to avoid the generation of examples like (35), repeated from (3) and (10) above.

(35) a. *The sum total you've got to do is bury your partner.
b. *The first act he does is put his arm around Larry.
c. *What we make is create Frankensteins.
d. ?*The first thing we try is make up a new name.

In short, while a few of our observations about the constraints on DBC are automatic consequences of the deletion analysis, others would remain unaccounted for.

In any event, a deletion analysis is not an option for us, since the ERG has no deletion mechanism. So we will not consider it further.

6 Analysis and Implementation

We have implemented one analysis of this construction, extending the ERG, the existing broad-coverage HPSG-based computational system cited above. Our analysis establishes a semantic dependency between a construction-specific verb *do* within the subject NP of a clause and a construction-specific verb *be* which has this NP as its subject. In addition to the new lexical entries for these two verbs, we define entries for the small class of nouns that can serve as the head of the subject NP, organized as a small type hierarchy to capture the commonalities among these seven words. With these entries in place, the existing standard inventory of feature principles and syntactic rules in the ERG will suffice to characterize the range of idiosyncratic constraints on grammaticality we have identified for this construction.

6.1 Lexical Entries

The lexical entry for this construction-specific verb *do* is unusual in that its single NP complement is obligatorily extracted, establishing one end of an unbounded syntactic dependency. Similar lexically licensed gaps are also found in the entries for adjectives such as *easy*, which select for an infinitival complement with an obligatory NP gap: *This problem is easy to solve.* The standard principles which account for the propagation of ordinary gaps (Lexical Slash Amalgamation and Head Feature Principles) ensure this NP gap will still be visible at the top of the relative clause which is sister to the head noun of the subject NP.

The feature structure for the lexical entry for the DBC *do* is shown in Figure 1, following the HPSG formalism of Pollard and Sag (1994, Ch. 9), where signs include constraints on both syntactic and semantic (SYNSEM, here SSM) properties, grouped into LOC(al) and NONLOC(al) features, the latter expressing constraints on long-distance dependencies such as in filler-gap phrases, wh-questions, and relative clauses. The local syntactic properties of a sign are grouped in the feature CAT(egory) and the semantic ones in CONT(ent), with the CAT features including both HEAD and VAL(ence) features. These groupings enable simple expression of general feature principles governing the propagation of constraints within phrases. Note that the valence features SUBJ(ect), COMP(lement)S, and SP(ecifie)R are (possibly empty) lists whose elements express the subcategorization requirements of the sign, with each element of these lists being again a *synsem* constraining both the syntax and semantics of these dependents. Modification in HPSG is treated as a dependency where the modifier constrains what it will modify, via the MOD attribute (here treated as a HEAD feature), whose value is again a *synsem* list, typically either empty or singleton.

The entry for *do* in Figure 1, then, expresses (i) the requirement for an ordinary subject NP: the value of the valence feature SUBJ, a singleton list whose HEAD value is *noun* and whose SPR feature is saturated (an empty list); (ii) no overt complements: an empty list as the value of COMPS; and (iii) an unusual lexically-introduced non-local dependency: a singleton list value for the SLASH feature, requiring a nominal phrase of a particular kind to be satisfied by a SLASH-discharging construction elsewhere in the clause containing this verb. The semantic index of this nominal phrase gap (the value of the feature IND) is constrained to have the idiosyncratic SORT value *do-event*, discussed below. Since the relative clause containing this verb *do* is obligatory in DBC, we cannot analyze it as a modifier of the head noun (assuming with Pollard & Sag that modification is by definition optional), so the small class of nouns

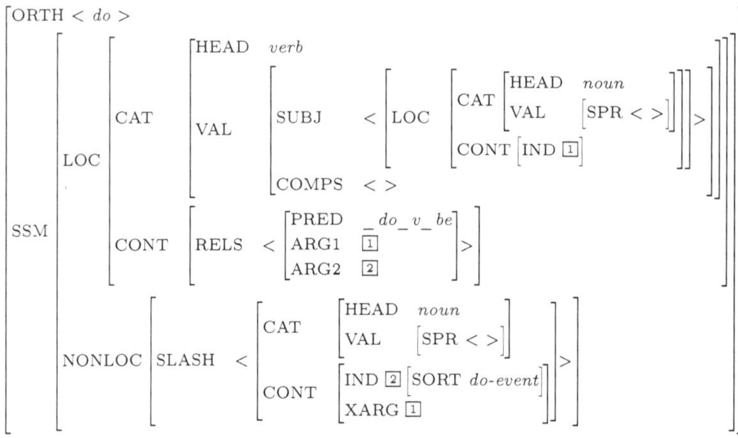

FIGURE 1 Feature structure for DBC verb *do*

that can head the subject NP is defined to instead select the relative clause as an obligatory complement. The head noun preserves the necessary information provided by the gap as part of the noun's semantic index, and propagates it to the top of the subject NP via the standard principles of semantic composition, so this information is visible when the full NP is combined as the subject of the *be* VP.

The seven lexical entries that can serve as the head of the subject NP in DBC have some properties in common, but also exhibit idiosyncrasies, which we express in a small hierarchy of lexical types, described in a following section. They all select for an obligatory complement which has the form of a relative clause, and they all preserve three pieces of information provided by the gap within the relative clause: the semantic index of the gap itself, the semantic index of the syntactic subject of the verb *do* within the relative clause, and (most surprisingly) the inflectional form of the verb *do*. These head nouns differ in whether the relative clause can be infinitival or finite, and whether a relative pronoun is possible, so appropriate subtypes of this noun class are defined that capture these differences.

We show in Figure 2 the feature structure of the lexical entry for one of these head nouns, *thing*. Note that this entry selects for an obligatory clausal complement (verbal head and saturated valence lists), which is a relative clause (non-empty MOD value) constrained to modify a noun with the DBC-specific SORT value *do-event*. The only such clauses admitted by the grammar are those which contain the lexical entry for the verb *do* shown above. The entry for *thing* also identifies its own

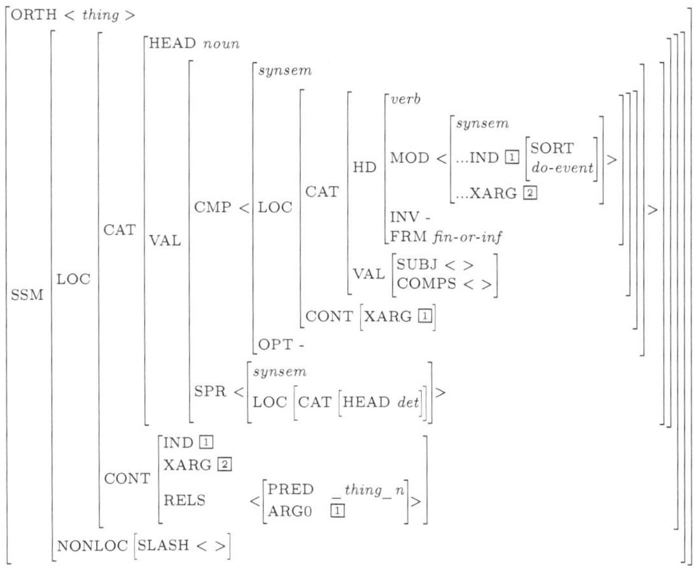

FIGURE 2 Feature structure for DBC noun *thing*

semantic XARG (external argument – its subject) value with that of its relative clause complement. It is via this identity that the relevant constraints are linked between internal properties of the relative clause: the semantic index of the subject of *do* in the relative clause, and the inflectional form of *do*.

The lexical entry for the DBC verb *be*, whose feature structure is shown in Figure 3, is unusual in at least two respects: (i) it requires a subject NP which is headed by one of the small class of seven permissible nouns (ensured by the SORT value of the subject's semantic index), and (ii) it requires a complement VP whose inflectional form and controlled semantic argument are both constrained by properties of that subject NP (via the XARG value of the subject NP, and the IFORM value of its index). However, the complement VP does not itself contain any construction-specific elements; it must only conform to the constraints imposed by the other elements of the construction.

Beyond the construction-specific lexical entries for *do*, *be*, and the seven head nouns, we added to the grammar's type hierarchy a new type of semantic index for the gapped NP, one which includes the surprising attribute IFORM which records the inflectional form of the governing verb *do*. The value of this attribute can thus be propagated using standard feature principles up through the relative clause and then further

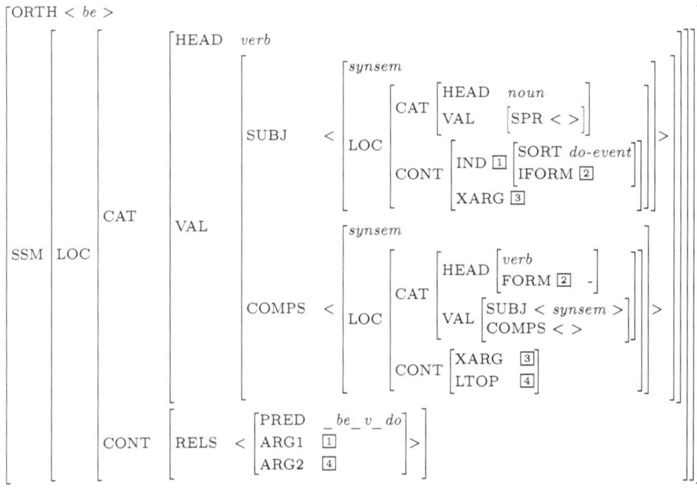

FIGURE 3 Feature structure for DBC verb *be*

to the full subject NP, so it is available to appropriately constrain the inflectional form of the VP complement of the verb *be*.

6.2 An Example

In Figure 4 we show a phrase structure tree summarizing the syntactic structure assigned by the ERG to an example sentence containing this construction. In this analysis the V/NP node above *did* indicates the NP gap lexically introduced by this *did* (via its non-empty SLASH value), a gap propagated on the dominating VP/NP and S/NP nodes via the Head Feature Principle. The verb *did* also records its own subject index as the external argument (XARG) value of the gap's semantics, so this index will be preserved up through the subject NP, to remain accessible to the verb *be*, as elaborated below. The unary rule with the S/NP as its daughter is the normal rule for *that*-less relative clauses, where the semantic properties of the NP gap in the daughter (the INDEX and the XARG values) are identified with those in the MOD value on the mother, and then unified with those of the head noun which is sister to the relative clause.

The head noun *thing* which selects this relative clause *he did* as a complement thus identifies its own INDEX and XARG values with those of the gap (the missing direct object of *did*); these values are then preserved as the noun is combined with the adjective *first* and the determiner *the*, since the modifier-head rule and the specifier-head rule both identify the mother's INDEX and XARG values with those of their

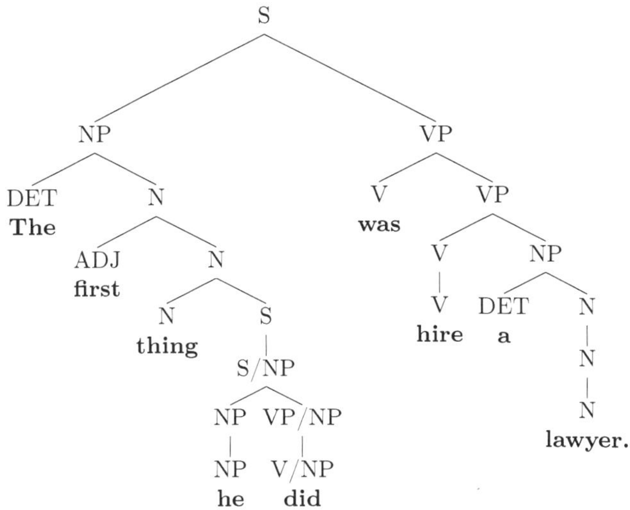

FIGURE 4 Syntactic structure for sentence exemplifying DBC

syntactic head daughter. As a result of the interactions among the new lexical entries for *thing* and *do*, and the standard feature principles and syntactic constructions already present in the grammar, the subject NP *The first thing he did* has as its INDEX value the newly added semantic type which includes an attribute recording the inflectional form of *did*, and this subject NP also has as its XARG value the index of the subject of *did*.

The lexical entry for *was* here introduces a two-place semantic relation denoting something like identity, where the value of the first argument in the relation is identified with the subject's INDEX value, that of *thing*, and the second argument of the relation is identified with the INDEX of the VP complement of *was*. The entry for *was* also identifies the XARG value of its subject with that of its VP complement, so the semantic index of *he* is constrained to also be the subject index of *hire a lawyer*, as desired. Finally, the inflectional form of *did* (finite) is visible to *was*, since it is stored as a property of the index of the subject NP, so it can be used by *was* to constrain the inflectional form of the head of the complement VP of *was*, here the base form *hire* which is typical when the form of *do* is anything other than a present participle, as noted above.

6.3 Some further details of the analysis

The other possible head nouns in DBC have corresponding lexical entries, sharing some properties with the entry for *thing* (and the closely related but separate entry for *something*), but they impose additional restrictions on their dependents, including the complement relative clause. All of these others require the relative clause to be finite, with the relative pronoun *that* optional except with *what*, where it is not possible. The entries for the superlatives *best, worst, most*, and *least* share with *thing* the selection for a determiner as their specifier, but unlike *thing*, they do not permit adjectival modification.

In order to avoid spurious ambiguity that would result from the two distinct analyses of an NP such as *the first thing that he did* (one with the ordinary entries for *thing* and *do*, and one with the DBC-specific entries), all verbs except for the DBC-specific *be* exclude subjects whose INDEX value is the newly added type that the DBC-specific nouns introduce. Thus the grammar will not assign two analyses to a sentence such as *The first thing he did surprised us.*

Finally, we observe in the corpus some subject noun phrases whose syntactic heads are not one of the seven nouns we have discussed, where one of these nouns is embedded in a partitive NP, as in the example *One of the things I want to do is make a movie.* Since partitives in general need to preserve some properties of the semantic index of the embedded NP, such as number and semantic type (for example the temporal/non-temporal noun distinction), the definition of the new DBC-specific index type also specifies the semantic sort of the index to be a DBC-specific type, and it is this semantic sort which the DBC verb *be* requires of its subject NP's INDEX value.

By making some additions to the existing lexical type hierarchy to accommodate the seven DBC nouns, as sketched in Figure 5, and defining DBC-specific variants of the transitive verb *do* and the identity-copula *be*, we can account for virtually all of the examples of DBC that we found in the corpus, without adding any new syntactic rules or feature principles. Of the 6331 well-formed sentences in our corpus (setting aside all examples with typos or other syntactic errors), the ERG (version 1111) successfully produces DBC analyses for 6283, leaving 48 sentences – less than one percent of our corpus –unanalyzed or only parsed without an occurrence of a DBC construction. The DBC parsing results are summarized by sentence length in Table 1. Here, the corpus examples are aggregated by the number of tokens per sentence, with the columns showing, in turn, the number of sentences in each aggregate, the number of lexical items considered by the parser

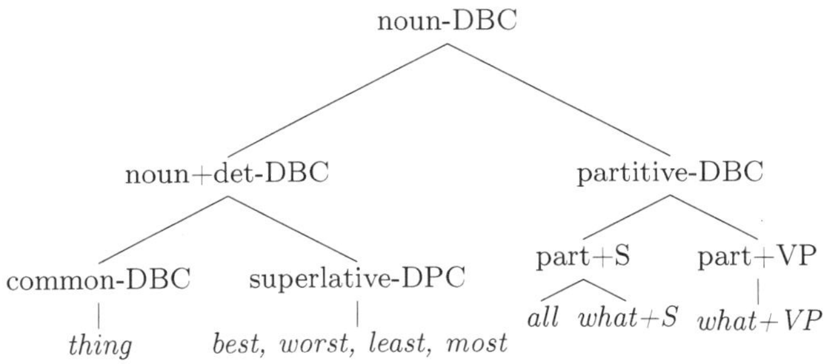

FIGURE 5 Hierarchy of lexical types for DBC nouns

Sentence length (in tokens)	number of sentences	lexical items	total parses	% parsed coverage
40–45	1	346.0	1	100.0
30–35	7	259.6	6	85.7
25–30	174	271.6	172	98.9
20–25	921	218.8	915	99.3
15–20	2469	180.8	2445	99.0
10–15	2040	136.5	2027	99.4
5–10	719	96.9	717	99.7
Total	6331	165.2	6283	99.2

TABLE 1 Parse results on the well-formed examples in the DBC corpus

per sentence (including inflected variants), the number of successfully parsed sentences[9], and these results expressed as percentages.

Of the 48 unparsed grammatical DBC examples in our corpus, 19 fail to parse due to unrelated shortcomings of the ERG, such as a robust treatment of inserted quoted expressions as in this example:

(36) all he had to do was remember those mandatory NASA Thou shalt not! lectures to squelch it

More interestingly, the remaining 27 unparsed sentences reveal a handful of inadequacies in our current implementation that are related to the DBC analysis. First, since we treat the relative clause within the subject NP as a complement of the head noun, the grammar should allow at least some optional modifiers to intervene, as seen in the four

[9] A successful parse means that the sentence was fully analyzed using the ERG and at least one of the parses included the correct DBC analysis, though this analysis may not have been ranked as the most likely reading.

corpus sentences below, but it does not, since it is not yet clear how freely such modifiers can appear.

(37) a. the last thing in the world you want to do is come in and get together
b. the last thing on earth I would do is kill the remaining dull tool that I had
c. last thing in the world I want to do is agree with Scott
d. the only thing left for you to do is go out

The second handful of problematic examples present the subject phrase of DBC as something other than an NP headed by one of the seven words identified in §4 above or a partitive noun such as *one* or *some*. While it remains our hypothesis that one of these seven nouns always serves as the semantic head of the subject phrase, this notion will need some further refinement in the implementation in order to admit the following three corpus examples, where the subject in the first two is syntactically a prepositional phrase headed by *among*, and in the latter two, it is an NP headed either by the common noun *part* (modified by the adjective *big* and with the overt determiner *a*), or by the word *something* again with an overt determiner *the*.

(38) a. among the things we've got to do is see to it that there are options
b. among the things bishops and other ecclesiastical teachers do is teach
c. a big part of what we do is give them the wind field on the entire storm
d. the something that we should be doing is supporting the SADC process

The other 19 corpus examples that remain unanalyzed by our implementation are all sentences which we are inclined to treat as disfluencies, where a full clause is followed by what would be the finite verb phrase of ordinary DBCs. We present a few typical examples:

(39) a. that's all you can do is be depressed
b. that's what we've been trying to do is get the money back
c. it's what we did is put in a very strict set of preconditions for them

In the process of adding DBC to the ERG, one other variation on the theme emerged in the corpus, and is now accommodated in the implementation. While the complement of the head word in the subject NP of a DBC is almost always a (finite or infinitival) relative clause, here is one example where what follows the head word *what* is a finite VP containing the required *do* (a variant not possible with *thing* or *all*):

(40) what's left for us to do is achieve

In the implementation, given the hierarchy of lexical types to capture the generalizations that hold for DBC, and also the fine-grained idiosyncrasies that we have described and exemplified, this additional variant is implemented by adding a second lexical entry for the DBC *what* which selects for a finite VP complement of the right kind, in place of the relative clause that is required by all of the other DBC head noun lexical entries.

7 Conclusion

The *do-be* construction presents interesting challenges to syntacticians considering the kinds of theoretical machinery required to provide comprehensive descriptions of natural languages. The constraints on DBC detailed in §4, involving syntax, semantics, and morphology, are just the sort of complex interdependencies that have led some linguists to propose including a notion of construction in the theory of grammar (e.g. Boas and Sag 2012; Croft 2001; Fillmore et al. 1988; Goldberg 1995). Two widely cited examples of constructions in English are the so-called *let alone* construction (Fillmore et al. 1988) and the *what's X doing Y* construction (Kay and Fillmore 1999). One major motivation for dealing with these in constructional terms is that they are subject to a special array of morphosyntactic constraints (Kay and Fillmore 1999, 4). As we have argued above, DBC has a remarkably rich array of such constraints.

In particular, the dependencies between the post-copula VP and the verb *do* in the subject involve elements that do not bear any kind of dominance or command relationship to one another, and this poses a challenge to any grammatical theory incorporating strong locality conditions. Our ERG implementation, however, shows that the standard feature-passing mechanisms of HPSG, together with a well-developed type hierarchy, are sufficient to handle the facts of DBC quite efficiently. Whether a fully constructional account would be preferable is a question we leave for future research.

Some might question the status of DBC as a distinct construction, given its shared properties with some other constructions (notably pseudoclefts), and the fact that our corpus studies found possible counterexamples to some of the properties we had used to characterize it.

The relationship to other constructions should come as no surprise. As Fillmore, Kay, Sag, and other construction grammarians have argued, languages have families of related constructions that can be represented with an inheritance hierarchy of construction types. Thus, for example, it would be natural to posit at least three subtypes of DBC, depending on whether the head of the subject is *what*, *all*, or one of the other five words. And sentences with specificational *be* might well constitute a construction of which DBC is a subtype.

The question of the status of DBC in light of the apparently non-categorical nature of the lexical constraints that characterize it is more difficult. Our corpus studies revealed that there are sentences very much like DBC but with nouns other than one of our seven heading the subject, and/or with another verb in place of *do* in the relative clause. But the number of examples we found that shared all of the properties A-H dwarfs the number of similar examples differing in these ways.

This sort of statistical convergence would be accepted as clear evidence of a real phenomenon in any of the social sciences, but most grammatical research has made categorical claims. This has been facilitated by the standard methodology of generative grammarians, which consists of testing hypotheses by inventing example sentences and introspecting on the sentences' acceptability. As the field moves from thought experiments to corpus studies and controlled experiments as its sources of data, the insistence on exceptionless generalizations becomes increasingly untenable. Clearly, this raises important and controversial methodological issues that are beyond the scope of this paper. We maintain, however, that the strong quantitative trends we found justify the claim that DBC is a distinct construction.

The constraints on DBC pose a challenge to developers of natural language processing systems trying to achieve broad coverage of English. The construction is common enough that such systems need to be able to handle it. The intricacy of the constraints on it, together with the unbounded character of the dependencies, suggest that it might create problems for systems relying entirely on statistical cooccurrence patterns. We have demonstrated that one grammar-based system can be readily extended to deal with DBC. We suggest that it may provide a good test of the versatility of any type of English-language NLP system.

Finally, as noted above, there are methodological lessons to be derived from our investigation into DBC. We relied crucially on both usage data (in the form of corpus examples) and invented examples, as well as introspective judgments about both. We contend that it is important for grammarians seeking to achieve descriptive adequacy to make use of all of these. We also made crucial use of a computational implementation to test our analysis. Languages are extremely complex systems, with so many interacting parts that it is typically difficult or impossible for people to keep track of all of the empirical consequences of any change to a grammar. Moreover, studies of different phenomena often make slightly different theoretical assumptions. Putting everything together into one computational system forces consistency in the analyses of distinct phenomena, and it makes possible reliable testing of what one's grammar predicts. In short, theoretical linguistics, at its best, should make use of a wide range of available methods for testing hypotheses.

Many open questions remain regarding DBC. How is it related to other similar constructions? In particular, DBC examples with *what* heading the subject are a species of pseudoclefts. But most DBC examples are not pseudoclefts, and most pseudoclefts are not instances of DBC. So how should the relationship between the two constructions be characterized? More generally, what properties of DBC follow from the fact that the copula in it receives a specificational interpretation? To what extent can the differences among the subtypes of DBC be explained semantically? When there are multiple choices for the form of the post-copula verb (that is, in all cases except where the form of *do* in the subject relative clause is present participle), what factors influence which one the speakers choose? How much variation is there in the use of DBC, both historically and across varieties of contemporary English? What other languages have similar constructions? We leave these and other questions for future research. We hope that our informal description of the construction and our description of the implemented analysis will be useful to those who investigate such questions.

Acknowledgments

We are grateful to Mark Davies for helpful advice regarding our corpus searches. Useful comments on earlier versions of this material were provided by Philip Hofmeister and an ostensibly anonymous reviewer (initials TFJ), as well as members of the audience at a talk in the Linguistics Department at Oxford University. Special thanks go to Rebecca Greene, not only for her careful and patient coding, but also for useful insights about the data she was annotating. Of course, we take full responsibility for any shortcomings in this paper.

References

Akmajian, Adrian. 1970. *Aspects of the Grammar of Focus in English*. Ph.D. thesis, MIT. Published in 1979 by Garland Publishing's Outstanding Dissertations in Linguistics series.

Boas, Hans and Ivan A. Sag, eds. 2012. *Sign-based Construction Grammar*. Stanford, CA: CSLI Publications.

Croft, William. 2001. *Radical Construction Grammar: Syntactic Theory in Typological Perspective*. Oxford University Press.

den Dikken, Marcel. 2005. Specificational copular sentences and pseudoclefts. In M. Everaert and H. van Riemsdijk, eds., *The Blackwell Companion to Syntax*, vol. IV. Hoboken, NJ: Wiley.

Faraci, Robert. 1970. On the deep question of pseduo-clefts. MIT.

Fillmore, Charles, Paul Kay, and Mary Catherine O'Connor. 1988. Regularity and idiomaticity in grammatical constructions: the case of let alone. *Language* 64(3):501–538.

Flickinger, Dan. 2000. On building a more efficient grammar by exploiting types. *Natural Language Engineering* 6(1):15–28.

Flickinger, Dan. 2011. Accuracy vs. robustness in grammar engineering. In E. Bender and J. Arnold, eds., *Language from a Cognitive Perspective: Grammar Usage, and Processing. Studies in Honor of Tom Wasow*, pages 31–50. Stanford, CA: CSLI Publications.

Gazdar, Gerald, Ewan Klein, Geoffrey K. Pullum, and Ivan A. Sag. 1985. *Generalized Phrase Structure Grammar*. Cambridge, MA: Harvard University Press.

Goldberg, Adele. 1995. *Constructions: A Construction Grammar Approach to Argument Structure*. Chicago: University of Chicago Press.

Halvorsen, Kris. 1978. The syntax and semantics of cleft constructions. Texas Linguistics Forum 11. The University of Texas Linguistics Department, Austin.

Jaeger, T. Florian. 2006. *Redundancy and Syntactic Reduction in Spontaneous Speech*. Ph.D. thesis, Stanford University.

Jaeger, T. Florian. 2010. Redundancy and reduction: Speakers manage syntactic information density. *Cognitive Psychology* 61(1):23–62.

Jaeger, T. Florian. 2011. Corpus-based research on language production: Information density and reducible subject relatives. In E. Bender and J. Arnold, eds., *Language from a Cognitive Perspective: Grammar, Usage, and Processing. Studies in Honor of Tom Wasow*, pages 161–197. Stanford, CA: CSLI Publications.

Kay, Paul and Charles Fillmore. 1999. Grammatical constructions and linguistic generalizations: The what's X doing Y? construction. *Language* 75(1):1–33.

Ladusaw, William. 1979. *Polarity Sensitivity as Inherent Scope Relations*. Ph.D. thesis, University of Texas, Austin. Published in 1980 by Garland Publishing's Outstanding Dissertaions in Linguistics series.

Levy, Roger and T. Florian Jaeger. 2007. Speakers optimize information density through syntactic reduction. In B. Schölkopf, J. Platt, and T. Hoffman, eds., *Advances in Neural Information Processing Systems (NIPS) 19*, pages 849–856. Cambridge, MA: MIT Press.

Pollard, Carl and Ivan A. Sag. 1987. *Information-based Syntax and Semantics; Volume 1 - Fundamentals*. No. 13 in CSLI Lecture Note Series. Stanford, CA: CSLI Publications.

Pollard, Carl and Ivan A. Sag. 1994. *Head-driven Phrase Structure Grammar*. Chicago: University of Chicago Press.

Ross, John R. 1972. Act. In G. Harman and D. Davidson, eds., *Semantics of Natural Language*, pages 70–126. Dordrecht: Reidel.

Ross, John R. 2000. The frozenness of pseudoclefts towards an inequality-based syntax. In A. Okrent and J. Boyle, eds., *Proceedings of the Thirty-Sixth Regional Meeting of the Chicago Linguistic Society*, pages 385–426. Chicago Linguistic Society, University of Chicago.

Ross, John R. 2008. An automodular perspective on the frozenness of pseudoclefts. Paper presented at the Pragmatics, Grammatical Interfaces, and Jerry Sadock Conference. University of Chicago.

Sag, Ivan A. 2010. English filler-gap constructions. *Language* 86(3):486–545.

Sag, Ivan A. 2012. Sign-based Construction Grammar: An informal synposis. In H. Boas and I. Sag, eds., *Sign-based Construction Grammar*, pages 69–202. Stanford, CA: CSLI Publications.

Wasow, Thomas, T. Florian Jaeger, and David Orr. 2011. Lexical variation in relativizer frequency. In H. Simon and H. Wiese, eds., *Expecting the Unexpected: Exceptions in Grammar*. Berlin: Mouton de Gruyter.

3

Agreement Between Scylla and Charybdis

Elizabeth Coppock

Although Steve, Ivan and I never played in Dead Tongues (n.b.: no definite article) at the same time, we are all Dead Tongues at some level of representation, so it feels somehow natural that I sing the first verse of this tune before Steve takes it away with his solo, while Ivan provides the underlying harmonic structure for it all. In this short introduction, I will briefly summarize the HPSG theory of agreement and its motivations, and try to explain why it is brilliant. This should not replace reading the HPSG book (Pollard and Sag 1994), which is more of an orchestral masterpiece. If you haven't read it, I highly recommend it, regardless of where you stand on the existence of empty categories. (It was one of the main reasons I wanted to go to Stanford for graduate school.)

The distinctive and powerful thing about the HPSG theory of agreement is that it ties agreement together with reference, hence, with semantics. The theory centers around the notion of an INDEX, which can be thought of either as a discourse referent in Discourse Representation Theory or as a parameter ($\approx$ free variable) in situation semantics (Barwise and Perry 1983). The idea is that the agreement features person, number and gender are features of INDICES, rather than of syntactic phrases, as was traditionally thought. The indices in question here are the same ones that play a central role in HPSG's non-configurational binding theory, its approach to subcategorization, and its storage-based approach to quantifier scope ambiguity, so the notion of index is im-

The Core and the Periphery.
Philip Hofmeister and Elisabeth Norcliffe (eds.).

portantly tied to multiple aspects of interpretation (and grammar). Making agreement features properties of indices thus results in a tight link between agreement and semantics.

This connection has a number of useful empirical consequences. A purely syntactic theory of agreement would have trouble with the following contrast, illustrating the phenomenon of REFERENCE TRANSFER:

(1) a. The hash browns at table nine are/*is getting cold.
  b. The hash browns at table nine is/*are getting angry.

SINGULAR PLURALS, which will be discussed in Wechsler's paper, constitute another case that is tough for a purely syntactic theory of agreement:

(2) Eggs is my favorite breakfast.

(3) Doing phonology problems and drinking vodka makes me sick.

The singular/plural ambiguity of COLLECTIVES, especially in British English, illustrates another problem for a purely syntactic theory of agreement:

(4) The faculty are all agreed on this point.

These facts can be accounted for by connecting the agreement features to the semantic index of the noun phrase.

While avoiding the Scylla of a purely syntactic theory of agreement, however, this theory steers clear of the Charybdis of a purely semantic theory. This makes it possible to account for data that does not seem compatible with either extreme.

(5) a. The faculty is voting itself a raise.
  b. The faculty are voting themselves a raise.
  c.*The faculty is voting themselves a raise.
  d.*The faculty are voting itself a raise.

(6) a. That dog is so ferocious, it even tried to bite itself.
  b. That dog is so ferocious, he even tried to bite himself.
  c.*That dog is so ferocious, it even tried to bite himself.
  d.*That dog is so ferocious, he even tried to bit itself.

(7) a. The ship lurched, and then it righted itself.
  b. The ship lurched, and then she righted herself.
  c.*The ship lurched, and then it righted herself.
  d.*The ship lurched, and then she righted itself.

If agreement were purely semantic, then all four variants of these examples should be acceptable. The partly syntactic theory in HPSG accounts for these restrictions, by mediating the agreement relation through indices and requiring that pronouns and their antecedents share an index.

Polite pronouns such as German *Sie* and French *vous* evince another advantage of the HPSG theory over a purely semantic theory. These involve a mismatch between semantic number and grammatical number:

(8) Vous êtes l'amour de ma vie.
you.FORMAL be.PRES.2PL the:love of my life.
'You (formal) are the love of my life.'

If agreement were purely semantic, then it should not be possible for a plural verb to agree with a semantically singular subject.[10]

Let's consider how the theory captures this data. In HPSG, unlike in many other theories, pronouns and common nouns have the same semantic type. The semantic value of both is essentially a pair consisting of an index and a restriction on that index. The elements of the pair have labels and are standardly represented in AVM format as in 9a, where the semantics of a commoun noun like *pancake* is shown. The boxed number indicates structure-sharing, which entails token-identity. Removing the labels gives us the pair in (9b), where u is the object that serves as the value of both the INDEX feature and the INST feature.

(9) a.
$$\begin{bmatrix} \text{INDEX} & \boxed{1}\begin{bmatrix} \text{PER} & \mathit{3rd} \\ \text{NUM} & \mathit{sg} \\ \text{GEND} & \mathit{neut} \end{bmatrix} \\ \text{RESTR} & \left\{ \begin{bmatrix} \text{RELN} & \mathit{pancake} \\ \text{INST} & \boxed{1} \end{bmatrix} \right\} \end{bmatrix}$$

b. $\langle u, \{\mathit{pancake}(u)\}\rangle$

[10] However, as discussed by Pollard and Sag (1994, 96) polite pronouns participate in a phenomenon that remained somewhat puzzling under this view, namely MIXED AGREEMENT, exemplified in *Vous êtes belle* 'you.FORMAL be.PRES.2PL pretty.SG'. In this case, the verb displays plural agreement and the adjective displays singular agreement. Evidently, predicative adjectives in French do not reflect the INDEX number feature of the subject but rather the fact that the subject is semantically singular. It is in this connection that Wechsler and Zlatić (2003) and Wechsler (2011) made an important contribution using two distinct feature bundles, INDEX and CONCORD.

The semantics of a pronoun is also a pair like this, except that the value of the RESTR feature is the empty set; in pair format, the semantics of a pronoun like *she* is $\langle u, \{\}\rangle$. The requirement that u is female is stated among the constraints on the context. Proper names also have this type, and come with a contextual constraint that u bears the relevant name.

What is the ontological status of the index u? Pollard and Sag tell us that we have at least two options: We can think of it either as a discourse referent or as a parameter in situation semantics. (Given that DRT can be embedded in situation semantics, maybe the latter is more specific than the former.) On the latter view, which is the one developed in more detail in Pollard and Sag (1994), the second member of the pair is a set of parameterized state of affairs (PSOA) as in situation semantics. If we think of u as a discourse referent, then the second element of the pair should be thought of as the bottom half of a Discourse Representation Structure (DRS) as in Discourse Representation Theory (Kamp and Reyle 1993), which is a set of CONDITIONS. So the semantics of a common noun can be seen as a pair consisting of a discourse referent and a set of DRS-conditions. (It's almost like a DRS; if the first element of the pair were a *set* of discourse referents, then it would be.)[11]

The representation in (9a) says a bit more about the index u than the representation in (9b) though. (9a) also tells us that u is 3rd person, singular, and neuter. These features are not mereological parts of the index, of course; they are properties of the index. So another way of thinking about this is that there is some function, call it π, whose domain is the set of indices and whose range is the set of possible person values (e.g. *1st*, *2nd*, and *3rd*), and $\pi(u)$ =*3rd*. Thus the HPSG theory of agreement is a general idea that can be implemented in any framework that has a notion of index and a function that assigns agreement features to indices.[12]

Subject-verb agreement comes about through constraints imposed by inflected verb forms requiring token-identity of indices (hence, of

[11]Note that if indices are discourse referents, then the semantic value of a word like *pancake* is a pair of terms in a representation language that must then be interpreted with respect to a model and an assignment function. For example if g is an assignment function and M is a model and $g(u) = a$, then it would be natural to assume that $[\![u]\!]^{M,g} = a$. Semantic values in HPSG thus contain what might be referred to as *representational objects*, i.e., objects that represent the world rather than actual entities in a model.

[12]One would have to be careful when undertaking such an enterprise, as HPSG indices can be non-referential; the English expletives *it* and *there* have non-referential indices and it is not clear whether they introduce discourse referents.

person, number and gender features). A verb like *succeed* will have as its semantic content something which can be thought of either as a PSOA or a DRS-condition, e.g. *succeed(u)*. The index u must also be the index of the subject. This identity requirement relates to the syntactic information associated with the verb (stored under the CAT features) as illustrated in (10).

(10)
$$\left[\begin{array}{ll} \text{CAT} & \left[\begin{array}{ll}\text{HEAD} & \textit{verb}[\text{FIN}] \\ \text{SUBCAT} & \left\langle \left[\text{LOC} \left[\begin{array}{ll} \text{CAT} & \left[\begin{array}{ll}\text{HEAD} & \textit{noun}\\ \text{SUBCAT} & \langle\rangle\end{array}\right] \\ \text{CONT} & \left[\text{INDEX}\ \boxed{1}\left[\begin{array}{ll}\text{PERS} & \textit{3rd}\\ \text{NUM} & \textit{sg}\end{array}\right]\right]\end{array}\right]\right]\right\rangle\end{array}\right] \\ \text{CONT} & \left[\begin{array}{ll}\text{RELN} & \textit{succeed}\\ \text{INST} & \boxed{1}\end{array}\right]\end{array}\right]$$

The semantic value of the verb is the value of its CONT[ent] feature, and this is a PSOA or DRS-condition which can be rewritten without labels as *succeed(u)*. The index u serving as the argument of the *succeed* relation must be token-identical to the index of the subject, the first argument of the verb's SUBCAT[egorization] list.

This theory of agreement can be contrasted with the one in for example Kamp and Reyle (1993), which is purely syntactic, despite the availability of discourse referents as part of the theory. There we have involving rules like the following, where α is a variable over different possible feature values (p. 30):

(11) $\text{S}_{Num=\alpha} \rightarrow \text{NP}_{Num=\alpha}\ \text{VP}_{Num=\alpha}$

Notice that number is treated as a feature of a syntactic *phrase* in this framework. Plural nouns are lexically specified as plural via rules like the following:

(12) $\text{N}_{Num=pl} \rightarrow$ books, hash browns, ...

This set-up entails that the reference transfer-type cases will be ruled out as ungrammatical. By treating agreement features as features of indices, which are tied to semantics, the HPSG theory of agreement gets the leeway it needs to deal with reference transfer, singular plurals, and collectives.

Like subject-verb agreement, pronoun-antecedent agreement also relies on indices according to the HPSG binding theory. A reflexive pronoun, for example, must share an index with its antecedent. This explains why the (c) and (d) examples in (5d)-(7d), in which there is a mismatch between a reflexive pronoun and its antecedent, are unacceptable. A purely semantic theory would allow these kinds of mismatches, since it would allow any pronoun whose features correspond to some possible conceptualization of the referent. In contrast, agreement features are still part of the grammar under the HPSG theory, even though they are connected to semantics. In this way, the HPSG theory navigates the tricky passage between Scylla and Charybdis.

I would like to underline the point that the HPSG theory of agreement is a general idea that can be implemented in any framework that has a notion of index, as one has in every framework that makes use of discourse referents. The sign-based nature of HPSG makes it particularly suited for an implementation of this type of theory, as constraints crossing the border between form and content can easily be stated as constraints on signs. But all one really needs beyond a notion of index is a function that assigns agreement features to indices, and a way to relate these functions to verb forms. Even if you don't do HPSG, if you have these things, then you too can make all of these lovely predictions.

Take it away, Steve.

References

Barwise, Jon and John Perry. 1983. *Situations and Attitudes*. Cambridge, MA: MIT Press.

Kamp, Hans and Uwe Reyle. 1993. *From Discourse to Logic*. Dordrecht: Kluwer Academic Publishers.

Pollard, Carl and Ivan A. Sag. 1994. *Head-Driven Phrase Structure Grammar*. Chicago: University of Chicago Press.

Wechsler, Stephen. 2011. Mixed agreement, the person feature, and the Index/Concord distinction. *Natural Language and Linguistic Theory* 29(4):999–1031.

Wechsler, Stephen and Larisa Zlatić. 2003. *The Many Faces of Agreement: Morphology, Syntax, Semantics, and Discourse Factors in Serbo-Croatian Agreement*. Stanford: CSLI Publications.

3

The Structure of Swedish *Pancakes*

STEPHEN WECHSLER

Vodka, det drikker Ivan.[1] — Norwegian example sentence, Enger (2004, 9).

1 Introduction

A recurring theme of Ivan Sag's work is the important insight that not all complex grammatical structure should be represented as complex phrase structure.[2] Silent phrase structure, when posited in order to explain syntactic or semantic phenomena, is possible in principle, but generally viewed with suspicion. For example Ivan has argued that extraction does not leave a phonologically empty trace (Sag and Fodor 1994). Significantly, Ivan *argues*; he does not assume. The question of syntactic structure is an empirical question, to be answered by following the facts wherever they lead. To take a different example, Pollard and Sag (1994) floats an analysis of relative clauses that involves a silent functional head; but the analysis in Sag (1997) does without the silent head.

Grammatical agreement is another area of syntax that has been analyzed in terms of constituent structures without audible words at the terminal nodes. Such structures have often been posited to explain special situations in which agreement does not operate in the usual

[1] 'Vodka, Ivan drinks it.'

[2] I am grateful to Elizabeth Coppock and an anonymous reviewer, for comments on an earlier draft; and to Östen Dahl, Kersti Börjars, Inga Marie Carmel and Anna-Sara Malmgren for Swedish grammaticality judgments and discussion of the data.

The Core and the Periphery.
Philip Hofmeister and Elisabeth Norcliffe (eds.).

way. For example, when a subject or other agreement controller fails to trigger agreement in the usual way, this has been explained as a consequence of a silent phrasal shell around the subject that blocks the normal agreement relation, or places a special set of agreement features on the subject. This paper investigates this phenomenon as it applies to certain Scandinavian sentences called 'pancake sentences', which are roughly similar to English sentences like *Steroids is big business*, in which the verb appears in the singular despite a plural subject. Following Ivan's lead, I take it as an empirical question whether or not this phenomenon involves a silent phrase structure shell around the subject. I argue against positing silent phrase structure, and in favor of an analysis in terms of logical metonymy.

2 Scandinavian pancake sentences

Swedish predicate adjectives normally agree with their subjects in gender and number:

(1) a. Orm-en är grön.
snake-DEF.COM.SG be.PRES green.COM.SG
'The snake is green.'

b. Hus-et är grön-t.
house-DEF.NT.SG be.PRES green-NT.SG
'The house is green.'

c. Orm-ar-na/ Hus-en är grön-a.
snake-PL-DEF / house-PL.DEF be.PRES green-PL
'The snakes/ The houses are green.'

Swedish nouns are classified into two genders, neuter (NT) and common (COM), the latter term referring to the gender held in common between masculine and feminine. As shown in (1), a predicate adjective is inflected for number, and, in the singular, for gender, and agrees with its subject. But in sentences like (2), the adjective appears in the neuter singular form, regardless of the number and gender features of the subject. This example has a plural, common gender subject, but the adjective is neuter singular (Faarlund 1977; Enger 2004; Josefsson 2009):

(2) Pannkak-or är gott.
pancake-PL be.PRES good.NT.SG
'Situations involving pancakes are good.' (e.g. 'Eating pancakes is good.')

As suggested by the translation, the predicate adjective applies semantically in a subtly different way when it fails to agree with the subject.

The sentences in (1) attribute properties directly to the subject denotation: the snake(s) and the house(s) are green. But (2) attributes goodness not to the pancakes themselves but to a pancake-related situation – most plausibly, an event of eating them. Anticipating the analysis proposed below, we may consider this a case of LOGICAL METONYMY in the sense of Pustejovsky (1995): the pancakes as entities are metonymic for the eventuality that involves them. Following the practice of some of the literature on Swedish, we call such sentences PANCAKE SENTENCES, and the subject of a pancake sentence will be called a PANCAKE NP or PANCAKE SUBJECT. The main question addressed in this paper is why the adjective in a pancake sentence fails to agree with its subject in the usual way, and how that difference of agreement relates to the observed logical metonymy.

The following minimal pair (from Wellander 1955, 380) further illustrates this connection between the special agreement pattern and the metonymic interpretation:

(3) a. En ny utrikesminister skulle inte vara
COM new.COM foreign.minister[COM] would not be
så dum-t.
so dumb-NT.SG
'(Getting) a new foreign minister would not be so dumb.'

b. En ny utrikesminister skulle inte vara
COM new.COM foreign.minister[COM] would not be
så dum.
so dumb.COM
'A new foreign minister would not be as dumb (e.g. as the current one).'

Example (3a) is a pancake-sentence: the predicate adjective appears in the neuter singular form, despite the common gender of the subject; and it has a metonymic interpretation: lack of dumbness is not attributed to the new foreign minister himself but rather to the idea of having a new one. This example also shows that the lexical gender of the head noun *utrikesminister* 'foreign minister' determines common gender concord within the NP, as evidenced by the forms of the indefinite determiner *en* and the attributive adjective *ny* 'new'. So our analysis must reconcile the non-agreement of the predicate adjective with the fact that those features are clearly present in the noun, and grammatically potent, as they determine concord within the NP.

Pancake-NPs tend to be indefinite, but grammatically definite NPs can appear in this agreement pattern if the semantic conditions are right, as observed by Josefsson (2009), from which these examples are taken:

(4) a. Väska-n på ryggen är modern-t i år.
bag.COM.DEF on back.DEF be.PRES modern.NT.SG in year
'It's modern to have the bag on the back this year.'

b. Den där bukett-en till svärmor i lördags
that bouquet-COM.DEF to mother.in.law on Saturday
var slug-t.
be.PST cunning-NT
'(Giving) those flowers to your mother-in-law last Saturday was cunning.'

Like the previous examples, the sentences in (4) have the metonymic 'related situation' reading, as suggested by the English translations. In addition to such cases, we also sometimes find the non-agreeing neuter singular predicate adjective with kind-denoting NPs (examples from Widmark 1966, 98):

(5) a. Halm är gult / gul.
straw[COM] be.PRES yellow-NT.SG yellow.COM.SG
'Straw is yellow.'

b. Ros-or är vacker-t / vackra.
roses-COM.PL be.PRES pretty.NT.SG pretty.PL
'Roses are pretty.'

Regarding the two alternatives in (5a), Widmark (1966, 98) observed that 'For myself I prefer the construction *Halm är gul* to *Halm är gult*, but the latter expression seems to be the more natural one for some people.'[3] She goes on to suggest that variation also depends on the adjective. Note that *halm* 'straw' is a mass noun, hence singular, so it is variation in the gender that is at issue. As for the plural count noun *rosor* 'roses' in (5b), Widmark (1966, 96) observes that with the plural adjective, 'we want to draw attention to each flower's beauty', while with the singular 'we give a judgement about roses in general.'[4]

We have seen pancake NPs of two semantic types, those denoting an eventuality related to the entity normally denoted by the NP; and those denoting a kind. Some pancake NPs are difficult to classify, per-

[3]Själv skulle jag föredra konstruktionen Halm är gul framför Halm är gult, men det senare uttryckssättet tycks vara det naturligare för somliga människor.' (Widmark 1966, 98, fn. 5)

[4]'I förra fallet vill vi dra uppmärksamheten till varje blommas skönhet, i senare fallet avger vi ett omdöme om rosor i allmänhet.'(Widmark 1966, 96)

haps because they belong to both types. Consider this example from Josefsson (2009):

(6) Kvalitet-en är viktig-t.
quality-COM.DEF be.PRES important-NT
'Quality is important.'

The subject *kvaliteten* (literally, 'the quality') appears to be kind-denoting: in Swedish as in English, definite NPs can sometimes denote kinds (although this is not possible for the English phrase 'the quality'). But at the same time, it is not clear whether (6) is saying that quality is inherently important, or rather that 'having quality' is important. In this paper I focus primarily on the metonymic type of pancake sentence, although there is some further discussion of the kind-denoting type as well.

A last property of pancake sentences, noted by Josefsson (2009), concerns case marking. Swedish distinguishes case only on personal pronouns, not common or proper nouns. The subject of a finite verb appears in nominative case; in all other syntactic contexts accusative case is used. Interestingly, when the subject of a pancake sentence is headed by a pronoun, that pronoun can appear in accusative, not nominative, despite serving as the subject of a finite verb (example from Josefsson 2009):

(7) [One cannibal to the other:]
[Henne med senap och ketchup] vore läcker-t.
her.ACC with mustard and ketchup would.be delicious-NT
'(To get/have/eat) her with mustard and ketchup would be delicious.'

According to Josefsson, using a nominative pronoun precludes the special 'related-situation' interpretation and the special agreement:

(8) Hon med senap och ketchup är läcker.
she.NOM with mustard and ketchup be.PRES delicious.COM
'She with mustard and ketchup is delicious.'

In short, a finite verb normally assigns nominative case to its subject, as in (7), but in a pancake sentence the subject can appear in accusative case instead.

Summarizing, these are the main properties of the pancake construction:

- The adjective appears in the neuter singular form, regardless of the apparent gender and number features of its subject.

- The clause has a metonymic 'situation-related-to-NP' interpretation, which is facilitated by the use of generic or indefinite NPs, but possible with definites too; or the subject denotes a kind.
- If the subject is headed by a pronoun, that pronoun can appear in accusative case, even when the verb is finite.

3 Locating the problem within the grammar

What is it about the grammar of Swedish that allows for pancake sentences? For concreteness we may cast the problem in historical terms. Apparently the pancake type agreement pattern is a relatively recent innovation in the history of Scandinavian, appearing for the first time only about 100 years ago (Widmark 1966). So the grammars of some Scandinavian languages underwent a change of some sort. What aspect of the grammar changed?

A priori several possibilities present themselves: (i) *The DP changed.* There was a change in the grammatical properties of the subject constituent, whereby *pannkakor*, for example, acquired a new meaning, 'situation involving pancakes', with special agreement and case properties. (ii) *The adjectives changed.* The neuter singular forms of predicate adjectives acquired a special new specification, whereby *gott* can mean 'good to eat/drink/do something with/etc.' and, on that meaning, it fails to agree with its subject.[5] (iii) *The sentence rule changed.* The language acquired a special new sentential construction. There are reasons for adopting the first alternative, locating the problem within the DP, and rejecting the second and third.

Telling against the third alternative, of a special clausal construction, is the fact that the same non-agreement pattern occurs in other syntactic constructions, as long as the AP has a subject, and the AP and its subject are semantically appropriate. Hellan (1986) cites the following Norwegian examples of non-agreement. In (9a) the subject *tran* 'cod liver oil' is a masculine mass noun, but the predicate adjective *sunt* 'healthy' appears in neuter singular (Hellan 1986, 95, examples 10a and 11a). Example (9b) has the same agreement and interpretation:

(9) a. Tran er sunt.
cod.liver.oil[M] be.PRES healthy.NT.SG
'Cod liver oil is healthy (to drink).'

[5]In many cases this meaning difference is all but neutralized: why else would pancakes be good, if not because they are good for some use such as eating? Cases allowing only the old (non-pancake) interpretation include *Livet är gott* ('Life is good.') and *Gud är god* ('God is good.').

b. Fabrikantene gjorde tran sunt.
producer.DEF.PL made cod.liver.oil[M] healthy.NT.SG
'The producers made cod liver oil healthy (to drink).'

In the latter example the adjective phrase *sunt* 'healthy' functions as a predicate complement, predicated of the direct object *tran* 'cod liver oil'. Thus this phenomenon is not associated with clausal syntax per se, but rather with the subject-predicate relation between the nominal and the adjective. Hence if a special construction type is responsible for this phenomenon, then it is not tied to the constituent structure of the clause; rather, it must be abstract enough to apply to secondary predication as in (9b). Hellan concludes that 'These facts make it unreasonable to associate the dis-agreement with a specific structural configuration per se. The crucial properties seem rather to reside in the T-expression [*the 'Term', i.e. the nominal—S.W.*] itself ...' (Hellan 1986, 95).

It may seem that alternative (ii) could fill the bill: one could posit special non-agreeing adjective forms such as *gott*, with the meaning 'good to do something with'. Then this would apply to both main clauses and secondary predicates. The form with that special meaning would be homophonous with the neuter singular but would not determine agreement features on its subject. However, the case facts are problematic for such an account. Nominative case is assigned by the finite verb, not the adjective: normally all finite verbs require a nominative subject, except in this construction, which allows accusative case despite the presence of a finite verb. It is hard to see how anything in the specification of the adjective alone could be responsible for blocking the assignment of case by the verb.

This leaves us with alternative (i): the grammar changed to allow an NP like *pannkakor* to mean 'a situation involving pancakes' and, on this meaning, to resist the normal agreement and case relations. Indeed previous accounts have focused on the NP. Next we consider two types of analysis of the NP: analyses involving silent phrase structure surrounding the NP; and analyses involving logical metonymy.

4 Silent phrase structure or logical metonymy?

Now we will contrast two different approaches to the analysis of pancake sentences, beginning with the SILENT PHRASE STRUCTURE approach. On this type of analysis the pancake subject consists of the word *pannkakor* (for example) embedded in some larger covert phrase structure that is intuitively similar to an infinitive or clause. The inspiration for this approach is the fact that when the subject is an infinitive or a clause, the predicate adjective appears in the neuter singular form:

(10) a. [Att äta pannkakor] är gott.
to eat pancakes be.PRES good.NT.SG
'Eating pancakes is good.'

b. [Att det snöade] var konstigt.
that it snowed be.PST strange.NT.SG
'That it snowed was strange.'

Since grammatical agreement features are normally head features, as long as the real head of the subject phrase is some silent element such as a silent verb, and not the noun that appears to be the head, then the gender and number features of the noun will be trapped within that embedded NP and are not expected to affect the form of the predicate adjective. Faarlund (1977) proposed the underlying structure in (11) for the Norwegian equivalent of (2) above:

(11) Faarlund's (1977) structure:

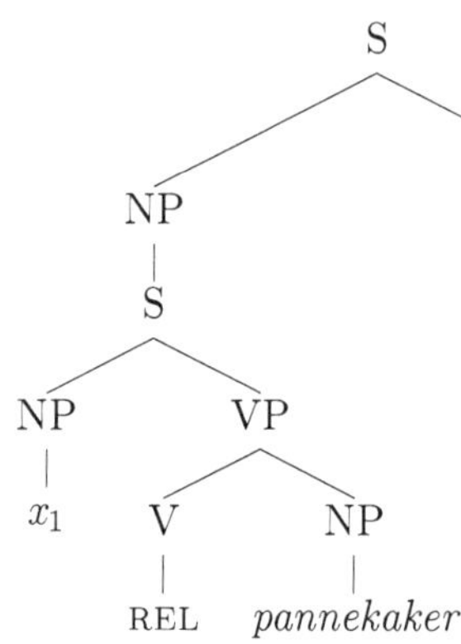

Faarlund's REL (for 'relation') is 'an abstract verb with a very general meaning ... a transitive verb that covers the relationship, of whatever kind, that we find underlying the subjects' of pancake sentences (Faarlund 1977, 246). The subject of this abstract verb is an empty category (cp. PRO in later theories).

Josefsson's (2009) version includes a silent light verb designated by HAVE, as shown in (12), the structure proposed for the bracketed subject of (13).

(12) Josefsson's (2009) structure:

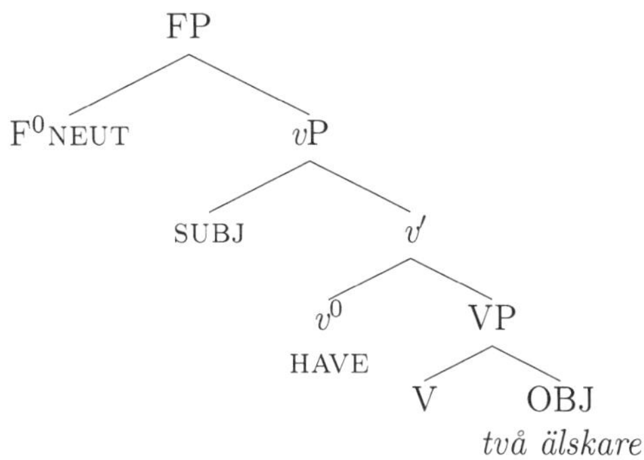

(13) [Två älskare] är omoralisk-t.
two lovers be.PRES immoral-NT.SG
'(Having) two lovers is immoral.'

For both Faarlund and Josefsson, the idea behind positing silent phrase structure is to encapsulate the NP by embedding it in a larger, partially covert structure. It is encapsulated both syntactically and semantically: syntactically, in that the features of the NP are unable to escape the subject and affect agreement on the predicate adjective; and semantically, in that the entity denotation of the NP (viz., 'pancakes') is embedded within some eventive or situational meaning for the subject as a whole (viz., 'eating pancakes'). So this brings together the main syntactic and semantic properties of this construction in a unified account.

Note, however, that the success of that unified account does not actually depend upon any of the details of the phrase structures posited above by Faarlund and Josefsson. All that is needed is a DP structure with the right meaning and where *pannkakor* fails to project its phi and case features. Robin Cooper (1984) proposed a simple unary branching structure for such NPs, generated by the phrase structure rule in (14) (Cooper 1984, 134), and the semantic interpretation rule in (15) (Cooper 1984, 139):[6]

[6] In Cooper's analysis the projection level of the mother node is higher than that of the daughter; in current terms they might be DP and NP, respectively. That correctly allows for bare NPs in this construction, as in *Bil vore utmärkt*, lit. 'Car would-be excellent', while NPs headed by singular count nouns are not normally permitted to serve as subjects. Our reformulation of Cooper's unary rule in Sec. 5 below does not explain the bare singular count NPs, but does correctly allows for

$$\begin{array}{ll} & N^2 \quad\; N^1 \\ (14) & [\alpha] \rightarrow [\beta] \\ & \text{where either } \alpha = [-\text{utr}, -\text{pl}], \text{ or } \alpha = \beta \end{array}$$

(15) $[\![\ [\ \mathrm{N}^1\ ]\ ]\!] = \textsc{prop}([\![\ \mathrm{N}^1\ ]\!])$

The feature [utr] is for *utrum* 'common gender', hence [−utr] means 'neuter'; and [−pl] is singular number. So the mother node is either neuter singular, or it matches the daughter. If we wish to maintain the convention that morphological features like gender and number are shared between a phrasal node and its head daughter (the Head Feature Principle), then we must say that the structure is technically exocentric (headless), at least when the features of the mother and its sole daughter do not match. In the semantic translation rule in (15), the single square brackets indicate phrase structure constituency, hence [N^1] is a constituent (namely N^2) with a single daughter labeled N^1. The double square brackets indicate semantic interpretation, hence [[X]] is the interpretation of constituent X. The function PROP(X) gives an unspecified propositional content related to X, such as 'eating pancakes', where X is pancakes. As in Faarlund's and Josefsson's silent phrase structure accounts above the noun *pannkakor* is encapsulated both syntactically and semantically.

The main idea unifying the silent phrase structure analysis and the unary branching analysis is that the entity-denoting NP is encapsulated within a larger, partially covert structure, and so the phi and case features of the embedded NP are shielded from processes outside that larger structure. The two analyses differ, however, in where they take their inspiration, so to speak. On the Silent Phrase Structure analysis the covert structure is syntactic, taking the form of a (mostly silent) verbal projection. The subject of the pancake sentence is effectively elliptical, an infinitival or clausal structure in which only the object of the verb is pronounced. For example, Josefsson (2009) motivates the silent light verb (see (8) above) by pointing out another Swedish construction that apparently involves a silent light verb, namely so-called *gå*-deletion (go-deletion), as in the following sentence, where *gå* can be omitted:

(16) Jag ska (gå) til skolan. 'gå-deletion'
I shall go to school
'I will go to school.'

On the most general level, then, the basis for the Silent Phrase Structure analysis is the claim that languages sometimes allow unpronounced

---

pancake-type subjects with determiners (see 4 above, for example).

constituents, and more specifically, the claim that Swedish allows certain unpronounced verbs with a general or 'light verb' meaning.

On the unary branching analysis, the covert structure is semantic. I suggest it is a consequence of the very general phenomenon of metonymy, where a part stands in for the whole. Pustejovsky (1995) observed that metonymy often occurs in contexts where the logical type of a constituent does not match its compositional semantic context. The NP *a novel* denotes an entity, but as the complement of an aspectual verb like start, this NP can be coerced to represent an event involving a novel:

(17) I started a novel.
$\Rightarrow$ 'I started reading a novel / writing a novel / etc.'

Pustejovsky called this phenomenon logical metonymy since the logical type of the object is changed, in this case from entity to event.

In the next section, I propose an updated version of the logical metonymy analysis informed by research on agreement over the past 20 years. Then I will argue that this analysis is better than the silent phrase structure analysis.

5 Index agreement and metonymy

A logical metonymy account of pancake sentences turns out to be very natural within the theory of Index agreement that originates in the work of Pollard and Sag (1994). Pollard and Sag observed that agreement often tracks the *referential index* of the agreement controller, as opposed to the controller's grammatical HEAD features. This can be seen in pronoun binding, where a bound anaphor must share its index with that of its antecedent, and also must match its antecedent in person, number, and gender features. Pollard and Sag posited that the index itself, modeled as the value of the feature attribute INDEX, bears those phi features. This is captured in the following feature declaration (from Wechsler and Zlatić (2003)), where *png-index* is the type of index (the value for the feature INDEX) associated with nouns and other elements that introduce phi features:

(18)
$$\textit{png-index:} \begin{bmatrix} \text{PERSON } \textit{person} \\ \text{NUMBER } \textit{number} \\ \text{GENDER } \textit{gender} \end{bmatrix}$$

Applied to pancake sentences, the basic idea is that normal agreement with a pancake subject fails because the referential index for the pancakes is necessarily distinct from the one for an event of eating them.

Now let us sketch a formal analysis. First of all, the lexical entry for the noun *pannkakor* is just the usual one, abbreviated here:

(19)

$$\textit{pannkakor:}\ \begin{bmatrix}\text{HEAD } \textit{N} \\ \text{SEM} \begin{bmatrix}\text{INDEX } i\text{: } \begin{bmatrix}\textit{3rd, com, pl}\end{bmatrix} \\ \text{RESTR } \left\{\textit{pancakes(i)}\right\}\end{bmatrix}\end{bmatrix}$$

We can use Sign-Based Construction Grammar (Sag 2008) to reformulate Cooper's unary branching phrase rule as a construction type, which I call *metonymy-ctx* ('metonymy construction'):

(20)

$$\textit{metonymy-ctx:}\ \begin{bmatrix}\text{MTR} \begin{bmatrix}\text{SYN } \textit{NP} \\ \text{SEM} \begin{bmatrix}\text{INDEX } \text{s}_{unm} \\ \text{RESTR } \left\{\text{INVOLVES(S,I)}\right\} \cup \boxed{1}\end{bmatrix}\end{bmatrix} \\ \text{DTRS} \left\langle \begin{bmatrix}\text{SYN } \textit{NP} \\ \text{SEM} \begin{bmatrix}\text{INDEX } i\text{: } \begin{bmatrix}\textit{3rd, com, pl}\end{bmatrix} \\ \text{RESTR } \boxed{1}\end{bmatrix}\end{bmatrix} \right\rangle\end{bmatrix}$$

This rule licenses structures like the following:

(21)

$$\text{NP}_{s[unm]}\text{:[RESTR } \{\textit{involve}(\text{s,i}),\ \textit{pancakes}(\text{i})\}]$$
$$|$$
$$\text{NP}_i[3rd, com, pl]\text{:[RESTR } \{\textit{pancakes}(\text{i})\}]$$
$$|$$
$$\textit{pannkakor}$$

The noun *pannkakor* comes with an index marked with the features [PERSON 3rd], [GENDER com], and [NUMBER pl], which, by the Semantics Principle, are therefore shared with the index of the lower NP, shown in (21) as *i[3rd,com,pl]*.

Wechsler and Zlatić (2003) posited that some referential indices, such as those introduced by verbs, lack phi features. This is modelled with two subtypes of the type *index*.

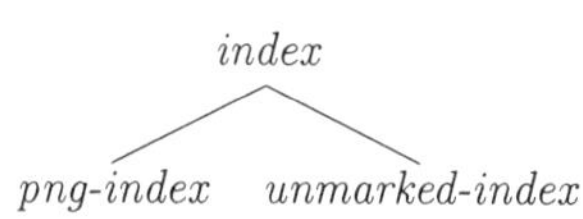

FIGURE 1 Type hierarchy of index types

The feature declaration in (18) applies to indices of type *png-index*, while those of type *unmarked-index* are atoms. The referential index of the higher NP in (20), abbreviated s_{unm}, is an unmarked index. In the semantic interpretation, the index i (on the lower NP) is restricted by the pancakes predicate in the usual way, while the index s (on the higher NP) is anchored to some situation 'involving' pancakes, hence the restriction *involve(s,i)*.

The predicate adjectives are inflected for the number and gender features of their subjects, with the neuter singular form also serving as the default used with subjects that lack a *png-index*. This is illustrated with the predicate adjective meaning 'good', in its common-singular, plural, and neuter-singular/default forms, respectively:

(22) Forms of the Swedish predicate adjective meaning 'good'

$$\textit{god:} \begin{bmatrix} \text{HEAD } \mathrm{A} \\ \text{SPR } \left\langle \text{NP: } \begin{bmatrix} \text{INDEX } i\text{: } \begin{bmatrix} com,sg \end{bmatrix} \end{bmatrix} \right\rangle \\ \text{SEM } good(i) \end{bmatrix}$$

$$\textit{goda:} \begin{bmatrix} \text{HEAD } \mathrm{A} \\ \text{SPR } \left\langle \text{NP: } \begin{bmatrix} \text{INDEX } i\text{: } \begin{bmatrix} pl \end{bmatrix} \end{bmatrix} \right\rangle \\ \text{SEM } good(i) \end{bmatrix}$$

$$\textit{gott:} \begin{bmatrix} \text{HEAD } \mathrm{A} \\ \text{SPR } \left\langle \text{NP: } \begin{bmatrix} \text{INDEX } i\text{: } \begin{bmatrix} nt,sg \vee unm \end{bmatrix} \end{bmatrix} \right\rangle \\ \text{SEM } good(i) \end{bmatrix}$$

The neuter singular form *gott* is thus used with any clausal or infinitival subjects—recall (10)—as well as the special nominals licensed by the metonymic construction type in (20).[7]

Much like the structures with silent heads posited by Faarlund and Josefsson, this analysis has the effect of encapsulating the basic entity-denoting NP both syntactically and semantically. The verb and predicate adjective impose constraints on the agreement and case features of the mother node, but not the daughter; while the features introduced by the words within the NP constrain the daughter but not the mother. This basic idea of encapsulation follows straightforwardly from the notion of index agreement: normal agreement with a pancake subject fails because the referential index for the pancakes is necessarily distinct from the index for an event of eating them.

[7]See §7 below for further discussion.

6 Evidence against the Silent Phrase Structure and for Logical Metonymy

If indeed the Silent Phrase Structure and the Logical Metonymy analyses both capture the basic facts, then is there any rational basis for choosing between them? As we will see, the evidence favors the latter.

What is the main difference between these two approaches? On the Silent Phrase Structure approach the covert structure is syntactic phrase structure. But on the Logical Metonymy approach the covert structure is almost entirely semantic, involving a metonymic extension of an entity-denoting NP. Specifically, we posited that the referential index of the event-denoting subject does not match that of its entity-denoting head noun. There is also a concomitant *syntactic* difference between a pancake subject and a normal subject, since the features of that referential index are grammatical features. It is the distinction between the grammatical features of the embedded entity-index and those of the situation-index that is responsible for the agreement facts.

The two approaches make rather different predictions. On the Silent Phrase Structure approach, pancake-NPs are predicted, *ceteris paribus*, to have the distribution of VP/infinitive/clause/vP type structures, as depicted in (23a):

(23) a. [v pannkakor]$_{vP}$ är gott.
b. [Att äta pannkakor] är gott.
(to eat) pancakes be.PRES good.NT.SG

After all, as noted above, such analyses are inspired by the putative parallel with infinitival subjects such as (23b).

But on the Logical Metonymy approach, pancake-NPs are predicted to have the distribution of event nominals, and not the distribution of verbal projections. Here the inspiration comes from the more generally attested phenomenon of logical metonymy. As in the English example (17) above, this phenomenon is found in Swedish too:

(24) a. Har du börjat (med) pannkakorna?
have you begun (with) pancake.PL.DEF
'Have you started (eating / cooking / ...) the pancakes?'

So the question is whether the pancake subjects have the external syntax of nominals or verbal projections. As it turns out, the evidence clearly favors the former: the pancake subjects behave in every respect like nominals and not like verbal projections of any kind.

A *pannkakor*-type singular-triggering, event-denoting phrase has the syntactic distribution of an NP (or DP), and never a clause, VP, infinitive phrase, vP, or anything else of that ilk. Swedish syntactic contexts that allow infinitives and clauses but disallow nominals uniformly reject phrases like *pannkakor*. In the pseudo-complement construction, a clausal or infinitival subject is replaced with the expletive pronoun *det* and extraposed, as shown in (25).

(25) a. [Att det snöade] var förvånande.
that it snowed be.PST surprising
'That it snowed was surprising.'

b. Det var förvånande [att det snöade].
it be.PST surprising that it snowed
'It was surprising that it snowed.'

Like clauses, infinitival subjects can also be replaced by an expletive and post-posed in the pseudocomplement construction:

(26) a. [Att äta pannkakor] är gott.
to eat pancakes be.PRES good.NT.SG

b. Det är gott [att äta pannkakor].
it be.PRES good to eat pancakes

(27) a. [Att ha två älskare] är omoraliskt.
to have two lovers be.PRES immoral

b. Det är omoraliskt [att ha två älskare].
it be.PRES immoral to have two lovers

In contrast, DP/NP subjects cannot be extraposed:

(28) a. Snön var förvånande.
snow.DEF be.PST surprising
'The snow was surprising.'

b. *Det var förvånande snön.
it be.PST surprising snow.DEF
(lit. *'It was surprising the snow.')

Like the nominals, and unlike the clauses and infinitives, pancake-subjects cannot be postposed:

(29) *Det är gott pannkakor.
it be.PRES good pancakes

(30) *Det är omoraliskt två älskare.
it be.PRES immoral two lovers

Under the Silent Phrase Structure analysis, the putative structures are like this:

(31) Det är gott [SUBJ v pannkakor]$_{vP}$.

This would leave us with no ready explanation for the unacceptability of such structures.

A similar contrast is found with verbs such as *fortsätta* 'continue', verbs that select verbal complements but reject NP/DP complements. Such verbs reject pancake-NPs, as shown in (32b):

(32) a. Jag fortsatte (att) äta pannkakor.
I continued (to) eat pancakes
'I continued to eat pancakes.'

b. *Jag fortsatte pannkakor.
I continued pancakes
'I continued pancakes.'

Adjectives such as *villig* 'willing' also select verbal complements but reject nominal complements. Once again, the pancake NPs cannot occupy this position:

(33) a. Jag är villig [att äta pannkakor].
I be.PRES willing to eat pancakes
'I am willing to eat pancakes.'

b. *Jag är villig [pannkakor].
I be.PRES willing pancakes
(*'I am willing pancakes.')

Similarly, nouns like *lust* 'desire' select verbal complements but reject NP complements, and pancake NPs behave just like other NPs in refusing to appear in such positions:

(34) a. Jag har lust [att äta pannkakor].
I have desire to eat pancakes
'I want to eat pancakes.'

b. *Jag har lust [pannkakor].
I have desire pancakes
('I want to eat pancakes.')

Finally, certain modal verbs like *kunna* 'be able to' select verbal complements but reject NP complements. Not surprisingly, the pancake NPs cannot appear there either:

(35) a. Jag kan inte [äta pannkakor].
I can not eat pancakes
'I cannot eat pancakes.'

b. *Jag kan inte [pannkakor].
I can not pancakes
('I cannot (eat, etc.) pancakes.')

All of the above contexts allow verbal projections and none of them allows a pancake-NP. Indeed, pancake-NPs seem to have exactly the same distribution as any other NPs, whether entity-denoting, event-denoting, etc. It is hard to see why this would be the case if the phrase structure of a pancake-NP differs so radically from that of a normal NP, as the Silent Phrase Structure analysis would have it.

Conversely, in syntactic contexts that allow an NP/DP but not a verbal projection, a pancake-subject is perfectly acceptable. For example, recall the secondary predicates pointed out by Hellan (1986). In Hellan's Norwegian example in (9b) above, repeated here as (36a), the lexical causative 'make' construction takes the form [*make* NP AP]. The object of causative *gjorde* 'made' must be an NP, not an infinitive, as shown in (36b).

(36) a. Fabrikantene gjorde tran sunt.
producer.DEF.PL made cod.liver.oil[M] healthy.NT.SG
'The producers made cod liver oil healthy (to drink).'

b. *Fabrikantene gjorde [å drikke tran] sunt.
producer.DEF.PL made to drink c.l.o. healthy.NT.SG
lit. 'The producers made [to drink cod liver oil] healthy.'

An example like (36b) can be 'rescued' using expletive replacement and postposing of the infinitive, since the expletive is itself a (pro)nominal:

(37) Fabrikantene gjorde det sunt [å drikke tran]
producer.DEF.PL made it healthy to drink c.l.o.
'The producers made it healthy to drink cod liver oil.'

Unlike the subject position in a matrix clause, which allows either a nominal or an infinitive (or clause), the subject of the secondary predicate in this lexical causative construction can only be a nominal. But an NP such as *tran* 'cod liver oil' can appear in either position. Thus the putative parallel between event-denoting metonymic subjects and verbal projections, which seems to be witnessed in the matrix clause, is illusory. In fact there is no parallel. If *tran* 'cod liver oil' were really a covert infinitival, then it should be unacceptable in (36a). If, on the other hand, it is exactly what it looks like, namely a nominal, then its behavior follows immediately.

Summarizing, the non-agreement-triggering *pannkakor* type word strings uniformly appear in syntactic contexts that permit NPs, while they are rejected from contexts that do not permit NPs but do allow verbal projections such as vP, VP, infinitives, and clauses.

To complete the picture, we must also consider, in addition to nominal projections (non-agreement triggering *pannkakor*) and verbal projections (*att äta pannkakor* 'to eat pancakes'), a third alternative: PPs headed by *med* 'with'. The 'with pancakes' construction in (40b) is very common and is often offered by informants as a paraphrase for the pancake sentences like (38a):[8]

(38) a. [Pannkakor] är gott.
pancakes be.PRES good.NT.SG

b. *Det är gott [pannkakor].
it be.PRES good pancakes

(39) a. [Att äta pannkakor] är gott.
to eat pancakes be.PRES good.NT.SG

b. Det är gott [att äta pannkakor].
it be.PRES good to eat pancakes

(40) a. *[Med pannkakor] är gott.
with pancakes be.PRES good

b. Det är gott [med pannkakor].
it be.PRES good with pancakes

These three options, NP, infinitive phrase, and *med*-PP, are illustrated in (38)-(40), respectively, with the phrase of each type appearing in the subject position in the (a) examples, and extraposed in the (b) examples. All examples mean roughly 'It's nice to have pancakes'. As discussed above, the NP cannot be extraposed (38), while the infinitive undergoes optional extraposition (39). To these two we now add the med-PP, which undergoes 'obligatory extraposition' (40).

Josefsson relates this obligatory extraposition of the PP to a more general fact about Swedish: 'It is a well-known fact that PPs cannot be subjects in Swedish.' (Josefsson 2009, 63). More generally, reviewing the three types of phrase, we find that each type occurs in the syntactic positions that are independently known to allow phrases of its type in Swedish: nominals can serve as subjects but not as complements of adjectives; infinitive phrases occur in both positions; and PPs cannot be subjects but can be complements of adjectives. This straightforward pattern follows as a trivial consequence of standard phrase structure grammar, which imposes local constraints on the combination of phrasal types. But it becomes hard to explain if we assimilate one or

[8]The exact string *Det är gott med kaffe* (literally 'it is good with coffee' but meaning 'It is nice to have coffee') garnered 33,500 Google hits. Needless to say, this sentence is heard very often in Sweden.

more syntactic type on the basis of the similarity of meaning. Every effort to make the pancake NP resemble a verbal projection by building a silent phrase structure around it has the unintended effect of erasing the very differences that would account for the distribution of the different phrase types.

It might be objected that on the right Silent Phrase Structure analysis, the exact structure posited for a pancake subject would differ in some crucial way from that of an infinitive or other verbal projection. Perhaps the topmost functional projection in that phrase, labeled FP in (12) above, turns out to have exactly the same distribution as an NP. But that would mean that the grammar of Swedish does not distinguish such an FP from an NP. In that case FP just is NP. And if the Swedish language presents us with no syntactic evidence for the other intervening shells (VP, vP, etc.), then apparently those parts of the diagram are not really representing syntactic structure.

Josefsson (2009, 43), arguing for a Silent Phrase Structure analysis, notes that pancake-NPs can contain reflexive pronouns, which normally require a subject antecedent:

(41) [Hemfärd till USA utan sin dotter]
hometravel.COM to USA without REFL daughter.COM
var omöjlig-t, tyckte Sally F.
was impossible-NT thought Sally F.
'Returning to the USA without her daughter was impossible, Sally F. thought.'

Josefsson cites this as evidence for the PRO subject of a silent 'light verb' within the bracketed phrase: the PRO binds the possessive reflexive *sin*. The conditions on the binding of such reflexives within NPs are complex and have been studied in some detail (Hellan 1988; Lødrup 2007, inter alia). For example, Josefsson (2009, 76, fn. 21) cites examples of possessive reflexives bound within NPs lacking a verb, including the following:[9]

(42)
Kvinnan med sina barn försvann i lördags.
woman.DEF with REFL children disappeared in Saturday
'The woman with her children disappeared last Saturday.'

In any case, on the theory assumed here, binding is defined on the ARG-ST (argument structure) list, not on the phrase structure. So if it turns out that entity-to-event logical metonymy licenses such bind-

[9]To explain the binding Josefsson (2009) suggests that such *med*-PPs are 'clausal'.

ing, then this would provide evidence regarding the ARG-ST list of the mother node dominating a pancake subject. But it would not bear on the question of silent phrase structure, unless it could be shown independently that the ARG-ST and the phrase structure systematically covary in the appropriate way.[10]

7 Neuter singular: default form or semantic agreement?

Having established that the pancake subject does not involve silent phrase structure, we turn to a second question: Why does the adjective in a pancake sentence appear in the neuter singular form in particular, and not some other form? Two general hypotheses will be considered. The first is that the neuter singular is the default or 'elsewhere' form. An alternative view, taken by Enger (2004) among others, is that the neuter singular form of the adjective arises through semantic agreement. In what follows I will give provide some evidence for the default hypothesis. However, it is important to first clarify what I mean by default agreement and semantic agreement, and what is at stake in this distinction, from my point of view. It is not clear, for example, that my proposal actually conflicts with that of Enger (2004).

There are three different ways in which the form of an agreement target may be determined by a grammar:

- grammatical (or formal) agreement: The target form depends on the controller's formal phi features.
- semantic 'agreement': The target form depends on the controller's meaning.
- failure of agreement: The target fails to agree and hence takes its default form.

Consider grammatical and semantic agreement first. In grammatical agreement the controller is grammatically specified for certain features

[10]Regarding the accusative pronoun in the pancake-subject in (7) above, an anonymous reviewer observes that the pronoun can be nominative instead if it is understood as the subject of the implicit action. The reviewer cites this example:

(43) [Hon som solist] vore oacceptabel-t.
she.NOM as soloist would.be unacceptable-NEUT
'Her (singing/playing/etc.) as soloist would be unacceptable.'

The pronoun's case is presumably assigned by the silent verb, on the the silent phrase structure view, or by the metonymy rule, on the logical metonymy view. This may complicate the metonymy analysis but it does not weaken any of the above arguments that the bracketed subject is a nominal rather than a clause. I leave this issue for future research.

as a consequence of the words making up the controller phrase: for example a nominal may be marked for a gender as a consequence of the lexical gender of the head noun. In semantic agreement the target is sensitive to the meaning of the controller instead of its formal features. According to the AGREEMENT MARKING PRINCIPLE (Wechsler 2011), semantic agreement arises when the controller lacks the formal grammatical features to which the target would normally be sensitive. For example, a French predicate adjective normally agrees with the formal features of its subject, as in (44a), where the feminine participle reflects the grammatical gender rather than the biological sex of the subject. But in (44b) the subject Dupont lacks a formal gender feature, so the semantic value of the predicate's gender marking is activated.

(44) a. La sentinelle à la barbe a été prise / *pris en otage.
the.F sentry bearded AUX been taken.F.SG / taken.M hostage
'The bearded sentry was taken hostage.'

b. Dupont est compétent / compétente.
Dupont is competent.M.SG / competent.F.SG
'Dupont (a man/a woman) is competent.'

The adjective in (44b) does not exactly 'agree' with the subject (hence the apologetic quotation marks around the word 'agreement' in the bulleted definition of semantic 'agreement' above). Rather, the gender feature of the adjective specifies some semantic information regarding the sex of the subject. This effect follows fairly straightforwardly in a unification based formalism such as HPSG: the adjective contributes certain semantic and syntactic features to its subject, and those features unify with the features contributed by the subject nominal itself. If the semantics specified by these two sources are inconsistent then the sentence is semantically anomalous, although it may be perceived as ungrammatical rather than anomalous if it can be fixed simply by substituting a different form from the agreement paradigm. This arises, for example, if a standard female name such as *Isabelle* replaces *Dupont* in (44b) and is understood to be referring to a woman, but the adjective appears in the masculine form.

If the Swedish neuter singular adjective is showing semantic agreement with its pancake-subject then the neuter singular features of the adjective bear some meaning that gets applied to the subject. However, semantic interpretation involves its own defaults, a consequence of paradigmatic blocking. The word *paper-cutter* is normally understood to refer to any device for cutting paper except for scissors. Scissors are called *scissors* instead. Similarly, a French feminine plural target, when applied to some controller that lacks a formal gender feature (such as *les Duponts* 'the Duponts'), indicates a group of females. Otherwise masculine plural is used, whether for a group of males or a group of people of mixed or unknown sex. In this example masculine is a semantic default: one consults the denotation of the controller phrase to see if it matches the semantics of the marked form(s); if not then the unmarked, or default, form is used. Returning now to the adjective in a pancake sentence, we can distinguish two possibilities regarding the neuter singular adjective, both of them 'semantic agreement' in some sense: (i) the neuter singular features have semantic content which matches the semantics of the pancake subject; or (ii) the neuter singular is a semantic default, used when the subject does not semantically satisfy the conditions set by the common gender or plural forms.

Yet another possibility is the failure of agreement, where the lack of agreement leads to the selection of a default form. On that analysis one does not consider the meaning of the subject at all.

Summarizing, we have the following theoretical possibilities:

(45) Procedure for determining agreement:

a. grammatical agreement: If the controller is marked for formal phi features, then the target should match those features.
b. semantic agreement: If the controller lacks the formal phi feature, then consult the semantics of the controller:
   (i) Select a target form and apply the semantic content of its agreement feature to the controller;
   (ii) If the controller is semantically inconsistent with any of the semantically marked target forms, use the semantically unmarked (default) form.
c. Failure of agreement: The target fails to agree and hence takes its default form.

Now let us consider the neuter singular adjective in a logical metonymy pancake sentence like (2) above. We consider number first, then gender.

By way of comparison, consider number agreement in English and French. English verbs normally show grammatical agreement with a (non-coordinate) NP subject: *His clothes are/*is dirty*, but *His clothing is/*are dirty*. But when the subject lacks a formal phi-feature, then semantic agreement becomes possible (Wechsler 2009). An example is semantic agreement with coordinate clausal subjects. In (46a) the verb is singular while in (46b) it is plural (examples from McCloskey 1991):

(46) a. [That the position will be funded and that Mary will be hired] now seems likely.
b. [That the president will be reelected and that he will be impeached] are equally likely at this point.

McCloskey (1991, 564-5) observes that singular is used for 'a single complex state of affairs or situation-type' (as in (46a)), while plural is possible for 'a plurality of distinct states of affairs or situation-types' (as in (46b)). The latter sort of interpretation is facilitated by the use of the adverb *equally*.

A similar situation is observed in French verb and adjective agreement with infinitival subjects (examples from Wechsler 2004, 262):

(47) a. Manger équilibré et faire du sport sont bons/?est bon
eat.INF balanced and do.INF sports are good.PL/is good
pour la santé.
for the health
'Eating a balanced diet and doing sports is good for you.'
b. Dormir dans un hôtel romantique et faire
sleep.INF in a hotel romantic and do.INF
des ballades en gondole sont/ *est inclus dans le prix.
the ballads in gondola are/ *is incuded in the price
'Sleeping in a romantic hotel and (doing) gondola ballads are included in the price.'

In that paper, I observed that 'Coordinate VPs often trigger singular agreement, since the conjunction of two propositions (habits, events, etc.) can often be lumped together into a single (conjoined) proposition (habit, event, etc.). But they trigger plural agreement as long as the meaning is readily conceptualized as an aggregate' (Wechsler 2004, 261-262).

But Swedish predicate adjective agreement appears to be rather different. In ordinary Swedish boolean coordination, the adjective appears in the plural form as expected:

(48) Jenny och Janna är (lika) snäll-a.
Jenny and Janna be.PRES equally nice-PL
'Jenny and Janna are (equally) nice.'

But when the subject is a clause or infinitive then the adjective appears in the (neuter) singular form, even if that subject is a coordinate structure and the sentence is heavily biased towards an aggregate reading. Clausal and infinitival subjects are illustrated in (49) and (50), respectively.

(49) Att det regnade och att det snöade var lika
that it rained and that it snowed was equally
konstigt /*konstiga.
strange.NT.SG / strange.PL
'That is rained and that it snowed were equally strange.'

(50) Att läsa och skriva är lika viktigt / *viktiga.
to read and write is equally important.NT.SG / important.PL
'Reading and writing are equally important.'

Even the use of adverbials like 'equally' or 'both', which force an interpretation as 'a plurality of distinct states of affairs or situation-types' (quoting McCloskey above), does not succeed in facilitating a plural adjective. The same applies to logically metonymous pancake-subjects:

(51) a. Våfflor och pannkakor är lika gott / (*)goda.
waffles and pancakes are equally good.NT.SG / good.PL
'Waffle and pancake situations are equally good.'

b. Både pannkakor och våfflor är gott / (*)goda
both pancakes and waffles are good.NT.SG / good.PL
'Both pancake and waffle situations are good.'

I have been unable to find a context in which speakers will assent to a plural adjective, when the subject involves coordinated, metonymic nominals. No matter how much we bias the sentence so that it will be interpreted as 'a plurality of distinct states of affairs', singular agreement is still favored.

Kind-denoting terms are similar, although there seems to be a little room for variation. The noun betong 'concrete' is a common gender noun: the definite form is *betongen* 'concrete.COM.DEF', not **betonget* 'concrete.NT.DEF'. As usual, it can occur in a kind-type pancake sentence, with a neuter singular adjective:

(52) Betong är tungt.
concrete[COM] be.PRES heavy.NT.SG
'Concrete is heavy.'

What about coordinated kind terms? Let us try to form a heterogenous aggregate of the sort that strongly favors plural agreement in English: *Concrete and sand are/??is equally heavy.* In Swedish such sentences do not force plural agreement. On the contrary, it is barely even possible to get plural agreement:

(53) a. Sand och betong är lika tungt.
sand and concrete are equally heavy.NT.SG

b. *Sand och betong är lika tunga.
sand and concrete are equally heavy.PL
'Sand and concrete are equally heavy.'

Out of four speakers surveyed, all four found (53a) acceptable. Three out of four found (53b) unacceptable. The fourth was slightly unsure, indicating at first that it is OK but 'perhaps not so likely to be uttered', and later speculating that it 'is theoretically possible but is usually avoided'. In any case, there appears to be an overall preference for the singular adjective in such cases.

As noted already, this situation contrasts sharply with number agreement in English, where plural is strongly preferred for predicates of the form BE equally AP when agreeing with conjoined kind-denoting mass nouns.

(54) a. When gin and tonic are/*is mixed, quinine and the flavor molecules from the juniper berries combine to make a perceived flavor that is different than just the sum of the individual parts.

b. For me, gin and tonic is /*are only good with lime.

The English coordinated mass term subjects, like the English clausal and infinitival subjects, illustrate semantic agreement: subtle differences of interpretation affect the choice of number form for the verb.

By contrast, the Swedish pancake-sentences, like Swedish sentences with clausal and infinitival subjects, uniformly favor neuter singular. I conclude from this fact that the neuter singular found with these sorts of subjects is not a case of semantic agreement — not even default semantic agreement. In constructions of this kind, the competence grammar of Swedish does not involve inspecting the semantics of the subject to determine its cardinality. In the case of pancake-sentences, the grammar must provide for the semantic construction and interpretation of a pancake subject, whether the logical metonymy or kind-denoting type. Nonetheless, once the subject is classified into this type, the adjective simply fails to agree, and the (so-called) neuter singular is the default form in Swedish, designated for use when there is no agreement relation at all.

Now consider gender agreement. Obviously the pancake subject need not have a head noun with a formal neuter feature, so that eliminates grammatical agreement (45a). So is the neuter gender a consequence of semantic agreement (45b.i), a semantic default (45b.ii), or the failure of agreement (45c)? It seems unlikely that the Swedish neuter gender encodes some descriptive content that is satisfied by events denoted by the metonymy type pancake subjects. Such a subject denotes an event or other situation, such as an event of eating pancakes, but as far as I know the only descriptive semantic categories that are clearly encoded in the gender system of Swedish are animacy (in pronouns and adjectives), and sex (in the personal pronouns). For reference to people (or animals such as pets), one uses the pronouns *han* / *honom* 'he, him' or *hon* / *henne* 'she, her'; for everything else one uses *det* 'it.NT' (the more general form; see below) or *den* 'it.COM', in grammatical agreement with its antecedent. (The plurals *de*/*dem* 'they, them' can be used for any plurals, whether personal or impersonal.) Thus the Swedish pronoun system distinguishes between male, female, and 'other'. Eventualities such as pancake-eating events clearly belong in the 'other' category.[11]

This eliminates (45b.i), leaving two possibilities: neuter singular is either a semantic default (45b.ii) or used for the lack of agreement altogether (45c). To put it in operational terms, the question is what the grammar directs the speaker to do when the subject lacks a grammatical gender feature. Do we inspect the semantics of the controller, using the neuter form if it fails to satisfy the condition of being animate? Or do we ignore the semantics of the controller altogether and just use neuter? If we restrict our attention to pancake sentences then I know of no way of distinguishing these two, for gender.

In conclusion, the so-called neuter singular form of the predicate adjective is actually the grammatically unmarked or default form: it is the form used in the absence of any agreement relation at all. In a pancake sentence agreement is blocked because the features of the noun are encapsulated within a larger semantic structure that serves as the adjective's subject.

This means that we should analyze the Swedish neuter singular adjective form as a general form, and not, strictly speaking, a neuter singular. Of the three members of the paradigm of the adjective for 'good', *god* is for agreement with a common gender singular and *goda* is for a plural; on a true default analysis, *gott* would be considered the 'elsewhere' form, used whenever there is no trigger that matches the specifications of the other forms in the paradigm. Note that the analysis sketched in §5 above is not really an analysis of that kind, but it simulates the effect of one. It reifies the notion of an 'elsewhere' referential index by distinguishing a special type for indices that lack phi

[11]Regarding the neuter gender, Enger suggests that 'The controllers in pancake sentences are low on the individuation scale (Sasse 1993). This is also the reason why they are neuters.' (Enger 2004, 30) This observation may be true as a metacommentary but it seems unlikely that 'low on the individuation scale' belongs to the positively specified descriptive content of the neuter gender feature.

features. Common nouns are lexically specified for gender and inflect for number, and this is the source of the grammatical gender and number features of the nominals that they head. Clauses, infinitives, and any other constituents that lack such features bear a referential index of the type *unmarked-index*, an option which a neuter singular adjective specifies for its subject (along with the option of taking a neuter singular subject). A true default analysis could probably be formalized in HPSG by using persistent defaults (Lascarides et al. 1996), but I will not undertake that here.

8 Conclusion

A pancake subject is a nominal that would normally denote an entity, but exhibits logical metonymy, so that it denotes an eventuality that is related to the entity instead: the pancakes qua foodstuff stand in for an event of eating them. As we have seen, such transfers of meaning can affect grammatical agreement processes. I consider the effect of metonymy on agreement processes to be a significant and quite interesting aspect of the interaction between syntax and semantic interpretation, one that has been noted in the past (Nunberg 1995) and still merits further study. But while pancakes can stand in for a pancake-eating event, there is no evidence that *pannkakor* qua NP 'stands in' phonologically for a phrasal construction with a syntactic type normally associated with event denotations. With respect to syntax, such a phrase is just what it appears to be: a nominal. The temptation to assimilate the metonymic nominal's phrase structure to that of a clause should be resisted, not only because such nominals clearly pattern syntactically with other nominals and not with clauses, but also because such an approach prevents us from appreciating an interesting interaction between syntax and semantic interpretation.

References

Cooper, Robin. 1984. Svenska nominalfraser och kontext-fri grammatik. *Nordic Journal of Linguistics* 7(2):115–143.

Enger, Hans-Olav. 2004. Scandinavian pancake sentences as semantic agreement. *Nordic Journal of Linguistics* 27(1):5–34.

Faarlund, Jan Terje. 1977. Embedded clause reduction and Scandinavian gender agreement. *Journal of Linguistics* 13(2):239–257.

Hellan, Lars. 1986. The headedness of NPs in Norwegian. In P. Muysken and H. C. van Riemsdijk, eds., *Features and projections*, pages 89–122. Dordrecht, Netherlands: Foris Publications.

Hellan, Lars. 1988. *Anaphora in Norwegian and the Theory of Grammar*, vol. 32. Dordrecht, NL: Foris Publications.

Josefsson, Gunlög. 2009. Peas and pancakes: On apparent disagreement and (null) light verbs in Swedish. *Nordic Journal of Linguistics* 32(1):35–72.

Lascarides, Alex, Ted Briscoe, Nicholas Asher, and Ann Copestake. 1996. Order independent and persistent typed default unification. *Linguistics and Philosophy* 19(1):1–90.

Lødrup, Helge. 2007. Norwegian anaphors without visible binders. *Journal of German Linguistics* 19(1):1–22.

McCloskey, James. 1991. There, it, and agreement. *Linguistic Inquiry* 22(3):563–567.

Nunberg, Geoffrey. 1995. Transfers of meaning. *Journal of Semantics* 12(2):109–132.

Pollard, Carl and Ivan A. Sag. 1994. *Head-driven phrase structure grammar*. University of Chicago Press.

Pustejovsky, James. 1995. *The Generative Lexicon*. Cambridge, MA: MIT Press.

Sag, Ivan A. 1997. English relative clause constructions. *Journal of Linguistics* 33(2):431–483.

Sag, Ivan A. 2008. Feature geometry and predictions of locality. In G. Corbett and A. Kibort, eds., *Proceedings of the Workshop on Features*. Oxford, UK: Oxford University Press.

Sag, Ivan A. and Janet D. Fodor. 1994. Extraction without traces. In *West Coast Conference on Formal Linguistics*, vol. 13, pages 365–384.

Wechsler, Stephen. 2004. Number as person. In O. Bonami and P. C. Hofherr, eds., *Empirical Issues in Syntax and Semantics*, vol. 5, pages 255–274.

Wechsler, Stephen. 2009. Agreement features. *Language and Linguistics Compass* 3(1):384–405.

Wechsler, Stephen. 2011. Mixed agreement, the person feature, and the index/concord distinction. *Natural Language & Linguistic Theory* 29(4):999–1031.

Wechsler, Stephen and Larisa Zlatić. 2003. *The many faces of agreement*. Stanford, CA: Center for the Study of Language and Information.

Wellander, Erik. 1955. *Riktig Svenska: En Handledning i Svenska Språkets Vård, 3rd edition*. Stockholm: Svenska Bokförlaget, PA Norstedt & Söner.

Widmark, Gun. 1966. Den inkongruenta neutrala predikatsfyllnaden och dess plats i svenskans genussystem. *Nysvenska studier* 46:91–134.

3

Handel, Liszt, and Minimal Recursion Semantics

DAN FLICKINGER

In the early years of the LinGO (Linguistic Grammars Online) project at CSLI in the mid-nineties, our efforts to build a broad-coverage grammar of English led to the design and implementation of a formalism for semantic representation called Minimal Recursion Semantics, which fit well into the declarative, unification-based descriptions of linguistic signs motivated and employed in the then-recently published second HPSG book. One of the central desiderata of the MRS design was the ability to underspecify scope constraints, both for quantifiers and for scopal operators including negation. As the implementation of the English grammar proceeded, we found real benefit in this approach for quantifiers, which enabled reduction in syntactic ambiguity, but we did not encounter many constructions with scopal operators in core English phenomena where morphology or syntax interacted with scope in interesting ways. Since we were at the time working closely with grammar developers for German and Japanese, as part of the ambitious Verbmobil spoken language translation project, we did encounter more interesting scope interactions particularly with German negation and adverbs, which lent support for the generality of the relevant design decisions in MRS.

This paper by Bender and Lascarides is thus a welcome contribution to the body of work on MRS, first providing argumentation supporting the analysis of negation with syntactically fixed scope as implemented

The Core and the Periphery.
Philip Hofmeister and Elisabeth Norcliffe (eds.).

in the English Resource Grammar, and then examining applications of that analysis to phenomena in other languages. Using data from Turkish, Hausa and Inuktitut, the authors explore several alternative variations on the approach to negation used for the English grammar, along the way demonstrating shortcomings of this approach even for English. Their analyses lead to the proposed use of one particular kind of scope underspecification that was indeed also motivated by German data back in the days of Verbmobil, but is now clearly of broader cross-linguistic import.

Ivan has been at the heart of the creation and development of the MRS formalism, conspiring readily in the rather irreverent early naming conventions for the formalism and the main attributes of its data structures. We co-conspirators, including Ann Copestake, Rob Malouf, Susanne Riehemann, and Tom Wasow, initially gave elements of these structures labels that were reminders of our commitment to compositional semantics, including HANDEL and LISZT, which led to first naming the formalism Messianic Romantic Semantics. Even we could see that a name with more gravitas and transparency was preferable if this formalism was to be adopted more widely, so the acronym was soon repurposed to serve for Minimal Recursion Semantics, and (some considerable time later) the two central attributes were renamed to the more neutral HANDLE and RELS. Still, the small statues that Rob brought in of these two composers continue to grace the LinGO offices at CSLI, reminders that a little whimsy can be welcome in the midst of serious formal work.

4

On Modeling Scope of Inflectional Negation

EMILY M. BENDER AND ALEX LASCARIDES

1 Introduction

In this paper, we investigate the representation of negated sentences in Minimal Recursion Semantics (Copestake et al. 2005). We begin with its treatment in the English Resource Grammar (Flickinger 2000, 2011), a broad-coverage implemented HPSG (Pollard and Sag 1994), and argue that it is largely a suitable representation for English, despite possible objections. We then explore whether it is suitable for typologically different languages: namely, those that express sentential negation via inflection on the verb, particularly Turkish and Inuktitut.[1] We find that the interaction between negation and intersective modifiers requires a change to the way in which (at least) one of them contributes to semantic composition, and we argue for adapting the analysis of intersective modifiers.

More generally, this work can be seen as a case study of universality in semantic representation in surface-oriented compositional semantics. Such representations are necessarily somewhat language-specific: notably in lexical semantics, but also in cases where translational equivalents display differences in structural relationships and/or elements that are usually treated as logical constants.[2] Nonetheless, we still expect

[1]We use the term 'inflection' here broadly to refer to any morphological process, and are not concerned with contrasting 'inflection' and 'derivation'.

[2]For example, Korean expresses situational possibility via a noun *swu* ('way') in combination with an existential verb (Sohn 1994, 348; see also van der Auwera and

The Core and the Periphery.
Philip Hofmeister and Elisabeth Norcliffe (eds.).

to see many common structures in areas of semantics such as negation. As we strive to work with a surface-oriented, compositional framework, however, we must negotiate the surface-structural differences between languages so as to achieve those common semantic structures. Thus, a cross-linguistically appropriate semantic representation must not only capture meanings as they are used in different languages, but also be buildable on the basis of the diverse morphosyntactic scaffolding provided by the different languages.

2 Semantic representation of negation in the ERG

In this section, we review the semantic representation of negation in the English Resource Grammar (ERG, Flickinger 2000, 2011) using Minimal Recursion Semantics (MRS, Copestake et al. 2005). The representation is motivated by semantic scope ambiguities involving negation and quantifiers, but it is challenged by other phenomena, including the focus-sensitivity of negation (e.g. Fischer 1968) and 'neg-raising' (e.g. Horn 1978). Nonetheless, we will argue that the representation is appropriate for English.

To focus the discussion on the level of representation we are concerned with, we note that the MRS language and its model theory are designed to express the incompleteness of meaning that is revealed by linguistic form on its own, while capturing (very abstractly) those aspects of a linguistic phrase's content that are conveyed in *all* its possible discourse contexts. In general, then, an MRS must be a (perhaps partial) description of a fully specific and context-aware interpretation of the linguistic phrase that it represents. In particular, in those cases where even a syntactically disambiguated analysis of the phrase exhibits semantic scope ambiguities, its MRS must underspecify the relative semantic scope of the relevant constructors, while at the same time ensuring that the pragmatically preferred fully scoped reading satisfies the MRS's scope constraints.

Negation's scopal interaction with quantifiers is illustrated in (1). In (1), there are two readings, one in which the quantifier *some* is interpreted inside the negation (see (1a)), and one in which *some* is given wide scope (see (1b)):

Ammann 2011b):

(i) Halapeci-nun wuncenha-si-l swu(-ka) iss-usi-ta.
grandpa-TOP drive-SUBJ.HON-PRES way-NMLZ exist-SUBJ.HON-DECL
'My grandpa can drive.' [kor]

(1) Kim didn't read some book.

a. ∃x (book(x), ¬read(Kim,x))

b. ¬∃x (book(x), read(Kim,x))

Accordingly, it is appropriate to produce a semantic representation (i.e. a partial description of a fully specific logical form such as (1a) or (1b)) which treats both negation and the quantifier as scopal elements but underspecifies their relative scope. For reasons that we turn to below, we give negation a fixed scopal position in the sentence while allowing quantifiers to scope in between it and the predicate it embeds (*read* in our example). In MRS, this is handled by giving the elementary predication corresponding to the negation (neg) a scopal argument position which is related to the verb's predication, _read_v (corresponding in (1) to the predicate *read*), via a 'qeq' (equal modulo quantifiers) constraint. This constraint says that neg either directly outscopes _read_v, or outscopes one or more quantifier relations which in turn outscope _read_v. The MRS representation assigned to (1) by the English Resource Grammar (Flickinger 2000, 2011) is shown in Figure 1. Note how not only the scopal argument to negation is left underspecified, but likewise the formulae representing the restrictor and the body of the quantifier are also underspecified ($h_{15} =_q h_{16}$ and h_{14} in no expressed scopal constraints, respectively). The former handles scope ambiguities in noun phrases like *some chapters of every book* which do not concern us here. The underspecification of the body of the quantifier is desirable because the scope of quantifiers isn't fixed relative to other scopal elements (compare the different formulae representing the body of the quantifier in (1a) vs. (1b)). Roughly put, an MRS is satisfied by a fully scoped logical form if the following three conditions are met: (a) all scope constraints are satisfied; (b) each scopal argument (in other words, any label h that appears as an argument in Figure 1) is equated with a unique label of a predication (in other words, a label h' that is to the left of a colon, with a predicated formula to its right in Figure 1); and (c) all variables are within the scope of their associated quantifier, if there is such a quantifier (so, for example, this means that the body h_{14} of the quantifier some_q_indiv, which binds x_{12}, must outscope the label h_{11} of read_v). This interpretation of MRSs means that, abstracting away from quantifiers introduced by the proper names, the MRS in Figure 1 yields exactly two possible fully scoped forms: (1a) and (1b).

That the scope of sentential negation should be fixed with respect to other scopal modifiers by its position in the sentence seems uncontroversial in English. Consider (2), which arguably has the readings in

$$\langle h_1, \left\{ \begin{array}{l} h_3\text{:proper\_q}(x_5, h_4, h_6), \\ h_7\text{:named}(x_5, \text{Kim}), \\ h_8\text{:neg}(e_{10}, h_9), \\ h_{11}\text{:\_read\_v\_1}(e_2, x_5, x_{12}), \\ h_{13}\text{:\_some\_q\_indiv}(x_{12}, h_{15}, h_{14}), \\ h_{16}\text{:\_book\_n\_of}(x_{12}, i_{17}) \end{array} \right\}, \\ \{h_{15} =_q h_{16}, h_9 =_q h_{11}, h_4 =_q h_7\}\rangle$$

FIGURE 1 MRS for (1) from ERG

(2a-c) but not those in (2d–e). That is, (2) cannot be paraphrased as 'It is not the case that Kim deliberately read every book.'

(2) Kim deliberately didn't read every book.

a. ∀x (book(x), deliberately(¬read (Kim,x)))

b. deliberately(∀x (book(x), ¬read (Kim,x)))

c. deliberately(¬∀x (book(x), read(Kim, x)))

d. *¬deliberately (∀x (book(x), read(Kim, x)))

e. *∀x (book(x), ¬deliberately(read(Kim,x)))

These facts are compatible with an analysis, such as that implemented in the ERG, where the negative element in the sentence (here, the inflected form *didn't*) introduces the scopal neg, as well as the qeq constraint connecting its argument position to the local top handle of the VP *read every book.*

2.1 Neg-raising

An apparent counter-example to the above claim that the scope of negation is fixed relative to everything except quantifiers by its syntactic position is the phenomenon of *neg-raising* (Horn 1978).[3] In neg-raising, a certain class of predicates license a reading where negation appears to be interpreted semantically inside the clausal complement of the negated verb. For instance, the natural reading of (3) is paraphrasable as 'Kim believes Sandy isn't happy', as represented (in a simplified way) in the logical form (3a):

(3) Kim doesn't believe Sandy is happy.

a. believe(kim,¬happy(sandy))

[3]Neg-raising is so named because early accounts had the negative operator positioned in the lower clause in an underlying structure and then 'raised' to its surface position.

$$\langle h_1, \left\{\begin{array}{l} h_3\text{:proper\_q}(x_5,\ h_4,\ h_6),\\ h_7\text{:named}(x_5,\ \text{Kim}),\\ h_8\text{:neg}(e_{10},\ h_9),\\ h_{11}\text{:\_believe\_v\_1}(e_2,\ x_5,\ h_{12}),\\ h_{13}\text{:proper\_q}(x_{15},\ h_{14},\ h_{16}),\\ h_{17}\text{:named}(x_{15},\ \text{Sandy}),\\ h_{18}\text{:\_happy\_a\_with}(e_{19},\ x_{15},\ i_{20}) \end{array}\right\}, \\ \{h_{14} =_q h_{17}, h_{12} =_q h_{18}, h_9 =_q h_{11}, h_4 =_q h_7\}\rangle$$

FIGURE 2 MRS for (3) from ERG

$$\langle h_1, \left\{\begin{array}{l} h_3\text{:proper\_q}(x_5,\ h_4,\ h_6),\\ h_7\text{:named}(x_5,\ \text{Kim}),\\ h_8\text{:neg}(e_{10},\ h_9),\\ h_{11}\text{:\_believe\_v\_1}(e_2,\ x_5,\ h_{12}),\\ h_{13}\text{:proper\_q}(x_{15},\ h_{14},\ h_{16}),\\ h_{17}\text{:named}(x_{15},\ \text{Sandy}),\\ h_{18}\text{:\_happy\_a\_with}(e_{19},\ x_{15},\ i_{20}) \end{array}\right\}, \\ \{h_{14} =_q h_{17}, h_{12} =_q h_8, h_9 =_q h_{18}, h_4 =_q h_7\}\rangle$$

FIGURE 3 Alternative MRS for (3), not from ERG

The ERG produces the MRS shown in Figure 2 for sentence (3). In this MRS, the scopal argument of neg is related (via qeq, as always) to the label of _believe_v, which in turn takes the label of _happy_a_with as its second argument via a qeq. Figure 3 shows an MRS representation (not generated by the ERG) which would yield a fully scoped interpretation that is equivalent to (3a). The only change is in the handle constraints (qeqs). While the neg-raising examples appear to always have both readings (e.g. those represented by Figure 2 and Figure 3), the current analysis implemented in the ERG, which we are supporting here, only produces the first.

Our motivation for supporting an analysis that only produces representations of the type given in Figure 2 concerns the grounds for neg-raising readings. Gajewski (2005) argues, on the basis of NPI licensing facts, that neg-raising is best understood in terms of presuppositions. In particular, he argues that neg-raising predicates introduce a lexical presupposition of the assumption of the Excluded Middle. Because this presupposition can be canceled in appropriate contexts, two apparent readings emerge despite the lack of any semantic ambiguity. Gajewski's analysis posits only a semantic representation where negation attaches 'high' (as indicated by its surface position). While the ERG does not

$$\langle h_1, \left\{ \begin{array}{l} h_3{:}\_the\_q(x_5, h_6, h_4), \\ h_7{:}\_dog\_n\_1(x_5), \\ h_8{:}neg(e_{10}, h_9), \\ h_{11}{:}\_bark\_v\_1(e_2, x_5), \\ h_{11}{:}\_loud\_a\_1(e_{12}, e_2) \end{array} \right\},$$
$$\{h_9 =_q h_{11}, h_6 =_q h_7\}\rangle$$

FIGURE 4 MRS for (4) from ERG

currently handle the introduction and propagation of presuppositions (as would be required to implement Gajewski's analysis), it seems reasonable to assume that these would be handled separately from the MRS structure representing the constant semantic contribution of each sentence. As the MRS in Figure 2 represents the 'high' attachment of negation that Gajewski argues is appropriate, the ERG's current analysis should be compatible with a presupposition-based approach to neg-raising.

2.2 Focus sensitivity

Another potential objection to an analysis of negation as having fixed scope comes from examples like (4), which has all of the possible continuations (4a–d). It is tempting to assume that (4a), (4b) and (4c) respectively provide evidence that the negation can outscope only the adverb, only the verb, or both.

(4) The dog didn't bark loudly.

a. It was really quiet, actually.

b. It was whining loudly.

c. It was whining quietly.

d. That was a hyena that was barking.

The MRS generated by the ERG (shown in Figure 4), however, makes negation take scope over both _bark_v and _loud_a, as these two are required by the analysis of intersective modification to share the same scopal position (in other words, their respective predications are joined with a conjunction $\wedge$ in any fully scoped logical form).[4]

However, as noted by many authors (Fischer 1968; Jackendoff 1972; Karttunen and Peters 1979; McCawley 1998; Herburger 2000; Krifka 2006; Beaver and Clark 2008), negation (in English, at least) is focus sensitive. Beaver and Clark (2008) present a detailed analysis of focus

[4]The subject NP introduces a quantifier which can scope above or below neg.

sensitivity, and argue that it is essentially pragmatic for all focus sensitive items, although certain items are conventionally focus sensitive. Negation is not one of these. On Beaver and Clark's analysis, negation is only quasi-focus sensitive. A quasi-association with focus, on their account, produces defeasible implicatures, but no truth-conditional effects. Thus, we can say that the semantics of (4) is as in Figure 4, i.e. the claim that there was no barking situation in which the dog was the barker and the barking was loud. The information structure of the utterance (not represented in English orthography) sets up the relevant contrast set, which in turn sets up the possibility of each continuation in (4). If *loudly* bears the focus-indicating pitch accent, then the focus will be just *loudly* (the so-called narrow focus reading, where the contrast set is other kinds of barking situations with that dog), or the VP *bark loudly* (the wide focus reading, where the contrast set is other things the dog might have done), etc.

2.3 Summary

To summarize this section, we have reviewed evidence from English that negation is scopal, and that its scope is fixed by its syntactic position in the sentence. Furthermore, the desired semantic representations can be built compositionally by having the negative formative (the word *not* or the affix *n't*) introduce the neg and its associated qeq.[5] We explored two possible types of counterexamples — neg-raising and the focus sensitivity of negation — and found that they do not require any revisions to the ERG's analysis.

3 Inflectional negation

We next ask whether this analysis can be extended to other languages. In particular, we are concerned with languages that express negation as an affix on main verbs. This is a fairly common pattern, occurring in 417 languages of the 1159 language sample in Dryer 2011. A problem arises for these languages when we consider the interaction of negation with intersective modifiers. Intersective modifiers are handled in MRS via handle-sharing: recall from §2 that they share the scope of the head they modify, meaning that in any fully-scoped reading the predicate introduced by the modifier and that introduced by its modifiee are conjuncts in a conjunction. This is shown in Figure 4, the MRS produced by the ERG for (4). We argued above that the MRS in Figure 4

[5]Kim and Sag (2002) note the relative scope of modals and negation is lexically specific, and take this as evidence that both sentential *not* and the affix *n't* (cf. Zwicky and Pullum 1983) are introduced by lexical rules. The lexical rules in question can introduce the neg and assign its scope.

is a reasonable representation for the semantics of the English example (4). Assuming for the moment that an analogous representation is appropriate for the Turkish translation in (5), we face the problem of how to build it compositionally.[6]

(5) Köpek yuksek ses-le havla-ma-di.
dog loud voice-INST bark-NEG-PST
'The dog didn't bark loudly' [tur]

In (5), the intersective modifier is the phrase *yuksek sesle*, which bears instrumental case[7] licensing its use as an adverbial modifier. One analysis of such modifiers uses a non-branching rule to introduce a two place predication relating the NP and the VP (e.g. one called instrument). While the NP will presumably contain its own quantifier, the modifier as a whole will be treated as intersective, and as such we would want the instrument predication to share its label with that of the verb.

Meanwhile the negation is expressed by an affix on the verb (-*mA*, subject to vowel harmony).[8] The most straightforward analysis would be to have the negative affix attached via a meaning-contributing lexical rule, such as that sketched in (6).

(6)
$$\left[\begin{array}{ll}
\text{C-CONT} & \left[\begin{array}{ll}
\text{RELS} & \left\langle \left[\begin{array}{ll}\text{PRED} & \text{neg}\\ \text{LBL} & \boxed{1}\\ \text{ARG1} & \boxed{2}\end{array}\right]\right\rangle\\
\text{HOOK} & \left[\begin{array}{ll}\text{LTOP} & \boxed{1}\\ \text{INDEX} & \boxed{3}\end{array}\right]\\
\text{HCONS} & \left\langle \left[\begin{array}{ll}\textit{qeq} & \\ \text{HARG} & \boxed{2}\\ \text{LARG} & \boxed{4}\end{array}\right]\right\rangle
\end{array}\right]\\
\text{DTR} & \left[\ldots\ \text{HOOK} \left[\begin{array}{ll}\text{LTOP} & \boxed{4}\\ \text{INDEX} & \boxed{3}\end{array}\right]\right]
\end{array}\right]$$

[6] In order to show that the analogous representation is suitable for Turkish, we would need to find evidence of scope ambiguities between quantifiers and negation analogous to (1). We have found it difficult to elicit judgments from native speakers on such examples, and thus must leave this issue for later work. It seems plausible to us, however, that such scope ambiguities should occur across languages.

[7] Kornfilt (1997) refers to -*le* as an instrumental clitic. Its status as a clitic or an affix is orthogonal to the point at hand.

[8] Kornfilt (1997) notes that Lewis (1975) analyzes -*mA* as a clitic. Kornfilt argues that it is in fact an affix, on the basis of its position inside other affixes and its participation in vowel harmony.

This rule introduces the neg and its associated qeq constraint. The LTOP of the mother's C-CONT (constructional content) and thus of the mother itself is the label of the neg. The label of the verb's relation is related, via the qeq, to the ARG1 of the neg, but is not otherwise available for further combination.

This is problematic if we take the MRS in Figure 4 as the target for this Turkish sentence (modulo predicate names, which are language-specific, and the substitution of the equivalent of *with a loud voice* for *loudly*). The adverbial phrase *yuksek sesle* necessarily attaches outside the negative affix, unless we are willing to abandon the Lexical Integrity Hypothesis (Bresnan and Mchombo 1995). But once the negative affix is attached, per the rule in (6), the label of the verb's relation is no longer available, meaning that the adverb would be predicted to be outside of the scope of the negative operator.

Returning to English for a moment, we can construct examples where adverbs attach semantically outside of negation:

(7) Kim pointedly didn't reply to the question.

(8) Kim didn't reply to the question, pointedly.

Again, English uses syntax to establish the scope of negation. Note the contrast between (8) and (9):

(9) Kim didn't reply to the question pointedly.

Thus, we wouldn't want to say that negation is necessarily the highest scoping non-quantifier in its clause—such an analysis would also run into problems with (2).

To summarize, we sometimes need to allow intersective modifiers to take scope inside the negative operator. However, the morphosyntactic facts of Turkish require us to attach the negative operator first, if we wish to maintain Lexical Integrity. Furthermore, the mechanisms of semantic composition used in English, and adapted for Turkish, make the scopal position that the intersective modifiers would like to take inaccessible at the point at which they attach syntactically.

There appear to be two potential ways out of this puzzle: one involves changing the way we compose the semantics of negation; the other involves changing the way we compose the semantics of intersective modifiers. In the first, we could dissociate the morphological marking of negation from its semantic contribution. Alternatively, we could change the way that the label (LBL) of (intersective) modifiers relates to that introduced by the semantics of the constituent they attach to in syntax. These two alternatives are each explored in turn in §4 and §5.

4 Dissociation of morphology and semantics

We start with the first approach mentioned above: to dissociate the morphological marking of negation from its semantic contribution. We assumed in rule (6) that one and the same lexical rule attaches the affix and introduces the neg. The alternative is to take the affix as simply marking the verb as part of a negated clause, while relegating the introduction of the semantics to a higher construction—i.e. a non-branching phrase structure rule. This analysis is essentially the same as that proposed for Turkish modal affixes by Fokkens et al. (2009), in light of suspended affixation examples such as (10).

(10) Çocuk-lar film izle-yip pizza ye-meli-ler.
child-PL movie watch-COORD pizza eat-NEC-3.PL
'The children must watch a movie and eat pizza.' [tur] (Fokkens et al. 2009, 111)

This example illustrates how the affix *-meli* meaning 'must' can take scope over multiple coordinated VPs. Fokkens et al. (2009) argue against treating it as a phrasal affix and show that the Lexical Integrity Hypothesis (Bresnan and Mchombo 1995) can be maintained by adopting an analysis along the lines of Tseng's 2003 analysis of apparent phrasal affixes in French. On these analyses, the presence of the morphology is registered (either in HEAD, as in Turkish, or with an EDGE feature, in French) and used to trigger a non-branching construction higher in the tree.

Crysmann (2010) presents a similar constructional approach to negation in Hausa, arguing that neither of the two markers used in the discontinuous negation construction illustrated in (11) actually carries the negative force on its own. Rather, the markers signal the presence of a construction, in this case also a non-branching construction, which requires both left and right EDGE features encoding the presence of both of the negative markers.

(11) mā̀lāmai bà sù ji kōmē ba.
teachers NEG 3.P.CPL hear anything NEG
'The teachers did not hear anything.' [hau] (Newman 2000, 357)

However, Crysmann's arguments for a constructional account of this Hausa negation strategy show it to be different in important ways from negation in Turkish. In particular, Crysmann shows that both of the markers are attached as affixes to the words they are adjacent to and then observes that the semantics of negated sentences with VP coordination requires that the negative force must be integrated into the semantics 'high', rather than at the level of the morphological attachment of one or the other of the markers:

(12) Mammàn nē bài zō ajī ya dàuki
Mamman FOC NEG.3.S.M.CPL come class 3.S.M.REL.CPL take
jarràbâwā ba.
exam NEG
'It was *Mamman* who didn't come to class and take the exam.'
[hau] (Jaggar 2001, 166)

In Turkish, the case for constructional introduction of negative force lacks such motivation. For one thing, the negative marker is not one of the affixes that can be suspended in 'suspended affixation'. Our consultants accepted (13a), where both constituents are negated separately.[9] However, when we put the negation on just one of the conjuncts, as in (13b) and (13c), the consultants rejected the sentences and offered alternatives with a *but* conjunction (13d).[10,11]

(13) a. Çocuk-lar film izle-mi-yor ve pizza
Child-PL movie watch-NEG-CONT and pizza
ye-mi-yor-lar-dı.
eat-NEG-CONT-3PL-PST
'The children were not watching a movie and were not eating pizza.' [tur]

b. *Çocuk-lar film izli-yor ve pizza
Child-PL movie watch-CONT and pizza
ye-mi-yor-lar-dı.
eat-NEG-CONT-3PL-PST
Intended 'The children were (not) watching a movie and were not eating pizza.' [tur]

[9] However, our consultants also said this would be an uncommon way to express this meaning, preferring instead a *neither ... nor* type construction, illustrated in (i):

(i) Çocuk-lar ne film izli-yor ne de pizza yi-yor-lar-di.
Child-PL NEG movie watch-CONT NEG COORD pizza eat-CONT-3PL-PST
'The children were neither watching a movie nor eating pizza.' [tur]

[10] One consultant accepted (13b) and (13c), but only with a reading where only the verb bearing the negation marker is interpreted as negated.

[11] There are two coordination constructions in Turkish which both allow suspended affixation: affixal coordination with -*(y)ip* and coordination marked by the independent word *ve* (Fokkens et al. 2009). Only -*(y)ip* coordination appears to allow suspended affixation with scopal elements like -*mEli*. Interestingly, our consultants rejected constructed examples involving -*(y)ip* coordination and negation on either conjunct.

c. *Çocuk-lar film izle-mi-yor ve pizza
Child-PL movie watch-NEG-CONT and pizza
ye-yor-lar-dı.
eat-CONT-3PL-PST
Intended 'The children were not watching a movie and were (not) eating pizza.' [tur]

d. Çocuk-lar film izli-yor ama pizza
Child-PL movie watch-NEG-CONT but pizza
ye-mi-yor-lar-dı.
eat-NEG-CONT-3PL-PST
'The children were watching a movie but were not eating pizza.' [tur]

Thus, we find that negation is not subject to suspended affixation, and so suspended affixation cannot provide positive evidence for a constructional account of the introduction of the semantics of negation.

There is also evidence against a constructional account in Turkish, concerning the interaction of negation and the morphological causative. In particular, while in Turkish the order of these two morphemes is fixed, with negation attaching outside the causative, the semantics can go either way. That is, (14) can have either of the meanings given in (14a–b).

(14) Ebeveyn-ler çocuk-lar-ına meyve yedir-t-me-di-ler.
Parent-PL child-PL-DAT fruit eat-CAUSE-NEG-PST-3PL

a. 'The parents did not make (or force) the kids to eat the fruit.'

b. 'The parents made the kids not eat the fruit.' [tur]

The constructional account is even less appealing for morphological causatives, as they affect not only semantics but also argument structure and linking. The effect of a causative lexical rule is to introduce the cause predication and link its arguments to the stem's arguments and the stem's own semantic contribution, as illustrated in (15).[12]

[12]In a given language, there might also be constraints on the CASE value of the ARG-ST elements.

(15)
$$
\left[\begin{array}{ll}
\text{C-CONT} & \left[\begin{array}{ll}
\text{RELS} & \left\langle \left[\begin{array}{ll} \text{PRED} & \text{cause} \\ \text{LBL} & \boxed{1} \\ \text{ARG0} & \boxed{2} \\ \text{ARG1} & \boxed{3} \\ \text{ARG2} & \boxed{4} \\ \text{ARG3} & \boxed{5} \end{array}\right] \right\rangle \\
\text{HOOK} & \left[\begin{array}{ll} \text{INDEX} & \boxed{2} \\ \text{LTOP} & \boxed{1} \\ \text{XARG} & \boxed{3} \end{array}\right] \\
\text{HCONS} & \left\langle \left[\begin{array}{ll} \multicolumn{2}{l}{\textit{qeq}} \\ \text{HARG} & \boxed{5} \\ \text{LARG} & \boxed{6} \end{array}\right] \right\rangle
\end{array}\right] \\
\text{ARG-ST} & \left\langle \left[\text{INDEX}\ \ \boxed{3}\right] \right\rangle \oplus \boxed{7} \\
\text{DTR} & \left[\begin{array}{ll} \ldots\ \text{HOOK} & \left[\begin{array}{ll} \text{LTOP} & \boxed{6} \\ \text{XARG} & \boxed{4} \end{array}\right] \\ \text{ARG-ST} & \boxed{7} \end{array}\right]
\end{array}\right]
$$

In order to get readings like (14b), where the negation attaches inside the causative, the negative-force introducing rule (lexical or constructional) would need access to the stem's semantic information. At the same time, the causative-introducing rule (argued to be lexical) needs access to the negative-introducing rule's semantic information, as it should set up a qeq constraint between the ARG3 of the cause and the LBL of the neg. This is already somewhat problematic in the case where both are lexical rules: if lexical rules are non-branching productions applying in sequence, once the causative rule in (15) applies, the verb stem's HOOK information is no longer available for further combination. Conversely, once the causative rule has applied, its qeq is fixed (it is linked to the verb stem's LTOP; see the co-occurrence of $\boxed{6}$ in rule (15)) and can't be modified by the negative rule. However, if all the processes involved are lexical, the apparent ordering of the suffixes could be treated as a templatic morphology effect (Hyman 2003), essentially a morphophonological process which obscures the order of application of the morphosyntactic rules.[13] No such analysis would be available if the negative force were introduced constructionally.

[13] Alternatively, if the Turkish causative is ambiguous between a permissive reading ('allow') and a non-permissive one ('make' or 'force'), then both readings could

The case against dissociating the morphology and semantics of negation is even stronger for Inuktitut, where both orders are possible and the order of the morphemes reflects semantic scope (Elke Nowak, pers. comm., see also Nowak 2008):

(16) ani-nngit-tit-tara.
go.out-NEG-CAUSE-1S.3S.TR
'I cause him/her not to go out.' [ike]

(17) ani-tit-nngit-tara.
go.out-CAUSE-NEG-1S.3S.TR
'I did not make him/her go out.' [ike]

Even if it were possible to handle the causative and negative semantics both through syntactic constructions, the order of application of those constructions would have to mirror the order of the morphemes within the word. This, in turn, means that that order would have to be recorded somewhere.[14]

In summary, it seems that a syntactic introduction of negative force will not serve as a general solution to the problem of modifier scope in negated sentences in languages with negative inflection. We now turn to the other possible solution.

5 Modifier attachment

The second possible solution involves changing the way the attachment of intersective modifiers is handled in the composition. Recall that the problem is that we want the modifier to share the label of the verb (which is outscoped by negation), but that label is not 'visible' at the point where the modifier attaches. Here we explore the possibility of using handle constraints other than simple equality to circumvent this problem.[15]

While MRS in general allows for multiple different kinds of handle constraints, the ERG only uses the 'qeq' (equal modulo quantifiers) relation: $h_1 =_q h_2$ means that the scopal positions that h_1 and h_2 denote in any fully-scoped logical form (each such logical form being a model for interpreting MRS expressions) must have only 0 or more quanti-

involve the same relative scope of the negative and causative elements, namely, one which is consistent with their morphological realization.

[14]The syntactic approach to linking suggested by Haugereid (2004) (see also Goldberg 1995) might provide some wiggle room here. However, it would still be odd—and counter to lexical integrity in spirit, at least—to have the order of syntactic rules dictated by the order of morphological rules.

[15]We are grateful to Dan Flickinger for suggesting this strategy.

fiers intervening between them.[16] Another type that has been explored in other grammars is 'leq' (less than or equal to) (Schlangen 2003; Alahverdzhieva and Lascarides 2011). Thus, one possibility would be to have the quantifiers constrain their own handles to be 'leq' the handle of the constituent they attach to. In words, $h_1 \leq h_2$ means that the scopal position denoted by h_1 in any fully-scoped logical form is outscoped by or equal to that denoted by h_2. In practice, this means that the constructor C_1 that is labeled by h_1 in the MRS is either outscoped by the constructor C_2 denoted by h_2—thereby allowing scopal elements like negation and modals, as well as quantifiers, to intervene between them—or (if $h_1 = h_2$) C_1 and C_2 are conjuncts joined by $\wedge$. In essence, $h_1 \leq h_2$ is a notational variant of the dominance relation $h_2 \lhd^* h_1$ from Egg et al. 2001.

We will illustrate this first with an example from English: we show how to compose an MRS for *The dog didn't bark loudly*, using a semantic entry for *loudly* that introduces an leq constraint $l \leq h$. The semantics of *didn't bark* is what we would expect from above: in terms of the algebra from semantic composition from Copestake et al. 2001, we get (18).

(18) hook = <l1,e>
slot = <l4,x>
rels = l1:neg(h)
l2:_bark_v(e,x)
hcons = h $=_q$ l2

The *slots* in the semantic representations (also called *holes* in Copestake et al. 2001) record gaps in semantic form—in (18) the semantic gap will be filled by a subject NP. According to the rules of the algebra, slots are filled during semantic composition by being equated with the hook of the relevant constituent (note that these slots aren't shown in the more compact MRS notation in Figures 1 to 4, but rather the first element of the tuple in these figures corresponds to the label of the hook in the algebra notation, the second element to the rels, and the third element to the hcons).

Now we assume a structure in which *loudly* attaches high (i.e. to the VP *didn't bark*, instead of just *bark*). This isn't required for this English example, but it is what we would need for Turkish, as negation is part of the verb. As we just proposed, the semantics of *loudly* introduces an leq constraint as shown in (19): $l3 \leq h'$ will allow the label l3 of

[16]The Grammar Matrix (Bender et al. 2002, 2010), which aims to be able to create starter grammars for any natural language, currently follows the ERG in only using qeq constraints.

the _loud_a relation to fit lower in the scope tree than the label h′ of whatever constituent *loudly* attaches to syntactically.

(19) hook = <h′,e′ >
slot = <h′,e′ >
rels = l3:_loud_a(e″,e′)
hcons = $l3 \leq h'$

In particular, combining (18) and (19)—i.e. by equating the hook in (18) with the slot of (19)—yields the representation (20) for *didn't bark loudly*:

(20) hook = <l1,e>
slot = <l4,x>
rels = l1:neg(h)
l2:_bark_v(e,x)
l3:_loud_a(e″,e)
hcons = $h =_q l2$
$l3 \leq l1$

In other words, we are using the leq constraints to allow intersective modifiers to effectively 'tuck' their labels underneath the label of the constituent they attach to in the syntax, such that they can share scope with something lower in the syntax tree.

There are at least two potential problems with this approach. First, it may be the case that the 'equal to' reading isn't actually available. Consider (5), repeated here as (21):

(21) Köpek yuksek ses-le havla-ma-di.
dog loud voice-INST bark-NEG-PST
'The dog didn't bark loudly.' [tur]

Similarly to the translation, there is probably no reading of this sentence where _loud_a shares its scope with neg. Such a reading would have to mean that what was loud was the lack of barking.

On the other hand, the lack of this reading could be captured via a pragmatic anomaly at the level of speech acts in the coherent use of the sentence in context (and this anomaly could be specified in the separate model theory for the language and logic of fully-specific logical forms). Specifically, we could, in principle at least, stipulate that any coherent assertion that an event is loud must also assert that the event happened. This constraint on coherent assertions is violated by any fully-specific logical form where the modifier _loud_a shares its scope with neg.[17] This would also be useful in English. The ERG actually licenses two structures for (5), the one we want (with the adverb attaching low) and a second one where the adverb attaches to the higher VP (*didn't bark*). This second parse gives rise to the semantic representation that we argue should not be a part of any coherent interpretation of (5) in context.

The second, and potentially more serious objection, is that we must establish a lower bound for the 'less than' part of the leq. If the modified verb takes a clausal complement, what is to stop the adverb from attaching its handle down inside that complement? The word order facts of Turkish make it somewhat difficult to find the relevant examples, but (22) provides a starting point.[18] This and similar examples would need to be investigated more thoroughly, but assuming that this example in fact only has the reading where the adverb attaches semantically high (to *inanıyorum*), then we need to make sure that the leq approach does not license readings where it attaches semantically low, if these are not warranted.

(22) Başarılı ol-acağ-ınız-a inan-ıyor-um
Successful become-FUTPART-2PL-DAT believe-CONT-1SG
yürek-ten.
heart-ABL.
'I whole-heartedly believe that you will become successful.' [tur]

This can be handled via a constraint on the resolution of fully scoped MRSs from underspecified representations, analogous to the constraint that requires all variables to appear within the scope of their associated quantifiers (Copestake et al. 2005; see also the discussion in §2). In this case, we stipulate that the modifier may not take a position lower in the scope tree than the one associated with the predication that introduces the event variable it is modifying as its ARG0. In (22), that would be the elementary predication _believe_v introduced by *believe*. In other words, this constraint ensures that in any fully scoped form that satisfies the MRS (22), _firmly_a shares its scope with _believe_v.

[17]This distinction between consistent at the domain level but anomalous at the speech act level is also the basis for solving Moore's paradox (Hintikka 1962)—that one would never utter *It's raining but I don't believe it.* This is satisfiable, but it is never coherent to assert it.

[18]The post-verbal position of the adverb in this example is an attempt to remove the possibility of syntactic attachment of the adverb to the lower verb. However, it appears that Turkish has a construction that allows for displacement of constituents to the post-verbal position, suggesting that that adverb might have been 'extracted' from the lower clause anyway.

So far, we have only considered intersective modifiers. However, it is also important to make sure that the analysis of negation interacts properly with scopal modifiers. In contrast to the intersective modifiers, preliminary evidence suggests that scopal modifiers in Turkish cannot inject their labels into a lower position in the scope tree. Thus our consultants say that (23) can only mean (23a) and not (23b).

(23) Köpek muhtemelen havla-ma-di.
Dog probably bark-NEG-PST.
'The dog probably didn't bark.' [tur]

a. $\exists$x dog(x) $\wedge$ probably($\neg$ bark(x))

b. *$\exists$x dog(x) $\wedge$ $\neg$probably(bark(x))

Similarly in Inuktitut, a because-type modifier clause combining with a negated clause is outside the scope of that negation. That is, unlike its translation in English, (24) is unambiguous (Elke Nowak, pers. comm.):[19]

(24) qiurami qilunngittuq.
qiu-rami qilu(k)-nngit-tuq
be.cold-3S.CAUS.ITR bark-NEG-3S.ITR
'It does not bark because it feels cold.' [ike]

The English translation could either mean that the dog does not bark and the reason for that is that it is cold or that the dog is barking, but for some other reason. The Inuktitut sentence only has the former meaning.

This is consistent with the analysis we have given so far. For the scopal modifiers to attach (semantically) inside negation, they would need to not only constrain their labels to be leq the label of the constituent they combine with, but actually break the qeq constraint established by the negative morpheme and replace it with two of their own, such that the negation operator's argument is qeq the label of the scopal modifier (e.g. Turkish *muhtemelen* 'probably') and the scopal modifier's argument is qeq the label of the verb. In other words, we would need to create a partial MRS for *muhtemelen* 'probably' such that it could combine with the MRS in (25) to create the MRS in (26). Setting aside the problem of how to make the label of *havla-* 'bark' visible for combination, such a representation would at any rate be inconsistent with a monotonic approach to semantic composition, as it would

[19]It remains to be seen, of course, whether the typical HPSG head-modifier structure is an appropriate model for the way in which these two clauses are combined. We assume for the sake of the argument that it is, while acknowledging that this can't be known without more careful study of Inuktitut using HPSG.

have to remove information ($h2 =_q l3$). Leaving that qeq constraint in is not an option, as each of neg, _muhtemelen_a and _havla_v must their own position in the scope tree; $h2 =_q l3$ allows quantifiers to intervene between neg and _havla_v, but not fixed-scope elements like _muhtemelen_a.

(25) hook = <l1,e>
rels = l1:neg(h2)
l3:_havla_v(e,x)
hcons = h2 $=_q$ l3

(26) hook = <l1,e>
rels = l1:neg(h2)
l3:_havla_v(e,x)
l4:_muhtemelen_a(h5)
hcons = h2 $=_q$ l4, h5 = q l3

To summarize this section, it appears that adapting the way that intersective modifiers attach semantically to the constituents they modify allows us to compositionally construct the same type of semantic representations for Turkish (and by extension, for other languages with inflectional negation, such as Inuktitut) as we do for English, despite their differences in morphosyntax. Only intersective, and not scopal, modifiers appear to need this modification, which is furthermore another point in favor of the approach presented in this section and against that presented in §4. For example, assuming that *often* is a scopal modifier, thereby reflecting the fact that semantically it quantifies over times and/or events, our analysis of negation matches intuitions in that it yields just one reading for each of (27a) and (27b): namely, the one where the relative scope of often_a and neg in logical form matches the order of *often* and *n't* in the string.[20]

(27) a. We often don't open the window.
b. We don't often open the window.

Note, finally, that the modifications we propose are only in the deployment of a particular type of handle constraint. The leq constraint is not new (cf. Schlangen 2003; Alahverdzhieva and Lascarides 2011;

[20]Dan Flickinger (pers. comm.) points out that *often* does not pattern syntactically with other scopal adverbs in English. In particular, it can appear in a post-VP position with no pause in intonation and without prosodic stress on the modifier, and this is not generally possible for the others (Müller and Kasper 2000):

(i) We open the window often/*probably.

We leave this puzzle for future work.

Egg et al. 2001), just not previously deployed (to our knowledge) for this purpose. Furthermore, the analyses we propose for the semantic contributions of intersective modifiers are compatible with the existing algebra for MRS composition (Copestake et al. 2001).

6 Conclusion

In this paper, we highlighted a number of challenges in providing a unified analysis of negation both in languages (like English) where it is lexicalized and in languages (like Turkish) where it is a morphological suffix on the verb. We explored two different ways in which such an analysis might be achieved, and argued for a solution where the scope constraints introduced by intersective modifiers are 'relaxed': instead of the adverbial's semantic predicate *always* being joined via conjunction to its head's predicate in a fully-scoped logical form, it can optionally take a lower position in the scope tree. This allows negation to attach in the morphosyntax before the intersective modifier does, while still allowing the modifier to appear lower in the position in the scope tree—this is the desired effect, since in this way negation semantically outscopes the intersective modifier. Thus, we are able to maintain parallel semantic representations across the languages despite their divergent morphosyntax.

In future work, we would like to explore whether our proposed analysis would be useful for capturing the right scopal readings of other types of scopal elements that appear as bound morphemes in some languages or free morphemes in others, such as modals of situational possibility (van der Auwera and Ammann 2011b) or epistemic possibility (van der Auwera and Ammann 2011a). In addition, we plan to test these analyses and their compatibility with further interacting phenomena by adapting the Grammar Matrix (Bender et al. 2002, 2010) to reflect them.

Finally, our model of negation captures crosslinguistic data by relaxing only scope constraints on intersective modifiers. If one were also to relax the constraints that identify the event that is modified by an intersective modifier, then it may be possible to simplify the mapping between form and meaning for utterances with PPs. For instance, one could conceivably create a grammar which assigns just one syntactic analysis to (28), where the PP attaches high. In the MRS associated with this analysis, the ARG1 of on would be left underspecified. Then, constraints on the algorithm for resolving that MRS to complete and specific interpretations would yield exactly the two desired readings: one where the decision occurs on Tuesday, and one where the room is reserved on Tuesday.

(28) We decided to reserve a room on Tuesday.

However, achieving such an analysis would involve relatively radical changes to the algebra for composing semantic forms, and to the algorithms for listing fully scoped and specific meaning representations from the underspecified MRS, and so it is beyond the scope of this paper to pursue this line of analysis here.

Acknowledgments

We are grateful to Dan Flickinger, Ann Copestake, Stephan Oepen, Nicholas Asher, and Joshua Crowgey for helpful discussion of the ideas presented in this paper, to Elke Nowak for discussion of the Inuktitut data, and to Ozan Hafizogullari, Eren Ayça Efe-Hafizogullari, Muge Salmaner and Taner Sezer for sharing their judgments on Turkish sentences. Any remaining errors are solely the responsibility of the authors. This material is based upon work supported by the National Science Foundation under Grant No. 0644097 and European Research Council Grant No. 269427. Any opinions, findings, and conclusions or recommendations expressed in this material are those of the author(s) and do not necessarily reflect the views of the National Science Foundation or the European Research Council.

References

Alahverdzhieva, Katya and Alex Lascarides. 2011. An HPSG approach to synchronous speech and deixis. In S. Müller, ed., *Proceedings of the 18th International Conference on Head-Driven Phase Structure Grammar (HPSG)*, pages 6–24. Seattle: CSLI Publications.

Beaver, David I. and Brady Z. Clark. 2008. *Sense and Sensitivity: How Focus Determines Meaning*. Wiley-Blackwell.

Bender, Emily M., Scott Drellishak, Antske Fokkens, Laurie Poulson, and Safiyyah Saleem. 2010. Grammar customization. *Research on Language & Computation* 8(1):23–72. 10.1007/s11168-010-9070-1.

Bender, Emily M., Dan Flickinger, and Stephan Oepen. 2002. The grammar matrix: An open-source starter-kit for the rapid development of cross-linguistically consistent broad-coverage precision grammars. In J. Carroll, N. Oostdijk, and R. Sutcliffe, eds., *Proceedings of the Workshop on Grammar Engineering and Evaluation at the 19th International Conference on Computational Linguistics*, pages 8–14. Taipei, Taiwan.

Bresnan, Joan and Sam A. Mchombo. 1995. The lexical integrity principle: Evidence from Bantu. *Natural Language & Linguistic Theory* 13:181–254. 10.1007/BF00992782.

Copestake, Ann, Dan Flickinger, Carl Pollard, and Ivan A. Sag. 2005. Minimal recursion semantics: An introduction. *Research on Language & Computation* 3(4):281–332.

Copestake, Ann, Alex Lascarides, and Dan Flickinger. 2001. An algebra for semantic construction in constraint-based grammars. In *Proceedings of the 39th Annual Meeting of the Association for Computational Linguistics (ACL 2001), Toulouse, France.*

Crysmann, Berthold. 2010. Discontinuous negation in Hausa. In S. Müller, ed., *The Proceedings of the 17th International Conference on Head-Driven Phrase Structure Grammar*, pages 269–287. Stanford: CSLI Publications.

Dryer, Matthew S. 2011. Negative morphemes. In M. S. Dryer and M. Haspelmath, eds., *The World Atlas of Language Structures Online*. Munich: Max Planck Digital Library.

Egg, Markus, Alexander Koller, and Joachim Niehren. 2001. The constraint language for lambda structures. *Journal of Logic, Language, and Information* 10:457–485.

Fischer, Susan. 1968. *On Cleft Sentences and Contrastive Stress*. Cambridge, MA: MIT Press.

Flickinger, Dan. 2000. On building a more efficient grammar by exploiting types. *Natural Language Engineering* 6 (1) (Special Issue on Efficient Processing with HPSG):15–28.

Flickinger, Dan. 2011. Accuracy v. robustness in grammar engineering. In E. M. Bender and J. E. Arnold, eds., *Language from a Cognitive Perspective: Grammar, Usage and Processing*, pages 31–50. Stanford, CA: CSLI Publications.

Fokkens, Antske, Laurie Poulson, and Emily M. Bender. 2009. Inflectional morphology in Turkish VP coordination. In S. Müller, ed., *Proceedings of the 16th International Conference on Head-Driven Phrase Structure Grammar, University of Göttingen, Germany*, pages 110–130. Stanford: CSLI Publications.

Gajewski, Jon Robert. 2005. *Neg-Raising: Polarity and Presupposition*. Ph.D. thesis.

Goldberg, Adele E. 1995. *Constructions: A Construction Grammar Approach to Argument Structure*. Chicago: University of Chicago Press.

Haugereid, Petter. 2004. Linking in constructions. In S. Müller, ed., *Proceedings of the HPSG-2004 Conference, Center for Computational Linguistics, Katholieke Universiteit Leuven*, pages 414–422. Stanford: CSLI Publications.

Herburger, Elena. 2000. *What Counts: Focus and Quantification*. Cambridge, MA: MIT Press.

Hintikka, Jaakko. 1962. *Knowledge and Belief*. Ithaca, New York: Cornell University Press.

Horn, Laurence. 1978. Remarks on neg-raising. In P. Cole, ed., *Pragmatics*, vol. 9, pages 129–220. New York: Academic Press.

Hyman, Larry M. 2003. Suffix ordering in Bantu: A morphocentric approach. In G. Booij and J. van Marle, eds., *Yearbook of Morphology 2002*, pages 245–281. Kluwer Academic Publishers.

Jackendoff, Ray. 1972. *Semantic Interpretation in Generative Grammar*. Cambridge, MA: MIT Press.

Jaggar, Philip. 2001. *Hausa*. Amsterdam: John Benjamins.

Karttunen, Lauri and Stanley Peters. 1979. Conventional implicatures in Montague Grammar. In C.-K. Oh and D. Dineen, eds., *Syntax and Semantics II: Presupposition*, pages 1–56. New York: Academic Press.

Kim, Jong-Bok and Ivan A. Sag. 2002. Negation without head-movement. *Natural Language & Linguistic Theory* 20:339–412. 10.1023/A:1015045225019.

Kornfilt, Jaklin. 1997. *Turkish*. New York: Routledge.

Krifka, Manfred. 2006. Association with focus phrases. In V. Molnár and S. Winkler, eds., *The Architecture of Focus*, pages 105–136. Berlin: Mouton de Gruyter.

Lewis, Geoffrey. 1975. *Turkish Grammar*. New York: Oxford University Press, corrected edition, originally published in 1967 edn.

McCawley, James D. 1998. *The Syntactic Phenomena of English*. Chicago: University of Chicago Press, 2nd edn.

Müller, Stefan and Walter Kasper. 2000. HPSG Analysis of German. In W. Wahlster, ed., *Verbmobil: Foundations of Speech-to-Speech Translation*, pages 238–253. Berlin: Springer.

Newman, Paul. 2000. *The Hausa Language: An Encyclopedia Reference Grammar*. New Haven, CT: Yale University Press.

Nowak, Elke. 2008. *Inuktitut. Eine grammatische Skizze*. München: Lincom Europa.

Pollard, Carl and Ivan A. Sag. 1994. *Head-Driven Phrase Structure Grammar*. Studies in Contemporary Linguistics. Chicago, IL and Stanford, CA: The University of Chicago Press and CSLI Publications.

Schlangen, David. 2003. *A Coherence-based Approach to the Interpretation of Non-Sentential Utterances in Dialogue*. Ph.D. thesis, University of Edinburgh.

Sohn, Ho-min. 1994. *Korean*. Descriptive Grammars. London / New York: Routledge.

Tseng, Jesse. 2003. Phrasal affixes and French morphosyntax. In G. Jäger, P. Monachesi, G. Penn, and S. Wintner, eds., *Proceedings of Formal Grammar 2003*, pages 177–188. Stanford: CSLI Publications.

van der Auwera, Johan and Andreas Ammann. 2011a. Epistemic possibility. In M. S. Dryer and M. Haspelmath, eds., *The World Atlas of Language Structures Online*. Munich: Max Planck Digital Library.

van der Auwera, Johan and Andreas Ammann. 2011b. Situational possibility. In M. S. Dryer and M. Haspelmath, eds., *The World Atlas of Language Structures Online*. Munich: Max Planck Digital Library.

Zwicky, Arnold M. and Geoffrey K. Pullum. 1983. Cliticization vs. inflection: English *n't*. *Language* 59:502–13.

3

Questions about Questions

Jonathan Ginzburg

Until fairly recently, there were very few formal analyses of what have been called DECLARATIVE QUESTIONS or INTONATION QUESTIONS, uses of declarative sentences 'to ask questions', as in (1):

(1) a. Jean is happy these days?
    b. Everything is going along fine?

Even now, there are still not that many fragments with formal accounts of these cases.[21] This can possibly be explained, in part, by the influence of what some have referred to as the Frege–Searle Propositional Content Hypothesis, a long standing and often repeated assumption of Speech Act Theory (see e.g. Searle 1969), which in fact originates with Frege (1918). It assumes that assertions, polar queries, and commands differ on the level of illocutionary force, but share the same descriptive/propositional content. Applied, for instance to (2), the claim amounts to saying that the declarative, the interrogative, and the imperative have the same content, namely some proposition p, when uttered in the same context. On this view, the difference between these potential utterances is that (2a) will be used to assert p, whereas (2b) will be used to ask p, and (2c) to command p:

(2) a. Bo will go away.
    b. Will Bo go away?
    c. Go away Bo!

[21] For some references, see the paper by Abeillé, Godard, and Marandin.

The Core and the Periphery.
Philip Hofmeister and Elisabeth Norcliffe (eds.).

In Ginzburg and Sag (2000), Ivan Sag and I argued against the Frege–Searle Propositional Content Hypothesis. We suggested that, in fact, the semantic ontology provides distinct abstract entities called, respectively, propositions, questions, and outcomes, which figure as the contents of assertions, queries, and commands and also as the arguments of distinct classes of predicates, as exemplified in (3):

(3) a. Kim believes that Bo will go away.
    b. Sandy asked whether Bo will go away?
    c. Merle ordered Bo to go away.

In particular, we argued, together with much of the literature on the semantics of interrogatives that both a 'whether' clause, and a polar interrogative denote a semantic entity $p?$ distinct from the corresponding proposition p. We argued that questions could be identified with the class of PROPOSITIONAL ABSTRACTS, entities that emerge from propositions via the semantic operation of abstraction and we identified $p?$ with the 0-ary abstract $\lambda\{\ \}p$. In the situation theoretic framework we developed 0-ary abstracts are distinct from the objects they abstract out—though the model theory was, as some people noted, somewhat complex.[22]

Back to declarative questions. What to say about them? They seem to behave very much like polar interrogatives: they give rise to disquotation patterns like those linking (3) and (4) and, of course, they trigger a similar range of responses:

(4) a. Charlie: Bo will go away?
    b. Charlie asked whether Bo will go away.
    c. Charlie: Bo will go away? Jean: Yes/No/Maybe.

When we were working on Ginzburg and Sag 2000, we did not initially have any elegant way of dealing with declarative questions. Polar interrogatives were a nice instance of constructional inference, with the lion's share of their properties falling out from their specification as Fillmorean subject-auxiliary-inversion clauses; the only stipulation required for the polar interrogative use was the 0-ary abstraction, which built a question out of a proposition. To the extent anyone bothered with specifying the rules for generating polar interrogatives (and since the heyday of Montague Semantics few people did), no one, we thought, had a simpler theory.

[22] Using an alternative view of abstraction, developed subsequently by Robin Cooper (Cooper 2012) in the framework of Type Theory with Records has enabled the idea of 0-ary abstraction to be simplified considerably. In TTR questions are identified with functions from records into propositions. 0-ary abstracts are, on this view, constant (propositional) functions.

Declarative questions, though, would not submit to such an analysis and in any case Ivan, despite his important grad school work on intonation with Mark Liberman (Liberman and Sag 1974), always gave the impression of being a skeptic about the importance of intonation and so probably thought we would just leave it.

We were working on reprise utterances, initially on cases where Kim repeats most of what Sandy says but replaces an 'unclear' constituent with a *wh*-word, as exemplified in (5). The analysis we developed could handle n *wh*–reprises, with $n \geq 1$:

(5) a. A: I like Vyachoslav Voinovich.
B: (Sorry,) you like WHO?
b. A: Who likes barack pálinka?
Who likes WHAT?
c. A: A video camera recorded absolutely every shaman priest from East Anglia.
B: What recorded WHO?

At some point we realized that because polar questions were 0-ary abstracts, if we were to allow the schema to apply to $n \geq 0$, our account would also capture LITERAL REPRISES, where a repetition expresses a clarification request:

(6) a. Sandy: Kim is angry.
Charlie: Kim is angry?!
b. Merle: Who do you like?
Kim: Who do I like?!

Given our analysis of reprise interrogatives, we could now demonstrate that English also possesses *in situ* unary interrogatives which express regular information questions, thereby contradicting a long asserted dogma of generative grammar:

(7) Michael Krasny [addressing a guest—WHO HAS NOT SAID ANYTHING YET—about the interim chief of the US Attorney's office]:
This is a position that is HOW IMPORTANT in your judgment, Rory?
[Forum KQED—July 29, 1998]
a. Lester: I've been working here for 14 years. You've been here for HOW LONG? A month? [from the movie *American Beauty*]

As with reprise interrogatives, our construction type for analyzing such cases was initially restricted to n *wh*-phrases, with $n \geq 1$. But when we saw the benefits of allowing $n = 0$ for the reprise case, we realized that $n = 0$ in this instance would yield directly an account of declarative questions. Ivan was quite elated.

Although we didn't explicitly formulate the presupposition, the idea was that there should be a commonality in contextual background between these and in situ *wh*-interrogatives. Now, given that in English uses such as (7) involve a rather strong presupposition, though one that has been difficult to characterize precisely, this would mean that declarative questions would, in contrast, to polar interrogatives, carry a certain bias (in favor of the positive option, for unnegated declaratives).

This is some of the background for the very subtle and empirically rich paper by Abeillé, Godard, and Marandin, who for French, argue *against* the analysis of declarative questions as denoting questions. This is a productive area, which will, I believe, yield much important work for at least two reasons. First, there seems to be much cross-linguistic variation: both English and French possess multiple means of expressing polar questions, whereas other languages, e.g. Hebrew and, apparently Spanish and Portuguese, at least in spoken variants, have only declarative questions. Sorting out the range of presuppositions and denotations across these various languages requires much careful work. A second reason to follow this area closely is the rise of probabilistic semantics (e.g. Goodman et al. 2008). This should enable research to more precisely formulate the presuppositions associated with such constructions.

References

Cooper, Robin. 2012. Type theory and semantics in flux. In R. Kempson, N. Asher, and T. Fernando, eds., *Handbook of the Philosophy of Science*, vol. 14: Philosophy of Linguistics. Amsterdam: Elsevier.

Frege, Gottlob. 1918. Thoughts. In P. Geach and M. Black, eds., *Translations from the Philosophical Writings of Gottlob Frege, 3rd Edition*. Oxford: Basil Blackwell.

Ginzburg, Jonathan and Ivan A. Sag. 2000. *Interrogative Investigations: the form, meaning and use of English Interrogatives*. No. 123 in CSLI Lecture Notes. Stanford: California: CSLI Publications.

Goodman, Noah, Vikash Mansinghka, Daniel M Roy, Keith Bonawitz, and Joshua Tenenbaum. 2008. Church: a language for generative models with non-parametric memoization and approximate inference. In D. McAllester and P. Myllymaki, eds., *Proceedings of the Twenty-Fourth Conference on Uncertainty in Artificial Intelligence*, pages 220–229.

Liberman, Mark and Ivan A. Sag. 1974. Prosodic form and discourse function. In *Proceedings of the 10th Annual Meeting of the Chicago Linguistics Society*. Chicago: University of Chicago.

Searle, John. 1969. *Speech Acts*. Cambridge: Cambridge University Press.

5

French Questioning Declaratives in Question

ANNE ABEILLÉ, DANIÈLE GODARD AND JEAN-MARIE MARANDIN

1 Introduction

Ginzburg and Sag (2000) define the notion of clause type independently of illocutionary force: a clause type is a construction which associates a family of clausal forms and a content type. The content of a declarative clause is a proposition, and that of an interrogative is a question. Each clause type is further associated with constraints on the type of speech act it enables the speaker to perform when used in root sentences. A root declarative clause is used to make an assertion, a root interrogative clause is used to make a query (provided the felicity conditions of the speech act are met). In this respect, there is a class of utterances which raise a difficulty. On the one hand, they have a declarative form, on the other, they have been analyzed as interrogatives, or as conveying a query or as having the effect of a query. They are known under different labels: 'intonation question', 'rising declarative', 'declarative question', 'questioning declarative'. We examine the French version of such utterances, which we call 'Q-declarative'. In the French tradition, they are analyzed as interrogatives. Accordingly, French is said to have three ways of expressing a polar question (a.o. Borillo 1978; Hansen 2001; Marandin 2005): they use the complementizer *est-ce que* (1a), a verbal suffix identical to the subject prefix (or pronoun) (1b) and Q-declaratives (1c).

The Core and the Periphery.
Philip Hofmeister and Elisabeth Norcliffe (eds.).

(1) a. Est-ce que Paul sera là?
'Will Paul be there?'
b. Paul sera-t-il là?
c. Paul sera là?

We revisit the arguments that led to the analysis of Q-declaratives as interrogatives and propose that they are declaratives. Qua declaratives, they convey a proposition *p* and allow a dialogical move that steers the conversation to a stage where the addressee has to ratify (or reject) the proposition. Thus, proposition *p* ends up as a joint commitment of speaker and addressee by virtue of addressee's ratification of *p*. As for the effect that is currently described as 'questioning', we propose that it is related to the type of commitment of the speaker. The speaker's commitment to *p* is part of the use of root declaratives (a.o. Gunlogson 2003; Beyssade and Marandin 2006). However, building on the work of Gunlogson (2008), we distinguish between two types of commitment, which may be independent from the addressee's ratification or contingent on it. In the first case, the assertion results in a statement (or assertoric assertion), in the second, it results in a proposal. The act corresponding to a Q-declarative is a proposal.

In §2, we dismiss some received ideas about French Q-declaratives. In §3, we review a number of properties that undermine the hypothesis that Q-declaratives denote questions. In §4, we show that the moves allowed by Q-declaratives resemble more assertions than queries. In §5, we propose our analysis, according to which Q-declaratives are pragmatically proposals to the addressee, resulting (or not) in the grounding of *p* in the shared ground. Finally, we adduce results from a corpus study to substantiate and illustrate our claims (Abeillé et al. 2012).[1]

Given the three way distinction that we adopt from Ginzburg and Sag (2000) (form, meaning, force), we use the following labels:

- *declarative, interrogative, Q-declarative* refer to clause types or subtypes
- *proposition, question* refer to content types
- *assertion, statement, proposal, query* refer to speech acts or speech act varieties.

In the conversation domain, *response* refers to a type of turn, uptake to the content of the turn. *Ratification, rejection, answer* are types of content of turn.

[1]We base our analysis on several corpora: Hansen 2001 (= corpus PIII), the recorded dialogs of CID (Bertrand et al. 2008), and Microfusées (Laurens et al. 2013), and the radio corpora Ester (as in Beyssade et al. 2007) and EPAC which has been annotated for questions by Bazillon et al. (2011).

2 On some received ideas about French Q-declaratives

2.1 Intonation

The labels 'intonation question', 'rising declarative' or 'question intonation' all imply that the intonation contour is the factor that identifies—or even coerces—declaratives as interrogatives or as questioning. However, the common wisdom that rising intonation is correlated with interrogatives or querying or the attitude associated with querying (doubt, uncertainty or call on addressee) has been called into question and there is now a consensus that "it is not possible to identify tune types [= intonation contour] with sentence types in any simple way" (Ladd 1996, 9). Concretely, it has been shown on the basis of several corpora (everyday conversations and radio news) that intonation is not a reliable criterion for distinguishing between declaratives used to assert and declaratives putatively used to query (Beyssade et al. 2007). It is not always the case that declaratives used to make a statement (assertoric assertions) have a final falling contour, or that Q-declaratives have a final rising contour. Rather, the choice of the contour and its import in context cut across clause types and speech acts (see a. o. Beyssade and Marandin 2007 and references therein).

2.2 Use

In the literature on French, it is claimed (a) that the preferred construction for a polar query is the Q-declarative, (b) that Q-declaratives are the most frequent form in everyday interactions, (c) that they belong to the informal register while interrogatives with *est-ce que* or with a suffixed verb belong to a more formal register (see a.o. Borillo 1978; Šafářová 2007). We are still lacking the relevant quantitative surveys to seriously address those claims; nonetheless, we are in a position to shed some light on the data. The first quantitative study available (Hansen 2001) is based on a mixed corpus (4 hours and 35 minutes of recordings) comprising everyday dialogues, radio programs and school examinations. The raw distribution in that corpus seems to support claim (a): Q-declaratives greatly outnumber the two other constructions. However, the distribution is different when the discourse genre is taken into account: Q-declaratives are less dominant in radio debates (Table 1) and we show in §6 that they can outnumber *est-ce-que* questions (Table 3). In fact, as Hansen strongly suggests, the genre is not the relevant factor: the role Q-declaratives play in the conversation and more broadly in the interaction is much more relevant. In addition, she notes that the difference between the forms cannot be register dependent, since they can all occur in the same dialogue.

	Q-declaratives	*est-ce-que*-interrogative	suffix-verb-interrogative	Total
Whole corpus	204 (83%)	36 (14%)	7 (2%)	247
Radio debates	31 (61.5%)	16 (28%)	6 (10.5%)	53

TABLE 1 The distribution of the forms from (1) in Hansen's corpus

3 Are Q-declaratives interrogatives?

We examine diverse properties that establish a contrast between interrogatives and Q-declaratives. Although we do not have a full analysis of all the data, the general picture indicates that Q-declaratives differ semantically from interrogatives.

3.1 Morpho-syntactic properties

The three forms in (1) share the property of being main clauses. Polar embedded questions are expressed by a clause introduced by the complementizer *si* (construction (2b) with the complementizer *est-ce que* is possible, but non-standard). Thus, if Marie has used any of the forms in (1), her act is uniformly described by (2a). However, no conclusion can be drawn as regards the content of (1c), contra Ginzburg and Sag (2000, 287): it is the act which is reported, not the clause type used to perform the act. So, (2a) merely indicates that the move performed by the three forms can be described by the same verb *demander à quelqu'un si* p ('ask someone whether *p*'): the appropriateness of (2a) as a description of (1c) could be a hint of its force, not its content type.

(2) a. Marie a demandé si Paul allait venir.
'M. wondered if Paul was coming'
b. !M. a demandé est-ce que Paul allait venir.
c.*Marie a demandé Paul allait-il venir.

The same caution is in order regarding the use of the French noun *question*. Q-declaratives are not natural for the elaboration of this noun, as illustrated in (3)-(4).[2] However, the noun *question* can refer to the content or to the act, which undermines the value of this observation concerning the content type of Q-declaratives.

(3) a. Est-ce qu'il réussira? Telle est la question.
'Will he succeed? Such is the question.'
b. Réussira-t-il? Telle est la question.
c. #Il réussira? Telle est la question.

[2]Gunlogson (2003) makes a similar observation for the English noun *question*.

(4) a. Mais la question fondamentale est: est-ce qu'on peut faire des élections libres aujourd'hui, accessibles à tout le monde? (TS 08/13/2004)[3]
'But the fundamental question is, is it possible to organize free elections nowadays, open to everybody?'
b. La question fondamentale est: peut-on faire des élections libres aujourd'hui?
c. #La question fondamentale est: on peut faire des élections libres aujourd'hui?

No conclusion can be drawn either from the fact that (1c) shows no specific marking that could be associated with the interrogative clause type, since there is no homogeneous interrogative marking, as shown by the difference between (1a) and (1b). *Est-ce que* is a complementizer,[4] while (1b) contains a verb hosting a pronominal suffix identical to the subject prefix (Miller and Sag 1997) and can be used in contexts other than interrogatives (for example, with modal adverbs such as *peut-être* 'maybe', or discourse connectors such as *ainsi* 'thus'). Moreover, no conclusion can be drawn from *wh*-in-situ questions (5) (a frequent form used to make *bona fide* queries in French). Admittedly, they are declarative as to their clausal form, but their questioning value is overtly contributed by the *wh*-phrase (Ginzburg and Sag 2000).

(5) a. Tu vas où cet été?
'You are going where this summer?'
b. Il votera pour quel projet, à ton avis?
'He will vote for which project, in your estimation?'

3.2 Coordination

The two types of interrogatives (1a,b) can be conjoined with *et* ('and') together (6a,b) or with *wh*-interrogatives (7a,b). On the other hand, it is difficult to conjoin Q-declaratives with any of the interrogative types (6c), (7c) while it is often possible with an assertive declarative (6d). This is expected if Q-declaratives are of a different semantic type given the general constraint on symmetrical coordination (with *et*), which requires that the conjuncts be of the same semantic (ontological)

[3]TS refers to the daily popular radio program *Le téléphone sonne*. All data from this program come from the annotated corpus EPAC (see below).

[4]*Est-ce que* is originally an inverted verb (='is it (the case) that'); thus, there is a limited variation in tense in formal register (*serait-ce que vous avez décidé d'accepter la proposition?* lit. 'would it be the case that you have decided to accept our proposal'). We do not analyze *serait-ce que* as a complementizer, and it may be necessary to admit two analyses for *est-ce que*, at least in formal registers.

type. This is all the more striking given that there are limited cases of coordination of unlikes in clausal types on the basis of a similarity in role (Hobaek Haff 1987). Were Q-declaratives questions or querying, they should be amenable to coordination with other questions or querying utterances.

(6) a. **Est-ce que** tu es prêt et **est-ce qu'**on peut encore arriver à l'heure?
'Are you ready and can we still make it on time?'
b. **Est-ce que** tu es prêt et **peut-on** encore arriver à l'heure?
c. #{**Est-ce que** tu es prêt/Es-tu prêt} **et on peut** encore arriver à l'heure?
'Are you ready and you think we can still make it on time?'
d. Tu n'es pas prêt et tu penses qu'on peut encore arriver à l'heure?
'You're not ready and you think we can still make it on time?'

(7) a. **Pourquoi** reçoit-on cet avis **et doit-on** le rajouter aux revenus imposables? (TS 03/26/2004)
'Why do we receive this notice and must we add it to our taxable income?'
b. **Pourquoi** reçoit-on cet avis **et est-ce** qu'on doit le rajouter aux revenus imposables?
c.*__Pourquoi__ reçoit-on cet avis **et on doit** le rajouter aux revenus imposables?
'Why do we receive this notice and we must add it to our taxable income?'

3.3 Polarity subjunctive

Some predicates (verbs of communication, propositional attitude), which select indicative complement clauses, may, in certain non-positive environments, interrogatives among them, take a subjunctive clause. We illustrate this fact with a suffixed main verb (mood alternation is possible, but less frequent, with *est-ce que*, see Huot 1986) (8a). Q-declaratives differ from interrogatives: they do not license the subjunctive (8b).

(8) a. Et moi, croyez-vous que je $craigne_{subj}$ votre jugement?
'Do you think that I am afraid of your appraisal?'
b.*Et moi, vous croyez que je $craigne_{subj}$ votre jugement?

Broadly, in a semantico-pragmatic approach, the subjunctive mood is motivated in contexts where the interpretation requires taking into account alternative situations (to the one described in the sentence) (Farkas 1992; Godard 2012). An interrogative or a negated belief verb creates such an environment, hence the subjunctive in (8a). The fact that Q-declaratives do not license the subjunctive in the complement of a belief verb is an indication that its interpretation does not require alternative situations, as do interrogatives.

3.4 Epistemic adverbs

Q-declaratives as well as interrogatives may host epistemic adverbs. However, they belong to different classes. Both interrogatives and Q-declaratives are compatible with propositional adverbs expressing an alethic modality (*incontestablement, indubitablement*; corresponding to 'true without question') (9a, 10a). But only Q-declaratives are compatible with epistemic adverbs expressing the speaker's assessment of the truth of the proposition, either its probability (*peut-être* 'may be', *sans doute* 'no doubt') or his/her degree of confidence (*évidemment* 'evidently', *certainement, sûrement* 'surely'). The question in (9a) is equivalent to 'Is it indubitable that Paul has discovered the virus?', in the same way as *Est-ce que Paul va nécessairement trouver une solution?* means 'Is it obligatorily the case that Paul will find a solution?'. As for Q-declaratives, adverbs expressing a speaker's epistemic attitude towards p are better than propositional adverbs: *sûrement* is better than *vraisemblablement* 'probably'.

(9) a. Est-ce que Paul a indubitablement découvert le virus? / Paul a-t-il indubitablement découvert le virus?
'Has Paul indubitably discovered the virus?'
b. #Est-ce que Paul a sûrement envie de venir? / #Paul a-t-il sûrement envie de venir?
'Does Paul certainly feel like coming?'
c. #Est-ce que Paul a peut-être/apparemment découvert le virus? / #Paul a-t-il peut-être/apparemment découvert le virus?
'Has Paul perhaps/apparently discovered the virus?'

(10) a. Mais Paul, il a indubitablement découvert le virus?
'Paul, he has indubitably discovered the virus?'
b. Et Paul, il a sûrement envie de venir?
'And Paul, he certainly feels like coming?'
c. Et Paul, il a apparemment/peut-être découvert le virus?
'And Paul, he has apparently discovered/he may have discovered the virus?'

Q-declaratives are compatible with all sorts of markers expressing positive degrees of certainty, like *je crois, j'espère* (11), which are not felicitous in interrogatives. In this respect, Q-declaratives are closer to assertions than to queries.

(11) a. Marie a réussi, **je crois**?
'Marie has succeeded, I think?'
a'.*Est-ce que Marie a réussi, **je crois**?
'Has Marie succeeded, I think?'
b. Marie a réussi, **j'espère**?
'Marie has succeeded, I hope?'
b'.*Marie a-t-elle réussi, **j'espère**?
'Has Marie succeeded, I hope?'

3.5 Negative polarity items

Gunlogson (2003) said that NPIs are impossible in Q-declaratives in English, on the basis of the behavior of *any* and *ever*. If true for French, this would be a motivation to analyze them differently from interrogatives, which do allow for NPIs, as is well-known. Beyssade and Marandin (2006) observe that NPIs such as (positive) *jamais, quiconque, qui que ce soit* do not occur in Q-declaratives (12c, 13c) or declaratives (12d, 13d), as they do in interrogatives (12a,b, 13a,b).[5]

(12) a. Est-ce qu'il y aurait **qui que ce soit** pour nous aider?
'Would there be anyone to help us?'
b. Y aurait-il **qui que ce soit** pour nous aider?
c. #Il y aurait **qui que ce soit** pour nous aider?
d. #Il y aurait **qui que ce soit** pour nous aider.

(13) a. Est-ce que ces jeunes gens avaient **jamais** lu un roman classique?
'Had these young people ever read a classical novel?'
b. Ces jeunes gens avaient-ils **jamais** lu un roman classique?
c. #Ces jeunes gens avaient **jamais** lu un roman classique?
d. #Ces jeunes gens avaient **jamais** lu un roman classique.

However, the data are more complicated. A number of NPIs used in non positive contexts are felicitous in Q-declaratives as well as in interrogatives: predicates denoting a minimal quantity (*lever le petit doigt* 'to lift a finger', *avoir le rapport le plus lointain* 'to have the remotest

[5]Sentence (13c) is acceptable if *jamais* is taken to be the negation (without *ne*) rather than the NPI.

connection') (14a,b) vs (14c), or a maximal quantity (*si Adj que ça* 'so Adj as that') (15a,b) vs (15c).

(14) a. Est-ce que vous voyez **le rapport le plus lointain** entre les deux hypothèses?
'Do you see the remotest connection between the two hypotheses?'

b. Vous voyez **le rapport le plus lointain** entre les deux hypothèses?
'You see the remotest connection between the two hypotheses?'

c. #Les deux hypothèses ont **le rapport le plus lointain**.
'The two hypotheses have the remotest connection.'

(15) a. Est-ce que l'hypothèse est **si bête que ça**?
'Is the hypothesis that stupid?'

b. L'hypothèse est **si bête que ça**?

c. #L'hypothèse est **si bête que ça**.

Thus, the properties of NPIs do not constitute a clear-cut criterion for contrasting interrogatives with Q-declaratives, however tempting it may look at first.[6] The partition among NPIs remains an open question.

To sum up, we do not have semantic arguments supporting the hypothesis that Q-declaratives have the defining feature of the interrogative type: a question denotation. On the other hand, we have some indication that they resemble declaratives.

4 Are Q-declaratives questioning?

We turn to the illocutionary potential of Q-declaratives, which is the primary motivation for considering them as interrogatives: they seem to be in free variation with polar interrogatives in many contexts. For example, a physician who was called in during a cardiac emergency said (16a) when entering the apartment. He could very well have said (16b) or (16c) (Marandin 2005). So, is the behavior of Q-declaratives similar, or closer to that of assertoric declaratives or to that of interrogatives?

(16) a. Le Samu est prévenu?
'Emergency services have been alerted?'

b. Est-ce que le Samu est prévenu?

c. Le Samu est-il prévenu?

[6]Nor does it correspond to the division proposed for instance in Krifka (1995) between strong and weak NPIs.

4.1 Working assumptions

We briefly present the basic assumptions which we rely on to describe the illocutionary import of Q-declaratives as compared to other declaratives and interrogatives (Ginzburg 2003, 2012; Beyssade and Marandin 2006; Gunlogson 2003, 2008; Farkas and Bruce 2010; Farkas and Roelofsen 2012; Malamud and Stephenson 2011). We assume the following:

i. Speech acts should be analyzed along two dimensions: the commitment of the speaker and the projected conversational response of the addressee.[7]

ii. Epistemic speech acts (assertions and queries) are oriented towards the same goal when they are used in on-topic talk, that is, enriching the common ground, or the set of facts shared by the conversation participants for the purposes of conversation (Stalnacker 1978; Zaefferer 2001).

iii. Assertions and queries aim at enriching the common ground in a different manner. By asserting, the speaker proposes that a proposition be ratified by the addressee and added to the set of shared facts. On the other hand, by querying, the speaker proposes that a question be resolved by the addressee so that the chosen alternative gets added to the set of shared facts (if ratified by the questioner).

iv. Assertions and queries also differ in the way they commit the speaker. It is commonly accepted that assertions commit the speaker to the asserted content; we take it that queries commit the speaker to the issue raised by the query (Beyssade and Marandin 2006). The difference shows up when addressees react negatively. As Farkas and Bruce (2010) put it, a negative response to an assertion as in (17a) brings about a conversational crisis while it does not do so when it is used to answer a query (17b). In (17a), after Ben's rejection of Ann's proposition, the participants have to come to terms: either one of them revises his/her commitment or they agree to disagree. In some cases, no enrichment of the shared ground is feasible. Nothing of the sort occurs with a negative answer to a question: none of the participants have to revise and the shared ground may be updated with the resolving proposition.

(17) a. Ann: Sam is home.
Ben: No, he is not.
b. Ann: Is Sam home?
Ben: No, he is not.

[7] The projected conversational response corresponds to the call on addressee in Truckenbrodt (2004) and Beyssade and Marandin (2006).

v. Assertions must be ratified by the addressee in order to be successful.[8] Ratification has two facets: the assessment of p and the grounding of p among the facts shared by participants for the purposes of conversation. Assessment and grounding are distinct. Assessment (of the truth of p) is rooted in knowledge or belief, while grounding rests on the dominance relationships between the participants (as felt or played by the participants in a given interaction). Assessment belongs to the private sphere of each participant, while grounding is crucial for assertion as a move towards enriching the shared facts: speaker A proposes p to addressee B for grounding (A has his own basis to assess p), speaker B grounds (or not) p using his/her own basis of assessment.

4.2 Addressee's responses

The analysis of Q-declaratives as questioning moves is based on the observation that they call for a response from addressees and on the claim that responses to Q-declaratives are closer to those expected after queries (conveyed by interrogatives) than assertoric assertions (conveyed by declaratives). However, the data do not lead to such a definitive conclusion.

It is a fact that Q-declaratives are followed by explicit responses: this is the most robust and stable cue to recognize them as such, rather than as assertoric declaratives. Queries also call for an explicit response, that is, an answer or a reply related to the issue raised by the query; on the other hand, statements do not require an explicit response (although implicit ratification is necessary for the conversational working of assertions). However, requiring an explicit response does not imply that the response should be an answer—i.e. the resolution of a question. In other words, one cannot exclude the hypothesis that Q-declaratives convey a type of assertion requiring an explicit ratification.

Concerning the type of responses to Q-declaratives, the data are more intricate than what is commonly accepted:

- Responses with *oui, non, si* ('yes', 'no') are appropriate reactions to interrogatives, Q-declaratives or assertoric declaratives. Correlatively, we are led to assume that they convey either an answer (resolving a question) or a ratification (grounding a proposition). Those adverbs give rise to a gamut of phonetic realizations associated with several contours. We lack detailed empirical studies showing whether

[8] Accordingly, assertions in general are discourse contingent in Gunlogson's (2008, 128) sense: "a discourse move can be presented as linked to the outcome of a succeeding move, with the update of the first move carried out or accepted only if some contextually salient condition is met by the second".

those realizations make a systematic difference between queries and statements.

- Although reverse reactions with Q-declaratives are rare (see §6), they seem to pattern more like those to queries than to assertions: the addressee's reverse uptake is smoother with Q-declaratives than with assertoric declaratives.
- Assertoric declaratives, but not queries or Q-declaratives, can be responded to with such factive adjectives as *génial*, 'great' (18b,c). Assuming that these adjectives require the propositional content to be part of the common ground (Ginzburg and Fernandéz 2002), they are felicitous in (18a) with an implicit ratification of S1's assertion. They are not in (18b,c) if the proposition is not yet part of the common ground. Here, Q-declaratives side with interrogatives rather than with assertoric declaratives.[9]

(18) a. S1: Il va neiger demain.
'It will snow tomorrow.'
S2: Super/Génial!
(Great!)
b. S1: Est-ce qu'il va neiger demain?
'Will it snow tomorrow?'
S2: #Super/#Génial!
c. S1: Il va neiger demain?
S2: #Super/#Génial!

- Assertoric declaratives can be responded to with adverbs (*absolument* 'absolutely', *effectivement* 'indeed') (19a) conveying the speaker's agreement with the addressee's axiologic judgment (*être beau* 'to be handsome' in (19)). Those adverbs cannot be used to answer or reply to queries (19b), but they are felicitous with Q-declaratives (19c). In this respect, Q-declaratives resemble assertoric declaratives.

(19) a. S1: Il est beau, son nouveau copain.
'He is handsome, her new boyfriend.'
S2: Absolument/Effectivement.
'Absolutely/right.'
b. S1: Est-ce qu'il est beau, son nouveau copain?
'Is he handsome, her new boyfriend?'

[9] Note that factive adjectives are also felicitous when the declarative is interpreted as an offer as in the following dialog:
S1: Je fais des lasagnes ce soir? ('I'll cook lasagna tonight?')
S2: Super! ('Great!').

S2: #Absolument/#Effectivement.

c. S1: Il est beau, son nouveau copain?
S2: Absolument/Effectivement.

Clearly, Q-declaratives bear some resemblance to interrogatives. However, there is no decisive argument for analyzing the response as an answer and accordingly, Q-declaratives as questioning.

4.3 Felicity conditions

Queries are submitted to the following felicity condition: the resolving answer must not be in the common ground. According to Ginzburg (2012, 114), the constraint is even stronger: it should not be in his category 'facts', "the shared knowledge conversational participants utilize during a conversation".[10] This explains why (20a) is not felicitous. On the other hand, (20b), a Q-declarative, is perfectly natural; in fact, it corresponds to a prototypical use of Q-declaratives (see §4.4.1). Moreover, while assertions are assumed to behave like interrogatives in this respect (20c), we find that things are different: it is sufficient that the speaker add some sort of mirative marker (20d) to make the assertion felicitous. The same distribution holds with another prototypical use of Q-declaratives, when the content is inferred from what the addressee (or the speaker) has just said (21); in (21d), the marker *donc* is inferential.[11]

(20) [S1's addressee enters the room with his jacket soaking wet]
S1. a. #Est-ce que tu es mouillé? / #Es-tu mouillé?
'Are you wet?'
b. Tu es mouillé?
'You are wet?'
c. #Tu es mouillé.
'You are wet.'
d. Tiens/Dis donc, tu es mouillé!
'Well/hey, you are wet!'

(21) [Paul, S1 and S2 are friends; S1 and S2 know that Paul was in the hospital]
<1> S1: Paul vient d'arriver au bureau.
'Paul has just arrived at work.'
<2> S2: a. (Donc) il est sorti de l'hôpital?
'So, he is out of the hospital?'

---

[10]"The presence in facts of a resolving answer to the question vitiates the possibility of a successful interrogatory use" (ibid).

[11]The notation <n> in (21) and onwards indicates the turn for easier reference.

b. #Est-ce qu'il est sorti de l'hôpital? / #Est-il sorti de l'hôpital?
'Is he out of the hospital?'

c. #Il est sorti de l'hôpital.
'He is out of the hospital.'

d. Il est donc sorti de l'hôpital.
'He is out of the hospital, then.'

In general, a declarative with a given content is felicitous when used to reassert its content or combined with an explicit account of how the speaker became committed to the content; on the other hand, it is almost impossible to ask again a question whose resolution is given in the current context. In this respect, Q-declaratives are closer to assertions than to queries.

4.4 Q-declaratives in context

We now turn to Q-declaratives in a broader context, presenting two sets of contexts that afford their use: in the former, the content is given, in the latter it is discourse-new. We focus here on how Q-declaratives behave in comparison with interrogatives, declaratives and questioning *n'est-ce pas*.

4.4.1 Context 1: the content (*p*) is given

The content *p* (or the basis for asserting *p*) is given when it has been mentioned in the previous discourse or turn(s), or has just been grounded as the result of the current interaction. In addition, we assume that the situation where the conversation takes place provides participants with given content. In such contexts, polar interrogatives would be inappropriate, as well as declaratives associated with the questioning tag *n'est-ce pas*. On the contrary, assertoric declaratives with the same content and roughly the same conversational import would be appropriate providing that the redundant character of *p* is salvaged by a mirative, an inferential or an evaluative marker (20d). We illustrate each case in turn.

i. The content of the Q-declarative has just been mentioned. This corresponds to various forms of reprise. For example, in (22), at turn 3, S2 reprises S1's turn literally. In (23), at turn 2, the speaker reprises part of addressee's long turn; interestingly, the reprise concerns the speaker himself. In both cases, the use of *n'est-ce pas* would be utterly incongruous and that of an interrogative out of place.

(22) [S1 and S2 are two young men: they are making small talk about their experience as a recent father or father to be (corpus CID)]

<1> S1. Tu avais assisté à l'accouchement, toi, de...
'You were present, you, for the delivery of...'

<2> S2. Nan. J'ai pas voulu.
'Nah. I didn't want to.'

<3> S1. T'as pas voulu?
'You didn't want to?'

<4> S2. Nan nan.
'Nah nah.'
[silence]

<5> S1. T'avais eu...? C'était quoi? T'avais? [...]
'You had...? It was what? You had? [...]'

(23) [In a radio show, the expert answers questions about obesity. The host is the moderator of the show (TS 08/05/2004)]

<1> Host: Je voudrais revenir sur une phrase que j'ai pu lire dans la presse, euh une que vous avez prononcée professeur Patrick Tounian: vous avez dit euh à propos de cette progression de l'obésité: "nous assistons" vous dites "à une véritable épidémie d'une maladie que l'on peut qualifier de mortelle". Qu'est-ce que vous avez voulu dire par là?
'I want to go back to a sentence that I found in the newspaper, uh, something you said, Professor P. T., you said, uh, regarding this progression of obesity: "we are witnessing", you said, "a true epidemy of a disease which we can say is deadly". What did you mean by that?'

<2> Expert: C'est moi qui l'ai écrit?
'I wrote that?'

<3> Host: Oui oui oui oui j'ai lu ça.
'Yes, yes, yes, yes, I read it.'

ii. The basis for *p* has just been grounded, see for example (21) at turn 2 above. In (24), at turn 2, the host draws a consequence from the lengthy turn of the expert. The tag *n'est-ce pas* would be appropriate in (24), while it would sound odd in (21).

(24) [The expert answers questions about the rise of gas prices. The host moderates the show (TS 08/06/2004)]

<1> Expert: Dans le gazole (il) y a deux tiers deux tiers de taxes, de taxe intérieure et de TVA. En fait, sans les

taxes, le prix du gazole et le prix de l'essence sont à peu près identiques. C'est donc les taxes qui font le différence () qui font la différence, et dans des niveaux dans des niveaux très importants.
'In oil, there are two thirds of taxes, domestic tax and VAT. In fact, without taxes, the price of oil and the price of gas are roughly identical; thus it is taxes which make the difference, a big, big difference.'

<2> Host: Donc le gouvernement pourrait très bien euh réduire les hausses à la pompe, s'il le voulait?
'So the government could very well uh reduce the increase in price at the petrol station, if they wanted to?'

<3> Expert: Ah, le gouvernement pourrait effectivement très bien réduire les hausses à la pompe.
'Ah, yes, the government could very well reduce the increase at the petrol station.'

Q-declaratives are also felicitous when the basis for p has been elaborated by both participants during several turns: this corresponds to checking moves in the closing section of activities in conversations. In (25), at turn 4, the tutor closes the selection of the best rockets before choosing the best one; it has taken about 20 turns.

(25) [Mia (a teenager in a day camp) has ranked rockets under the supervision of a tutor. Yves' one is the last to be ranked (Corpus Microfusées)]

<1> Tutor: Et Yves, tu as mis quoi?
'And, Yves' [rocket], how did you grade it?'

<2> Mia: Yves? Haut aussi mais pas très loin.
'Yves? High too, but not very far.'

<3> Mia: Voilà.
'That's it.'

<4> Tutor: D'accord. Donc à ton avis, c'est celles-ci qui ont le mieux volé?
'OK, then, according to you, those are the ones that flew best?'

<5> Mia: Oui.
'Yes.'

<6> Tutor: D'accord. Et celle qui a le mieux volé?
'OK, and the one which flew best?'

iii. The basis for p is given in the situation of utterance: this is illustrated in (21) above.

4.4.2 Context 2: the content (p) is discourse new

Discourse-new content is not inferred from the situation or the previous conversation. Nevertheless, there is some connection between Q-declaratives and the ongoing conversation. In such contexts, assertoric declaratives with the same content are completely inappropriate, while interrogatives are most of the time felicitous, as well as declaratives with questioning tag *n'est-ce pas* for a subset of contexts. However, the use of an interrogative or *n'est-ce pas* would often change the type of interaction.

i. The speaker has some private basis to believe p. In fact, p corresponds to speaker-old information that is relevant for the ongoing conversation or activity. The proposition may refer to an event primarily known to the addressee or to an objective state of affairs (B-events or O-events in Labov and Fanshel 1977). In (26), at turn 3, an interrogative would be appropriate, but not the questioning *n'est-ce pas*. On the contrary, in (27), at turn 3, *n'est-ce pas* would be appropriate and the interrogative strange.

(26) [Mother and son are on the phone. Tony, a relative, has been taken to the hospital recently. Example noted by one of the authors]

<1> M: A propos, t'as téléphoné à Tony?
'By the way, did you call Tony?'

<2> S: Non, j'ai pas eu le temps.
'No, I didn't have time.'

<3> M: Tu dis toujours ça, t'avais dit que tu le ferais.
'You always say that, you said you would do it.'

(27) [S1 calls information at the Bourg railway station (constructed example on the basis of recordings of interactions at commercial counters)]

<1> S1: Bonjour, y a-t-il un train au départ de Bourg pour Thonon le dimanche matin?
'Hello, is there a train from Bourg to Thonon on Sunday mornings?'

<2> S2: Un moment. [...] Oui, il y en a deux; le premier part à 8h30 et le second à 11h.
'One moment. [...] Yes, there are two; the first one departs at 8:30am, and the second at 11am.'

<3> S1: Le billet coûte vingt euros?
'The ticket costs about twenty euros?'

ii. The speaker may have a private belief, but essentially he makes a guess. In both (28) and (29), the use of an interrogative or of *n'est-ce pas* would be appropriate, but would rely on a different conversational setting. In (28) at turn 1, the use of *n'est-ce pas* would mean that speaker has some non publicized reason to believe *p*, which would ruin the tentative character brought by the use of a Q-declarative. In (28), using an interrogative would narrow down the center of the discussion on the material and imply a greater asymmetry between the participants in resolving the issue.[12] In (29) at turn 2, the Q-declarative is only interpretable as a possible answer suggested by the questioner, while an interrogative would introduce another question whose answer could influence the resolution of the question *pourquoi*.

(28) [S1 and S2 are friends; they are looking at a Roman vase at le Louvre (example noted by one of the authors)]
<1> S1: C'est du bronze?
'It's bronze?'
<2> S2: Possible.
'Possibly.'

(29) [Example (59), Hansen's corpus]
<1> S1: ...j'étais allongée dans mon lit et je me suis endormie.
'I was lying in my bed and I fell asleep.'
<2> S2: Pourquoi? T'as pris un calmant?
'How come? You took a tranquilizer?'

4.4.3 Summary

The distribution of Q-declaratives with respect to the informational status of content is summarized in Table 2, and compared to the possibility of polar interrogatives, declaratives with a questioning tag *n'est-ce pas*, and assertoric declaratives.[13]

Three generalizations emerge from table 2.

1. The family of contexts affording Q-declaratives cuts across those affording interrogatives and assertoric declaratives. Interestingly, assertoric declaratives with given content are felicitous insofar as they bring information about the speaker's assessment of *p* (for example, it has just occurred to the speaker that *p*) (20)-(21).

[12] Use of quasi-tags like *tu penses, tu crois* ('you think/ believe') as in *c'est du bronze, tu crois?* are typical of that type of interaction.

[13] The notation '—' means impossible, and '(+)' means possible, but with a different import.

Status of content		Examples of Q-declarative	Polar interrogative	Questioning *n'est-ce pas*	Assertoric declaratives
Given	Reprise	22	−	−	+
		23	−	−	+
	Inferred from conversation	21	−	−	+
		24	−	+	+
		25	−	−	+
	In the situation	20	−	−	+
Discourse new	Speaker-old	26	+	(+)	−
		27	−	+	−
	Speaker-new	28	(+)	(+)	−
		29	(+)	(+)	−

TABLE 2 Distribution of Q-declaratives with respect to informational status of p

2. The family of contexts affording Q-declaratives does not coincide with those affording *n'est-ce pas*. Assuming that *n'est-ce pas* signals that speakers have an independent basis for assessing p, we may infer that Q-declaratives are felicitous whether speakers have or fail to have an independent basis for assessing p. This shows up most clearly when the content is discourse-new: p may be a speaker's presupposition or just a conjecture made on the fly. This is in keeping with the observation (see §3.4 above) that Q-declaratives are compatible with expressions of the speaker's state towards assessing p.
3. The family of contexts where the addressee is committed to p or to the basis for assessing p (given content) is a subset of those affording Q-declaratives (20)-(25). The family of contexts where speakers attribute p to addressees is also a subset (e.g. when p is a speaker's presupposition). Thus, the use of Q-declaratives does not require the addressee's previous commitment to p or attribution of p to the addressee.[14]

Generalization 1 leads us to reconsider the observation illustrated in (16) that there are contexts where the three forms in (1) are in free variation. It is not possible to simply claim that Q-declaratives are a sort of interrogative. Generalization 2 shows that Q-declaratives have felicity conditions and conversational import different from declaratives with tagged *n'est-ce pas?* They differ regarding the assessment of p:

[14]The quasi tag *c'est ça?* ('that's it?') signals attribution of p to the addressee. As it has other felicity conditions that are not clear to us, we do not include it here. But, clearly, contexts affording *c'est ça?* cut across those affording Q-declaratives.

n'est-ce pas presents the speaker as a potential source of assessment, while Q-declaratives leave the source of assessment underspecified. Generalization 2 is neutral with respect to the claim made for English in Gunlogson (2008) that Q-declaratives imply that the addressee is a better source of commitment than the speaker. Generalization 3 leads one to reject the claim made for English Q-declaratives (Gunlogson 2003; Malamud and Stephenson 2011) that the addressee's commitment to *p* (actual or attributed) is a felicity condition for Q-declaratives.

We conclude that there are no compelling arguments for analyzing Q-declaratives as queries or questioning. They convey a speech act of their own. We show in the next section that it is a variety of assertion.

5 Q-declaratives are *bona fide* declaratives

We are now in a position to propose our analysis of Q-declaratives as declaratives. First, their content is a proposition. Second, their illocutionary potential as root clauses is constrained: the speaker is committed to *p* and they steer the conversation to a stage where the addressee has to ratify (or reject) *p*. This goes a long way towards explaining their behavior in actual conversations. However, it does not explain why they are considered 'questioning'. We derive this effect from the type of commitment associated with Q-declaratives. Adopting the notion of contingent commitment proposed by Gunlogson (2008), we distinguish between two types of commitment. When a speaker uses a declarative with an independent commitment, the move is an assertoric declarative that carries a statement; when a speaker uses a declarative with a commitment contingent on the addressee's ratification, the move is a Q-declarative that carries a proposal.

5.1 Assertion behavior

Q-declaratives are root declaratives. As such, they abide by the usual constraints on their use:

- the speaker is committed to *p*, which means that speaker is liable for putting *p* under discussion;
- the conversation is steered to a state where the addressee has to ratify or reject *p*. By ratifying *p*, the addressee grounds *p* and commits himself to *p*.

Speaker's commitment to *p* is responsible for the bias of declaratives in favor of *p*. By using a declarative, the speaker excludes non-*p* or alternatives to *p* from discussion. Addressees may revive them, but this requires rejection of *p* as a first step. This explains why Q-declaratives are optimal in contexts where *p* is the only plausible option for discussion. The same contexts make the use of interrogatives out of place. Take (20): it is so obviously the case that it is raining outside that it would be vacuous to even consider other weather conditions. Accordingly, the speaker verbalizes the weather condition for reasons other than arriving at the truth about p. Hence the use of Q-declaratives as a strategy to start an interaction. Similarly in (25), the tutor, taking into account the fact that Mia had trouble choosing the best rockets, uses a Q-declarative to check whether they both agree on the selection, without reopening the discussion, which would trigger further hesitation on the part of Mia. The same bias effect holds even in contexts where alternatives to p have not been closed off, for example in (26-29). Such contexts make interrogatives possible, and correlatively also queries, but in those contexts, by using a Q-declarative instead of an interrogative, speakers narrow down the options left to addressees to just one.

Note that the dialogical commitment to p is different from the epistemic attitude towards p. In fact, the use of a declarative is compatible with the whole gamut of epistemic attitudes, from utter certainty to mere plausibility. But epistemic certainty does not correspond to a statement, or plausibility to a proposal. Consider (21). The speaker, using robust world knowledge, can be certain that Paul is not in the hospital any longer, but he is not in a position to ground the corresponding statement. On the other hand, the addressee is in such a position since he is the one who might know more about Paul's situation. By using a Q-declarative, the speaker yields to the addressee, leaving it to him to take the conversational responsibility of grounding p, and elaborating on it.

5.2 The questioning flavor

The questioning flavor which is associated with Q-declaratives lies in the nature of the speaker's commitment. Following Gunlogson (2008), the speaker may commit him/herself to p either unconditionally or tentatively pending the addressee's ratification of p.[15] This is what makes an assertion either a statement or a proposal. The contingency of the speaker's commitment on the addressee's ratification is central to the working of the pair 'Proposal/Ratification'. In particular, it explains one of the main properties of Q-declaratives: proposals, unlike statements, call for an explicit response by addressees. The role of the addressee as the key agent in making p a commitment shared by both par-

[15] "Contingent commitment criterion: an utterance of a declarative with content Φ is questioning to the extent that the speaker's commitment is understood as contingent on the addressee's ratification of Φ." (Gunlogson 2008, 129)

ticipants is the common feature between queries and proposals. In both cases, addressees play the key role in making individual commitments a joint commitment. But joint commitment is achieved differently. With an interrogative, it takes three turns (query + commitment to *p* by answerer + ratification of *p* by questioner), while it takes two with a Q-declarative (contingent commitment to *p* by speaker + ratification of *p* by addressee).

The fact that the commitment is contingent on the addressee's ratification is not specifically marked. One can speculate that some aspect of prosody provides the participants with cues for recognizing it, but this is still poorly understood for French.[16] Nevertheless, it should be inferable given the content of the clause, the speaker's relation to the addressee and the context of utterance: the speaker lets the addressee ground *p*. It has been proposed (Hansen 2001; Gunlogson 2008) that this is due to an epistemic asymmetry between the participants, the addressee being in a better position to ground *p* because s/he has more knowledge about *p*. We are not in a position to discuss Gunlogson's judgments about English. However, it is clear that, at least with some of her interrogative examples, Q-declaratives would be more appropriate in similar settings in French. Moreover, as already observed, Q-declaratives are felicitous in contexts where both participants are (potentially) equal in knowledge (25), (27), or ignorance (28). Take (27). At turn 3, both speaker and addressee may use the same source (say the website of the railway company), nevertheless the attendant is the only one that can publicize the price of the ticket. It has been noted that the content of Q-declaratives frequently refers to private states of the addressee (B-events). This may well be true, but it does not indicate that addressees are a better source of knowledge. Assessment of private matters involves intricate (and changing) politeness or face considerations that prevent making a public issue of private matters via the use of interrogatives. Thus, epistemic asymmetry is not the primary factor which affords the use and recognition of Q-declaratives in French.[17] The decisive factor for the use of Q-declaratives pertains to the grounding of *p*, rather than its assessment.

By using a Q-declarative, speakers step down in favor of their addressee for grounding a proposition. They achieve such a move by committing themselves conditionally, either because they cannot assess *p*, but are nonetheless ready to commit themselves to *p* (28), or because they can assess *p* but are not entitled to ground *p* in the situation or

[16] Gunlogson (2008) claims that rising intonation is such a cue in English.

[17] While it is the most relevant factor for the use of interrogatives.

the conversation (21), or because they can assess p but want the addressee to engage in conversation about p or in relation with p (21). As we will see in the next section, this type of move is put to use in the monitoring of conversation.

5.3 Types of assertions

The present analysis is true to form; it modifies one aspect only of the current theories of speech acts. It maintains that declaratives commit the speaker to p, but, following Gunlogson (2008), it proposes that commitment has two subtypes: it is either independent of the addressee's ratification of p or contingent on it. Such a divide gives rise to two speech acts that speakers perform by using a declarative: statements or proposals. In schema 1, we tentatively propose a classification of subtypes of proposals, which follows from the contextual status of the content (given *vs* discourse-new; speaker-old *vs* speaker-new).[18]

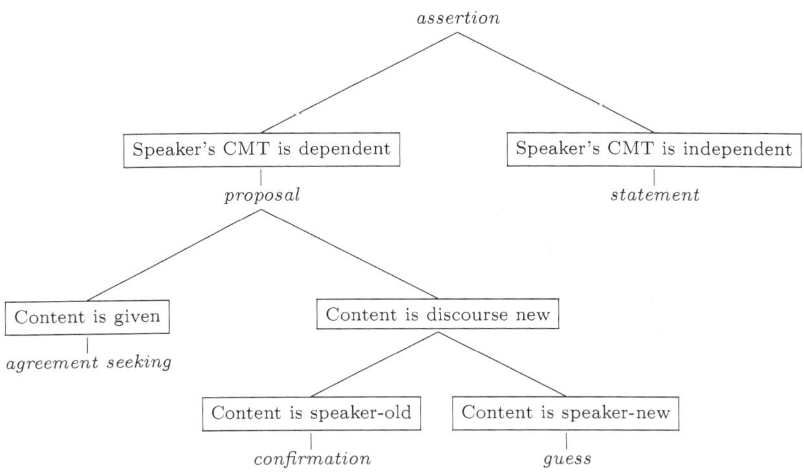

FIGURE 1 *Schema 1*: Types of assertion

6 Corpus-based support

We now adduce results from a corpus study to substantiate our proposal (Abeillé et al. 2012). First, we present some preliminary results of a pilot quantitative study aiming at describing the main patterns of use of Q-declaratives compared to polar interrogatives. Secondly, we focus on the conversational role of Q-declaratives compared to interrogatives in a specific conversational setting.

[18]CMT stands for 'commitment' in schema 1.

6.1 General description

We support the analysis by a study of the EPAC corpus (Bazillon et al. 2011), which corresponds to 20 hours of recording of a popular radio program *Le téléphone sonne* on the radio station France Inter in 2005. It has been annotated for interrogatives and Q-declaratives. We randomly extracted 227 annotated root clauses out of about half of the corpus (10 hours) and studied them along several parameters. The first main result is that the distribution of the three constructions in (1) is almost even in the corpus (see table 3). More importantly, the distribution is correlated with the role played by the speaker: the host produces around half of the 'questioning' moves (i.e. interrogatives + Q-declaratives) and among them, more than half are Q-declaratives.

Speaker	Q-declaratives	*Est-ce-que*-interrogative	Suffixed-verb-interrogative	Total
Host	61	51	144	256 (47%)
Callers	79	92	5	176 (32%)
Experts	74	11	29	114 (21%)
Total	214 (39%)	154 (28%)	178 (31%)	546

TABLE 3 Interrogatives and Q-declaratives by speakers (Bazillon et al. 2011)

Such a result does not support the claim that Q-declaratives belong to an informal register (see §2.2). Moreover, it strongly suggests that the use of Q-declaratives is correlated to specific roles in conversation. We may conjecture that the host uses Q-declaratives to perform the actions required by his moderating the interaction between the different conversation participants. Such a suggestion is supported when one observes that 45% of his Q-declaratives pertain to the monitoring of the conversation and that he uses most of the remaining 55% to manage the elaboration of topics by callers and experts.

Two other quantitative results are clear (Table 4):

- Q-declaratives are almost always followed by a response (only 15% are left without a response). Paradoxically, lack of response is much more common with interrogatives (46% of polar *est-ce que* and 23% of Suffixed-verb interrogatives are not followed by answers), which is explainable by the fact that this activity favors the use of self-addressed interrogatives as topic management devices (see below).
- Q-declaratives are most often followed by ratification (75% of them, whatever the polarity of the declarative).[19]

[19]Positive *est-ce-que* questions receive as many positive as negative answers and positive inverted questions only receive 36% positive answers.

	Same polarity answer	Reverse polarity answer	No direct answer	Total
Est-ce que Int	21 (23.8%)	26 (29.5%)	34 (38.6%)	88
Suff-verb Int	25 (39%)	24 (37.5%)	15 (23.4%)	64
Q-declaratives	56 (74.6%)	8 (19.6%)	11 (14.6%)	75

TABLE 4 Answers to interrogatives and Q-declaratives (total 227)

6.2 Conversation monitoring

Making conversation requires the participants to coordinate with each other at all levels of organization. As Clark (1994) stresses, cooperation should be optimal at all levels: from attention of the participants towards the conversation, to understanding the turns, grounding the contents and performing the activities-in-conversation. In particular, the participants anticipate problems of coordination, they try to prevent them and when they occur, they resort to strategies to repair them in order to restore the coordination. Preventing problems of cooperation is one of the main functions Q-declaratives are put to use for in everyday interactions.[20] They are used to check the attention of the addressee at the lowest level (30) as well as the intended meaning or intention of the addressee at the highest one (31).

(30) S1: Pierre?
[Pierre is looking blank]
S1: Pierre, tu m'écoutes?
'Pierre, are you listening to me?'

(31) S1: Il fait froid ici!
'It's cold in here!'
S1: Tu veux que je ferme la fenêtre?
'You want me to shut the window?'

Indeed, they are particularly well suited for such a use inasmuch as (a) the addressee is the only one to be entitled to ground a proposition describing his state towards the ongoing conversation, (b) Q-declaratives are not inquisitive (they do not make an issue out of a problem that has not arisen yet), and (c) participants accept the consequences of their ratification. Indeed, with the monitoring function, ratification amounts

[20] Mosegaard noted such a use under the label of 'next-turn repair initiator'.

to showing positive orientation towards the ongoing conversation and activity.[21]

In the EPAC corpus, the host uses Q-declaratives to monitor the conversation: to introduce the participants in the program (32), to check their attention and readiness for floor taking (33), to give the floor by proposing uptake by a participant (mainly the experts) (34), to clarify a caller's question (in order to prevent misunderstandings), etc.[22]

(32) a. Host to caller: Vous êtes je crois à Issy-les Moulineaux Fatiha? Bonsoir! (TS 03/25/2004)
'You are I think in Issy-les M. Fatiha? Good evening!'
Caller: Oui bonsoir.
'Yes, good evening.'

b. Host to caller: Xavier dans l'Isère en ligne. Vous êtes médecin aussi je crois? (TS 03/25/2004)
'Xavier in Isère on the phone. You are also a doctor, I think?'
Bonsoir Xavier!
'Good evening, Xavier!'
Caller: Euh bonsoir messieurs.
'Uh good evening sir.'

(33) a. Host to caller [on the phone from New York]: Vous avez entendu la question de Xavier? Vous l'avez compris? (TS 08/13/2004)
'You heard Xavier's question? You understood it?'

b. Host to caller [on the phone]: Vous vouliez poser une autre question? (TS 04/02/2004)
'You wanted to ask another question?'

c. Host to expert [in the studio]: Vous vouliez ajouter également quelque chose? (TS 05/02/2004)
'You wanted to add something else?'

(34) a. Host to expert [in the studio]: Vous confirmez, monsieur Doudrich? (TS 09/20/2004)
'You confirm, Mr Doudrich?'

---

[21]Declarative reprises are another paradigmatic example of this role: foreseeing that s/he is not ready to ratify the addressee's information, the speaker repeats the addressee's turn, which gives the latter the opportunity either to re-assert its content, or to elaborate on it in order to prevent speaker's potential rejection.

[22]Correlatively, they fulfill a role specific for such a setting: they describe what's going on to the audience that is listening to the radio. Media analysts independently have shown that media agents use the same strategies to moderate talk-shows, interviews, etc, as those used in everyday conversations (e.g. Léon 1999). That makes corpora of media interactions relevant resources for linguistic analysis.

b. Host to expert: Élisabeth Dupoirier, vous êtes euh (), vous partagez cette analyse? (TS 03/19/2004)
'E.D., you are, uh, you share this analysis?'

The host also, but much less often, uses interrogatives with the same conversational roles. Interrogatives are indeed possible since addressees are the relevant agents to solve the problems pertaining to their attitudes towards the ongoing conversation.

(35) a. Host to caller: Frédéric ne nous entend pas. Frédéric, est-ce que vous m'entendez bien là, Frédéric? Frédéric? Non, visiblement il ne nous entend pas. (TS 08/25/2004)
'F. does not hear us. F. do you hear me F.? F.? no, clearly, he does not hear us.'

b. Host to caller: Êtes-vous toujours là, madame? Non, elle n'est plus là. (TS 03/26/2004)
'Are you still there, madame? No, she is no longer connected.'

c. Host to expert: Est-ce qu'on peut en dire un mot? [...] Monsieur Dubois? [no answer] (TS 09/20/2004)
'Can we say a few words about it? [...] Mr. D?'

Crucially, there is a contextual difference between Q-declaratives and interrogatives: the host uses Q-declaratives when the conversation and the show unfolds smoothly, while he uses interrogatives (both forms of polar interrogatives) after trouble has occurred in order to characterize it and make it explicit to the participants and to the audience. This difference follows directly from the fact that a declarative steers the conversational flow to the ratification of one alternative (corresponding to what is expected from the participants), while the use of an interrogative puts on the table several options (corresponding to what is expected and what is impeding the normal course of the show). In other words, the appropriateness of Q-declaratives as a monitoring device preventing troubles crucially hinges on their being declaratives.

6.3 Topic promotion

The other typical use of Q-declaratives in everyday interactions is as a topic promotion device when the speaker is the topic initiator and addressee the main elaborator. Such topic promotion requires a fine-tuned cooperation: it involves selecting and highlighting a topic which the addressee is in a position to elaborate on, showing one's interest in it and checking that the addressee is also positively oriented towards elaborating on it (Button and Casey 1985). Q-declaratives are used for the first two steps. Take (20) and (21) above: the Q-declaratives initiate on-topic talk, that is, chatting about the weather in (20) and about

Paul's condition in (21). Declarative reprises may also be used with such a role. The speaker repeats the addressee's move, which results in highlighting its content or part of it. By handing it back to the addressee for confirmation, the speaker gives him/her the opportunity of showing his/her positive orientation towards its elaboration. The dialogue (22) above is an interesting example of such a strategy that misfires. At turn 3, S1 reprises S2's turn; at turn 4, S2 responds to p with an explicit ratification (same polarity *nan nan*), but shows no desire to elaborate on it. Thus, the conversation comes to a stop, which is marked by a long silence and a crisis: S1 is obliged to reinitiate the topic with explicit topic eliciting devices: *C'était quoi? T'avais?*

The host in EPAC consistently uses Q-declaratives in such strategies. He uses reprising with the same function: reprise in (36) below at turn 2 has the same role as that in (22), at turn 3. Similarly, he draws inferences from the addressee's turn to elicit or center on-topic talk: compare (21) at turn 2a with (24) at turn 2.

(36)<1>Expert: Alors ce numéro donc, cancer info service, au 818 118 121, **est un numéro qui a ouvert lundi** et qui est un numéro d'information pour le public sur le cancer [...] donc toute l'information et tous les services de proximité dont peuvent avoir besoin les gens sur les questions du cancer.
'So, this phone number, then, cancer info service, 818 118 121, is a number which started on Monday [...] thus all the information and services that people may need about cancer.'

<2> Host: **Il est d'ores et déjà opérationnel ce numéro?**
'It's already operational, this number?'

<3> Expert: Oui il est ouvert depuis lundi. (TS 03/25/2004)
'Yes, it's been in operation since Monday.'

As is well known, interrogatives also may be used by the participants to define and promote discourse topics. Once again, the conversational settings for the use of Q-declaratives and that of interrogatives are different. Here, we list a sample of settings where Q-declaratives are strongly dis-preferred and interrogatives optimal.[23]

- Q-declaratives are appropriate when the speaker is primarily interested in the ratification of p, while interrogatives are used when the

[23] From a broader perspective, conversational analysts distinguish two main strategies for topic promotion and management (see Button and Casey 1985). Either the participants select topics and sub-topics segregated from one another ('boundaried topic flow'), or they concatenate them, presented as if they evolved from one another ('stepwise topic flow'). Q-declaratives are the primary vectors of the second strategy, while *est-ce que* interrogatives are most often used for the first one.

question under discussion crucially hinges on the choice between p and its alternatives. While Q-declaratives project a course of discourse where on-topic elaboration is about p, interrogatives project one that is more specifically centered on the whereabouts of the choice itself (37).

(37)<1>Caller: Je voudrais savoir: je vis en concubinage et j'ai un enfant; c'est moi qui vais le prendre sur ma declaration. Je voudrais savoir si mon conjoint peut me verser une pension alimentaire? **Est-ce que** c'est légal? (TS 03/26/2004)
'I would like to know: I have a live-in companion, and I have a child. I am putting the child on my tax declaration. I want to know whether my companion can give me a maintenance allowance. Is this legal?'

<2> Host: **Est-ce** légal euh g() des concubins, un enfant, Frédéric Iannucci?
'Is it legal, uh, cohabiting companions, a child, FI?'

<3> Expert: euh s() la (en)fin la la réponse dépend un peu de la question de savoir si euh (en)fin la la personne que vous avez en () à charge [...]
'Uh, well, the answer somewhat depends on the question whether, uh, well, the person who is in your charge [...]'

- Interrogatives are preferred when the speaker initiates but does not elaborate on the topic and is not in a position to commit him/herself to one of the alternatives. This is typically the caller's strategy in (38). This is also the host's strategy when he is the mouthpiece of the callers and does not want to commit himself to the content of the question (39).

(38) Caller: J'aimerais connaître le point de vue de vos intervenants sur le plan du ministre de la Santé présenté il y a quelques jours [...] pour euh mieux diagnostiquer et prendre en charge la maladie. **Va-t-on** effectivement enfin dégager des moyens suffisants pour faire face à ce fléau? (TS 09/20/2004)
'I would like to know the position of your experts about the plan that the the Health minister presented a few days ago [...] in order to ensure a better diagnosis and treatment of the illness. Is it really the case that sufficient means will be released to counter this plague?'

(39)<1>Host: **Est-ce que** ce discours radical, donc c'est la question qui revient sans cesse sur France Inter point com, n'est pas là pour finalement euh donner un p() p() pour donner un sens

euh existentiel à un mouvement qui serait en train de décliner? (TS 08/23/2004)
'Is this radical talk, this is the question that comes again and again on France Inter dot com, not intended to finally uh give a, to give meaning to a movement which would tend to be on the decline?'

<2> Expert: Non, je ne le crois pas du tout.
'No, I don't think that at all.'

- Interrogatives are the only option when the speaker is the initiator and the primary elaborator of topic. This usage (often dubbed self-addressed question) is the primary strategy of experts. Q-declaratives are just impossible with such a use (40).

(40) Expert: Je constate qu'il n'y a pas le minimum requis pour faire des élections li() libres et dignes de ce nom-là. **Faut-il** les préparer sous supervision des Nations Unies? Oui. **Est-ce qu'il** y a aujourd'hui un danger que les islamistes i(ls) prennent le pouvoir par les élections? Euh oui c'est possible. Mais la question fondamentale est: **est-ce qu'on** peut faire des élections libres aujourd'hui, accessibles à tout le monde? J'en doute.
'I observe that the minimal conditions for organizing elections free and worthy of the name is not there. Should they be prepared under the supervision of United Nations? Yes. Is there today a danger that Islamists come into power following elections? Well, yes, this is possible. But the fundamental question is: is it possible to organize free elections today, open to everybody? That, I doubt.'

7 Conclusion

We have shown that there is no strong argument for analyzing French Q-declaratives as interrogatives or as having an impact resembling that of interrogatives. In fact, the analysis in terms of interrogative, question or query was plausible only as long as the interactive nature and discourse contingency of assertion was not fully recognized and the adjacency pair Question/Answer (inherited from conversational analysis) was the only format available for capturing the compelling nature of all speech acts or dialogical moves. Recognizing that assertions require a response of their own, even if it is not necessarily publicized, paved the way for our analysis. Conversely, analyzing Q-declaratives as *bona fide* declaratives led us to a simple account of their import and use.

Our analysis is in the same vein as previous 'true to form' analyses (Gunlogson 2003, 2008; Beyssade and Marandin 2006). Indeed, it brings support to their claim that clause types deterministically constrain the speech acts they allow when used by speakers in root clauses. It constrains the call-on-addressee: the declarative type requires the addressee to ratify (reject) the proposition which the asserter has selected and for which s/he projects the status of joint commitment. It commits the speaker to the propositional content. However, the speaker's commitment may either be independent of or dependent on the addressee's ratification. This gives rise to two subtypes of assertion: statements (the speaker is committed on his/her own ground) and proposals (the speaker is committed pending addressee's ratification). Q-declaratives are associated with proposals. There are different situations in which the speaker chooses a proposal rather than a statement. In particular, the addressee is more entitled than the speaker to ground the proposition, or the speaker gives way to the addressee for some interactive or conversational purpose.

Comparison of French Q-declaratives with their equivalent in English lies outside the scope of this paper. At first sight, French Q-declaratives have a broader spectrum of usage, but we lack an empirical study. Interestingly, the difference does not seem to lie in the semantics of declaratives or their use as assertion carriers, but rather in the conditions under which speakers can make a contingent commitment. The classification of contexts based on the discourse status of their content (Table 2) could be a good starting point for a systematic comparison.

Acknowledgements

We thank Jonathan Ginzburg, who read a first version, for raising good questions, and Claire Beyssade for sharing her analysis of biased questions (p.c.).

References

Abeillé, Anne, Benoît Crabbé, Danièle Godard, and Jean-Marie Marandin. 2012. French questioning declaratives: a corpus study. In *16th Semdial/Seindial Proceedings, Paris.*

Bazillon, Thierry, Benjamin Maza, Mickael Rouvier, Frederic Béchet, and Alexis Nasr. 2011. Qui êtes-vous? Catégoriser les questions pour déterminer le rôle des locuteurs dans des conversations orales. In *Proceedings of TALN (Traitement Automatique des Langues Naturelles).*

Bertrand, Roxane, Philippe Blache, Robert Espesser, Gaelle Ferré, Christine Meunier, Beatrice Priego-Valverde, and Stephane Rauzy. 2008. Le CID - Corpus of Interactional Data - Annotation et exploitation multimodale de parole conversationnelle. *Traitement automatique des langues (TAL)* 49(3):105–134.

Beyssade, Claire, Elisabeth Delais-Roussarie, and Jean-Marie Marandin. 2007. The prosody of interrogatives in French. *Nouveaux cahiers de linguistique française* 28:163–175.

Beyssade, Claire and Jean-Marie Marandin. 2006. The speech act assignment problem revisited: Disentangling speaker's commitment from speaker's call on addressee. In O. Bonami and P. Cabredo, eds., *Empirical issues in Syntax and Semantics 6*, pages 37–68. http://www.cssp.cnrs.fr/eiss6/index.html.

Beyssade, Claire and Jean-Marie Marandin. 2007. French intonation and attitude attribution. In P. Denis, E. McCready, A. Palmer, and B. Reese, eds., *Proceedings of the 2004 Texas Linguistics Society Conference: Issues at the Semantics-Pragmatics Interface*, pages 1–12. http://www.lingref.com/cpp/tls/2004/index.html.

Borillo, Andreé. 1978. Structure et valeur énonciative de l'interrogation totale en français. Thèse d'Etat, Université Aix en Provence.

Button, Graham and Neil Casey. 1985. Topic nomination and topic pursuit. *Human Studies* 8:3–55.

Clark, Herbert. 1994. Managing problems in speaking. *Speech communication* 15:243–250.

Farkas, Donka F. 1992. On the semantics of subjunctive complements. In P. Hirschbühler, ed., *Romance Languages and Modern Linguistic Theory*, pages 69–105. John Benjamins.

Farkas, Donka F. and Kim B. Bruce. 2010. On reacting to assertions and polar questions. *Journal of semantics* 27:81–118.

Farkas, Donka F. and Floris Roelofsen. 2012. Assertions and polar questions: the default case and beyond. Workshop Questions, Paris (ms).

Ginzburg, Jonathan. 2003. La sémantique et la grammaire dans le dialogue. Thèse d'habilitation, Université Paris 7.

Ginzburg, Jonathan. 2012. *The interactive stance: Meaning for conversation*. Oxford University Press.

Ginzburg, Jonathan and Raquel Fernandéz. 2002. A corpus study of non-sentential utterances in dialogue. *Traitement automatique des langues (TAL)* 43(2):12–43.

Ginzburg, Jonathan and Ivan A. Sag. 2000. *Interrogative Investigations*. Stanford: CSLI Publications.

Godard, Danièle. 2012. Indicative and subjunctive mood in complement sentences. In C. Piñon, ed., *Empirical Issues in Syntax and Semantics 9*, pages 129–148. http://www.cssp.cnrs.fr/eiss9/.

Gunlogson, Christine. 2003. *True to form: rising and falling declaratives as questions*. New York: Routledge.

Gunlogson, Christine. 2008. A question of commitment. *Belgian Journal of Linguistics* 22:101–136.

Hansen, Maj-Britt Mosegaard. 2001. Syntax in interaction. Form and function of yes/no interrogatives in spoken standard French. *Studies in language* 25(3):463–520.

Hobaek Haff, Marianne. 1987. *Coordonnants et éléments coordonnés*. Didier Erudition.

Huot, Hélène. 1986. Le subjonctif dans les complétives : subjectivité et modélisation. In M. Ronat and D. Couquaux, eds., *La grammaire modulaire*, pages 83–111. Paris: Minuit.

Krifka, Manfred. 1995. The semantics and pragmatics of polarity items. *Linguistic Analysis* 25:209–257.

Labov, William and David Fanshel. 1977. *Therapeutic discourse*. New York: Academic Press.

Ladd, D. Robert. 1996. *Intonational phonology (Cambridge Studies in Linguistics 79)*. Cambridge: Cambridge University Press.

Laurens, Fréderic, Cedric Patin, and Jean-Marie Marandin. 2013. Corpus Micro-fusées. Laboratoire de linguistique formelle (CNRS and Paris-Diderot).

Léon, Jacqueline. 1999. *Les entretiens publics en France, analyse conversationnelle et prosodique*. Paris: CNRS Editions.

Malamud, Sophia and Tamina Stephenson. 2011. Three ways of avoiding commitment: declarative force modifiers in the conversational scoreboards. In *Proceedings of Semantics of Dialogue*. Los Angeles, CA.

Marandin, Jean-Marie. 2005. Formatage de l'information: focus et contexte. In *Interpréter en contexte*, pages 31–80. Paris: Hermès.

Miller, Philip H. and Ivan A. Sag. 1997. French clitic movement without clitics or movement. *Natural Language and Linguistic Theory* 15(3):573–639.

Šafářová, Marie. 2007. Nuclear rises in update semantics. In M. Aloni, A. Buter, and P. Dekker, eds., *Questions in Dynamic Semantics*. Oxford/Amsterdam: Elsevier.

Stalnacker, Robert. 1978. Assertion. In P. Cole, ed., *Pragmatics*, pages 315–322. New York: Academic Press.

Truckenbrodt, Hubert. 2004. Sentence type meanings. http://www2.sfs.nphil.uni-tuebigen.de/ hubert/ Home/papers/.

Zaefferer, Dietmar. 2001. Deconstructing a classical classification: a typological look at Searle's concept of illocution type. *Revue internationale de Philosophie* (216):209–225.

≈ 3 ≈

Beyond the Core: The Road to Sign-based Construction Grammar

PAUL KAY

Sometime in the mid 1980s, Charles Fillmore proposed to me that if one were to marry the concept of construction as found in traditional grammars to a formalism like that of Martin Kay's (1984) Functional Unification Grammar, one might develop a formal (i.e. 'generative' in Chomsky's original sense) grammatical approach that could account for a wider range of linguistic data than was being considered in current generative-transformational work and could do so without having recourse to such uncomfortably unobservable entities and processes as empty categories and movement. I shared with Chuck a suspicion that the current concept of core grammar was motivated less by empirical observation than methodological convenience and agreed to join him in pursuing the idea of a 'unification-based' Construction Grammar. Part of the intuition was that large chunks of syntax often have meanings that appear to be non-compositional; or, to put less casually, that to maintain a compositional analysis in such cases it would be necessary to recognize a syntactically complex entity as a separate construction with a semantic rule of its own. A favorite example of Chuck's at the time concerned negative questions, like (1a). On a naively compositional reading, (1a) would convey a straightforward polar interrogation of (1b), as roughly indicated in (1c), but, in fact, negative questions like (1a) convey a suggestion that the speaker agrees with the contained affirmative proposition, e.g. (1d).

The Core and the Periphery.
Philip Hofmeister and Elisabeth Norcliffe (eds.).

(1) a. Isn't lutefisk delicious?
b. Lutefisk is not delicious.
c. Lutefisk is not delicious, true or false?
d. Lutefisk is delicious.

Shortly after this Mary Catherine O'Connor joined Chuck and me in working out a preliminary constructional analysis of *let alone* sentences, which we presented at a talk at Stanford, and which Ivan attended. Following this Ivan revealed to us – with characteristic enthusiasm – that the intuitions that had evidently motivated our analysis of *let alone* were things he had come to independently and that he had already begun introducing into HPSG. He immediately wanted to engage in a collaboration. I remember his saying sometime soon after that we ought to 'fly the same flag.'

It was a good many years before that flag found its Betsy Ross. In the meantime, discussions both organized and casual among various faculty and students at Stanford and Berkeley took place. During one quarter I attended a seminar of Ivan's at Stanford, where the group worked through the never-to-be-published Construction Grammar Course Book (Fillmore and Kay 1996), where I was particularly struck by problems with the Fillmore-Kay mechanisms that Ivan uncovered. (One example was a naïve and essentially incoherent notion of set unification that the Berkeley group was relying on to assemble complete argument structures for syntactically underspecified lexical entries.) During this period, Ivan pushed on with constructional HPSG, as particularly represented in Sag 1997 and Ginzburg and Sag 2000. Various groups of Stanford and Berkeley faculty and students met – sometimes regularly, sometimes occasionally – over a period of several years. Then in the early 2000s a group consisting of Ivan, Chuck, Laura Michaelis, and me began meeting regularly, adopting for our joint project the name Sign-Based Construction Grammar. As well as providing leadership with regard to formalism, Ivan led the group in many issues of substance. One example was his success in persuading the Berkeley group to abandon an approach to long distance dependencies based on an unconstrained recursion using the Kleene star notation in favor of an approach based on a sequence of local dependencies, in several details already familiar from GPSG and in spirit always present in the generative-transformational tradition. The current status of SBCG is represented in Ivan's long chapter (Sag 2012) in the recently released volume Sign-Based Construction Grammar (Boas and Sag 2012).

In the present chapter, Rui Chaves exploits two major properties of SBCG as represented in Sag 2012. RC argues that part-of-speech categories (N,V, etc.) can be dispensed with if one refers instead to the features that distinguish their behavior, adding that precision of prediction is thereby increased because universal definitions of parts of speech, applicable to all languages, were never empirically firm in the first place. In making this argument RC adroitly exploits the particular feature geometry proposed by Ivan in Sag 2012. As a demonstration of the advantage of an approach in which syntactic categories are replaced by specific features, RC shows that a great deal of the behavior of coordination of 'unlike categories' can be explained when features replace categories in the characterization of constituents. Since the array of features RC employs to this end includes both syntactic and semantic features, the fact – essential to SBCG – that signs comprise both syntactic and semantic information (along with phonological and contextual) plays an essential role.

References

Boas, Hans and Ivan A. Sag, eds. 2012. *Sign-Based Construction Grammar*. Stanford: CSLI Publications.

Fillmore, Charles J. and Paul Kay. 1996. Constructing grammar course book. Unpublished manuscript, UC Berkeley.

Ginzburg, Jonathan and Ivan A. Sag. 2000. *Interrogative Investigations: the form, meaning and use of English interrogative constructions*. Stanford: CSLI Publications.

Kay, Martin. 1984. Functional unification grammar: A formalism for machine translation. In *Proceedings of the 10th International Conference on Computational Linguistics*, pages 75–78. Association for Computational Linguistics.

Sag, Ivan A. 1997. English relative clause constructions. *Journal of Linguistics* 33(2):431–484.

Sag, Ivan A. 2012. Sign-based construction grammar: An informal synopsis. In H. Boas and I. A. Sag, eds., *Sign-based Construction Grammar*. CSLI Publications.

6

Grammatical Alignments and the Gradience of Lexical Categories

RUI P. CHAVES

1 Introduction

The notion of part of speech dates back at least to 5th century BC Sanskrit grammar (Matilal 1990, ch.3) and is adopted in one form or another by most current linguistic theories. In spite of this, no objective definition for standard part of speech labels has ever been put forth (Croft 1984, 2001; Langacker 1987; Aarts 2007). The present work explores the idea that parts of speech and their syntactic distribution may be the result of language-specific alignments of several linguistic aspects: meaning (in terms of actions, individuals, or properties), semantic function (i.e. predicates, arguments, and modifiers), and morphosyntactic properties. Since Sign-Based Construction Grammar (Sag 2010, 2012) is in an ideal position to capture such alignments in terms of fine-grained featural and constructional specifications, a grammar fragment of English is formulated along these lines, with the goal of obtaining a linguistic model where the various phrasal classes of English emerge without appeal to part of speech labels of any kind. Of special interest are the various environments which tolerate a wide range of syntactic categories, such as predicative structures and 'coordination of unlikes' phenomena.

It has long been recognized that one of the remarkable traits of predicative phrases is that they can be instantiated by a wide range of different categories. For example, verbs like *be* and *remain* allow for NP, AP, PP, and VP complements as shown in (1).

The Core and the Periphery.
Philip Hofmeister and Elisabeth Norcliffe (eds.).

(1) He is [tall]/[in Peru]/[a teacher]/[singing]/[endorsed by Nike].

As is well-known, this kind of syntactic flexibility is by no means limited to predicative environments. The complement of (2a) can be an NP or a PP, as long as it denotes a location, and the complement in (2b) can be an NP, an AdjP, or a PP, as long as it denotes a period of time. Similarly for the PP and the adjectival passive VP in (2c), which can be modified by *very* as if they were adjectival phrases instead.

(2) a. The magician emerged from [behind the curtain]/[the box]. (Huddleston and Pullum 2002, 599)
  b. The meeting lasted [two hours]/[much too long]/[until noon]. (attributed to Jane Grimshaw in Jackendoff 1985, 280)
  c. I didn't know about it [until [recently]/[May]/[the wedding]].
  d. I feel very [loved by everybody]/[in touch with myself]/[happy about that].

Similarly, English subject phrases allow a wide range of different categorial instantiations as illustrated in (3). For more data and discussion, see Crystal (1967), Ross (1972, 1973), Langacker (1987), Huddleston et al. (2002b, 1327), and Aarts (2007).

(3) a. [To prove the theorem] would be a pleasure.
  b. [That John quickly proved the theorem] astonished everyone.
  c. [For John to have quickly proved the theorem] made no sense.
  d. [John quickly proving the theorem] astonished everyone.
  e. [John's quickly proving the theorem] astonished everyone.
  f. [John's quick proving of the theorem] astonished everyone.
  g. [The proving of the theorem (by John)] astonished everyone.

These data suggest that sometimes selection is governed by semantics rather than by morphosyntax. In other cases, however, the role of semantics is smaller and more formal selection constraints are at work. This is illustrated by the contrast between (4) and (5). Even though these verbs are near-synonymous, the complementation patterns differ.

(4) a. Robin disposed *(of) the batteries.
  b. Robin discarded (*of) the batteries.

(5) a. Kim relies *(on) Robin.
  b. Kim trusts (*on) Robin.

Analogously, near-synonymous adjectives like *sick* and *ill* differ because of their morphosyntactic features: *sick* can be used in comparative and superlative forms, but *ill* cannot (e.g. **iller*, **more ill* and **illest*). Yet, both adjectives can be predicative and be suffixed by *-ness*. A similar disparity is observed in pairs like *alive*/*living* and *drunken*/*drunk*.

In general, one cannot determine the distribution of a sign solely as a function of its meaning. Morphosyntactic properties often play a crucial role. Some nouns have verbal semantics (e.g. *movement*, *kiss*, *earthquake*), and others have adjectival semantics (e.g. *strength*, *whiteness*, *size*). For example, the noun *hunger* (as in *the hunger for trivia*), and the homophonous verb (in *they hunger for trivia*) are essentially synonymous and yet differ in their distribution. This is determined by morphosyntactic properties, not by semantics. See Aarts (2007) for more examples in other lexical categories of English.

The point is that a balance between morphosyntactic and semantic constraints must be struck. Some environments impose mostly semantic constraints, others impose mostly morphosyntactic constraints, and others still impose a blend of both semantic and morphosyntactic constraints. This view is amply supported cross-linguistically. As Van Valin (2008) notes, although all languages have expressions for referring and expressions for predicating, they come with different alignments of syntactic, semantic, and morphological features. Some languages have sharply differentiated lexical categories because of little semantic/morphosyntactic feature overlap, while others do not.

Theories like Head-driven Phrase Structure Grammar (Pollard and Sag 1994) and Sign-Based Construction Grammar (Sag 2010, 2012) are in an ideal position to formalize the intuition that categories and fine-grained distributional patterns can be modeled via sets of morphosyntactic and semantic constraints, without resorting to part of speech labels. In this rather speculative paper, I explore such an approach, and show how such an account could be formulated.

1.1 Coordination of unlike categories

Ideally, a unified account of the data discussed above should also provide a handle on so-called coordination of unlikes phenomena. Consider for example (6) and (7), from Gazdar et al. (1985), Bayer (1996), Huddleston et al. (2002a) and others. Such data raise the old problem of determining what is the part of speech and categorial status of the bracketed constituents, as well as the properties that the coordination phrase retains from each conjunct.

(6) a. Kim is [alone and without money].
    [AP & PP]
  b. Pat is [a Republican and proud of it].
    [NP & AP]

c. Jack is [a good cook and always improving].
[NP & VP_{ger}]

d. What I would love is [a trip to Fiji and to win $10,000].
[NP & VP_{inf}]

e. That was [a rude remark and in very bad taste].
[NP & PP]

f. Pat was [awarded the Ig Nobel Prize and very upset about it].
[VP_{pas} & AP]

g. I am [expecting to get the job and of the opinion that it is a desirable one].
[VP_{ger} & PP]

h. Oprah is [a woman, rich, and in the lucky position of owning a castle].
[NP & AP & PP]

(7) a. Chimpanzees hunt [frequently and with an unusual degree of success].
[AdvP & PP]

b. I'm planning [a four-month trip to Africa and to return to York afterwards].
[NP & VP_{inf}]

c. I remembered [the appointment and that it was important to be on time].
[NP & CP]

d. I remembered [reading about you in the papers and that you lived in NY].
[VP_{ger} & CP]

e. [That Himmler appointed Heydrich and the implications thereof] frightened many observers.
[CP & NP]

f. [The danger involved and that the wiring had to be replaced] were clearly explained in the electrician's technical report.
[NP & CP]

It is clear that coordination does not simply compute the intersecting properties. As Jacobson (1987) pointed out, verbs like *remain* are compatible with both AdjP and NP complements whereas *grew* is only compatible with AdjPs. This is shown in (8). Crucially, however, the information associated with the phrase *wealthy and a Republican* somehow allows *grew* to detect the presence of the nominal, as (9a) illustrates, even when the verbs are coordinated, as in (9b–d)

(8) a. Kim remained/grew wealthy.

b. Kim remained/*grew a Republican.

(9) a. Kim remained/*grew [wealthy and a Republican].
b. Kim grew and remained wealthy.
c.*Kim grew and remained a Republican.
d.*Kim grew and remained [wealthy and a Republican].

A number of influential accounts in Type-logical grammar (Morrill 1990, 1994; Bayer 1996) have used one of the rules of inference from propositional calculus in order to deal with coordination of unlikes phenomena, namely, disjunction introduction (or addition): from P one can infer $P \vee Q$. Thus, by assuming that categories like NP, PP and so on can also be disjunctive, the grammar allows an expression of type 'NP' to lead a double life as an 'NP $\vee$ PP' expression, or the type 'AP' to be taken as an 'AP $\vee$ PP $\vee$ NP' and so on.[1] This account is only possible if one accepts the existence of part of speech labels in the first place. In this work, I follow Croft (2001), Van Valin (2008) and others in assuming that such labels are artificial and unnecessary. In that view, what is needed is a fine-grained characterization of categories in terms of independently motivated morphosyntactic and semantic properties. The goal is to identify what are the key linguistic factors that allow apparently different categories to be conjoinable.

1.2 On left-periphery ellipsis

Crysmann (2000), Yatabe (2002), Beavers and Sag (2004) and others argue that coordination of unlikes can be explained by a deletion operation that omits the left periphery of non-initial conjuncts. In that view, (6) and (7) are verbal coordinations where the verb (or the verb and the subject) has been deleted (e.g. *Kim is alone and ~~is~~ without money*). This analysis is independently motivated by data like (10).

(10) a. Tom gave a book to Mary, and ~~gave~~ a magazine to Sue.
b. He drinks coffee with milk at breakfast and ~~drinks coffee with~~ cream in the evening. (Hudson 1984)
c. There was one fatality yesterday, and ~~there were~~ two others on the day before.
(Chaves 2007, 339).
d. I see the music as both going backward and ~~going~~ forward.
[http://pdxjazz.com/dave-holland; 20 December 2010]

However, left-periphery ellipsis cannot fully explain coordination of unlikes phenomena. First, nothing explains the subject-verb agreement of (7f), repeated in (11).

[1] See also Daniels (2002), Sag (2002) and Yatabe (2004) for related accounts.

(11) [The danger involved and that the wiring had to be replaced] **were** clearly explained in the electrician's technical report.

Second, the data in (12) cannot be viewed as involving ellipsis.[2]

(12) a. Simultaneously shocked and in awe, Fred couldn't believe his eyes.
b. Both tired and in a foul mood, Bob packed his gear and headed North.
(Chaves 2006)
c. Both poor and a Republican, *no one* can possibly be.
d. Dead drunk and yet in complete control of the situation, *no one* can be.
(Levine 2011)

Further problems for an ellipsis account of coordination of unlikes phenomena are posed by the position of the correlative coordinators *both*, *either* and *neither* in (13).

(13) a. Isn't this both illegal and a safety hazard?
b. It's both odd and in very poor taste to have a fake wedding.
c. Who's neither tired nor in a hurry?
d. Isn't she either drunk or on medication?

If (13a) is an elliptical coordination like *isn't this both illegal and ~~isn't this~~ a safety hazard*, then the location of *both* is unexpected. Instead of occurring before the first conjunct, it is realized inside the first conjunct. Crucially, the non-elided counterparts are not grammatical, e.g. **isn't this both illegal and isn't this a safety hazard?* The same issue is raised by (13b,c). In an elliptical account one would have to stipulate that *both* can only float in the presence of ellipsis, which is unmotivated. In sum, left-periphery ellipsis does not offer a complete account of coordination of unlikes.

1.3 Goals of this paper

The main goal of this paper is to explore how linguistic categories can emerge implicitly – without part of speech labels – from independently motivated morphosyntactic and semantic constraints. For example, in this view, any sign with valent arguments that describes an eventuality and has the potential for verbal inflection will have verbal distribution. Similarly, any sign that describes entities conceptualized as entities, and that is capable of bearing case and of inflecting for number will have a

[2]Levine (2011) offers arguments against the coercion account of Chaves (2006), and against the existence of left-periphery ellipsis. See Yatabe (2012).

nominal distribution. Argument classes emerge as a consequence of the constraints imposed by the governing heads. For example, verbs like *devein* and *diagonalize* are well-known to impose extremely specific constraints on their valents, as shown in (14) from McCawley 1968.

(14) a. Mia deveined the shrimp / *duck.
  b. Tom diagonalized the matrix / *equation.

In contrast, verbs like *be* and *remain* impose very few morphosyntactic and semantic constraints on their valents and therefore can combine with many kinds of phrases. Hence, a wide range of phrases have similar distributions if they share the relevant morphosyntactic and semantic constraints that are required by the selecting head. The degree of cross-categorial distributional overlap in coordinate and in non-coordinate environments therefore follows from fine-grained morphosyntactic and semantic constraints that are associated to a sign.

The structure of the paper is as follows. In §2, I lay out a variant of Sign-Based Construction Grammar where grammatical labels play no role, and in §3, I focus on coordination of unlikes phenomena.

2 A grammar fragment

The feature geometry adopted in this work draws from Sign-based Construction Grammar (Sag 2010, 2012) with various modifications. Perhaps the most significant change is that various features that would be only appropriate for signs of a given part of speech are now appropriate for all signs. The advantage of this move is that all signs boil down to the same repertoire of features, and therefore will be able to conjoin as long as they have compatible information. The adopted feature geometry is shown in Figure 1. The adopted features are assumed to be appropriate for English, but not necessarily appropriate for other languages. As usual, the PHON(OLOGY) feature pertains to the representation of phonology and CONTEXT to pragmatics. These dimensions will not be addressed in the present work.[3]

2.1 Syntactic features

The feature SYN(TAX) specifies syntactic information. Let us first focus on the CAT feature. The grammar adopted here differs from previous HPSG/SBCG work in that there are no types for parts of speech and the features in CAT are appropriate for all signs. The type *category* is

[3]See Engdahl and Vallduví (1994), Kuhn (1996), Klein (2000), Koenig (1999), Orgun (2000), Haji-Abdolhosseini (2003), Gundel (2003), and Wilcock (2005). Also not discussed are unbounded dependencies; see Levine and Hukari (2006), Sag (2010), Chaves (2012) and references cited.

$$\begin{bmatrix} \textit{sign} & \\ \text{PHON} & \textit{list(phon)} \\ \text{SYN} & \begin{bmatrix} \textit{syn-obj} & \\ \text{CAT} & \begin{bmatrix} \textit{categorial} & \\ \text{AUX} & \textit{bool} \\ \text{INV} & \textit{bool} \\ \text{FORM} & \textit{form} \\ \text{CASE} & \textit{case} \end{bmatrix} \\ \text{VAL} & \textit{list(sign)} \\ \text{XARG} & \textit{arg-sign} \\ \text{SEL} & \textit{arg-sign} \\ \text{CRD} & \textit{crd} \end{bmatrix} \\ \text{SEM} & \begin{bmatrix} \textit{sem-obj} & \\ \text{LABEL} & \textit{label} \\ \text{INDEX} & \textit{index} \\ \text{FRAMES} & \textit{list(frame)} \end{bmatrix} \\ \text{CONTEXT} & \textit{context-obj} \end{bmatrix}$$

FIGURE 1 Feature geometry for signs

maximal, and therefore has no subtypes. This eliminates the problem of deciding what features are appropriate for the mother node of a coordination of unlike categories. All features are appropriate. Note that CAT information need not be explicitly enumerated in listemes. As usually assumed in HPSG, similar lexemes can be clustered in an Hierarchical Lexicon and their featural specifications can be determined by various principles with different generality.

Following Sag (2012), the feature AUX specifies if the sign occurs as the head of auxiliary constructions.[4] Since AUX provides information about the environment of the sign rather than about the sign itself, non-auxiliary verbs are always specified as [AUX–], and auxiliary verbs other than unstressed *do* are underspecified. The result is that the distribution of auxiliary and non-auxiliary verbs is distinct but overlaps in some cases. As hinted at above, all non-auxiliary verbs and all non-verbal signs are [AUX–].[5] The feature INV specifies if the sign occurs as

[4]That is, sentential negation, contraction, VP-Ellipsis or subject-auxiliary inversion constructions (Fillmore 1999), such as *Has he left?*, *Am I tired!*, *May you live long and prosper*, and *Had he been on time, John would have made it to the concert.*

[5]Allowing AUX to be available to non-verbal signs could provide a uniform account of VP/N-Ellipsis in terms of a single rule (Jackendoff 1971; Beavers 2003).

the head of certain inversion constructions. As Sag (2005) shows, all four combinations of [AUX+/] and [INV+/−] are attested in English. I assume that all signs other than certain non-auxiliary verbs are lexically specified as [INV−].[6]

The feature FORM identifies the tense/voice inflectional class of the sign. The type *form* has the usual subtypes *bare*, *fin*, *psp*, *inf*, *prp*, *pass*, and *none*. All *-ing* forms are systematically typed as *prp* (present participle) (Huddleston and Pullum 2002, 82). The type *none* is reserved for signs without any kind of verbal inflection. The value of the feature CASE can be *nom(inative)*, *acc(usative)*, *gen(itive)* or *none*. Nouns and gerundial forms are underspecified for CASE, and personal pronouns have inherent case along the lines of Levine et al. (2001). All other signs are [CASE *none*], and therefore cannot be assigned case. Thus, in this theory a sign can have a verbal suffix *-ing* and yet inflect for number and obtain structural case as in [*the sightings of UFOs*] *were too frequent to ignore*.

The VAL(ENCE) records the syntactic valents of the sign, and (E)X-(TERNAL) ARG(UMENT) singles out a distinguished argument that can be accessed from outside the projected phrase (Williams 1980; Sag and Pollard 1991; Meurers 1999). For example, in English there is strong evidence that subjects must be visible from outside their clause (Bender and Flickinger 1999; Levine 2001). See §2.5 for more discussion about XARG. The feature SEL(ECT) enables non-heads (such as modifiers and markers) to impose constraints on the heads they combine with. The type *arg-sign* subsumes the types *none* and *sign*. The former indicates that the feature value is null.

Finally, drawing inspiration from Beavers and Sag 2004, the marking feature CRD distinguishes coordinator lexemes like *and* and *or* (and signs marked by such markers) from all other signs. All coordinator lexemes have a specific CRD value, and all non-coordinate signs below are assumed to be specified as [CRD −].

2.2 Semantic features

The feature SEM(ANTICS) specifies semantic content and essentially follows the accounts proposed in Copestake et al. 2005 and Sag 2012. The type *frame* corresponds to a semantic predication formed by a relation feature called RELN and its arguments, as in Fillmore et al. 2003. The feature LABEL singles out the label of the main semantic frame

[6] In languages like Kiowa, however, determiners are underspecified for INV and therefore can occur to the right or to the left of the nominal (Adger et al. 2009, 8).

of the sign, and INDEX singles out the main index. For convenience, I abbreviate semantic representations as in (15).

(15) a. $[l : cat(x)]$ abbreviates $\begin{bmatrix} \textit{frame} & \\ \text{LABEL} & l \\ \text{RELN} & cat \\ \text{ARG} & x \end{bmatrix}$

b. $[l_1 : \forall x(l_2 \rightarrow l_3)]$ abbreviates $\begin{bmatrix} \textit{frame} & \\ \text{LABEL} & l_1 \\ \text{RELN} & \forall \\ \text{ARG}_0 & x \\ \text{ARG}_1 & l_2 \\ \text{ARG}_2 & l_3 \end{bmatrix}$

Following Pollard and Sag (1994), the value of INDEX is either a referential index *r-index* or a dummy *it* or *there* type. A referential index is essentially an unsorted variable that can in principle correspond to any kind of individual or eventuality. Crucially, it is assumed in this work that the difference between an eventuality and an individual is a matter of degree, and that indices can sometimes correspond to entities that have both individual- and eventuality-like properties. Alternatively, the reader may prefer to assume that referential indices are sorted in a fine-grained conceptual ontology like the one in Asher 2011. Some sorts are reserved for concrete individuals, other for abstract individuals, others for mixed individual-eventuality entities, and others still for various types of eventualities. The key point is that referential indices are assumed to correspond to a spectrum of entities with varying ontological status (see §2.3 below). Finally, I assume that agreement features are appropriate for all referential indices, but are lexically specified to be null for indices describing finite tense eventualities.

Finally, a clausal root can be defined as in (16), with no appeal to parts of speech. Basically, a root clause is an unmarked independent clause with finite verbal inflection, no case, no unsaturated valents, and no selected dependents. I assume that finite CPs cannot function as root clauses for semantic reasons, as discussed in §2.7.

(16) S_{root} abbreviates $\begin{bmatrix} \text{SYN} & \begin{bmatrix} \text{CAT} & \begin{bmatrix} \text{FORM} & \textit{fin} \\ \text{CASE} & \textit{none} \end{bmatrix} \\ \text{VAL} & \langle\,\rangle \\ \text{SEL} & \textit{none} \\ \text{CRD} & - \end{bmatrix} \end{bmatrix}$

2.3 Analytical metaphysics and semantic selection

Following Givón (1984, 51), Link (1998b) and others, I assume that the difference between individuals and eventualities is one of degree, based on the properties that the corresponding concepts individuate. This means that the linguistic indices used in semantic representations can correspond to entities which have both individual-like and eventuality-like properties. There is a long tradition of viewing concepts in terms of fine-grained primitives in linguistics (Wierzbicka 1972, 1996, 2006; Katz and Fodor 1963; Hjelmslev 1975; Andersen 1974; Keenan and Faltz 1985; Langacker 1987; Link 1998b; Croft 2001; Cruse 2004), in psychology (Collins and Quillian 1972; Rosch 1973; Rosch and Mervis 1975; Smith and Medin 1981; Medin 1989; McRae et al. 1997; Cree and McRae 2003; McRae et al. 2003, 2005) and in artificial intelligence (Minsky 1975; Norman and Rumelhart 1975).[7] One can view such primitives as features forming a conceptual space, as in the theory of conceptual representations of Gärdenfors (2001), the vector models of memory of Murdock (1982); Hintzman (1986), and current connectionist models of object recognition (Plaut 2002), word recognition (Harm and Seidenberg 2004), and semantic memory (Hinton and Shallice 1991; Plaut and Shallice 1993). For my purposes, it suffices to assume that lexical meaning is associated to particular regions in such conceptual space and that the emergent conceptual classes can overlap. To be clear, I am not concerned with the physical structure of the world here, but rather, with our thoughts about the world. All concepts are abstract by definition and therefore their conceptualization and individuation does not always reflect actual physical properties.

Following Givón (1984, 51), Link (1998b), and Gärdenfors (2001, 167, 193–195), I take two of the defining conceptual features of individuals to be *stability* and *reference*. Individuals are conceptualized as having intrinsic properties that apply continuously during their existence and which can be referenced by other linguistic expressions. In Link's terms, their existence is attributed to an intrinsic causal continuity, not to a series of individuals. Conversely, the persistence attributed to an eventuality is due to an iteration of eventualities.

Non-stative eventualities are conceptualized as dynamic manifestations which require intrinsic change. Such non-stative eventualities can sometimes be anaphorically referenced (e.g. *I cheated on the exam. That wasn't very wise. It caused me to fail the class*). Finally, states are stable manifestations, but cannot be referenced anaphorically (e.g.

[7] See Elman (2009, 2011) for a the view in which lexical elements are highly distributed and contextualized networks associated to fine-grained nonlinguistic cues.

*I know Danish. *It is a pleasure*). It is therefore assumed that the grammar can distinguish meanings that are stable and referential from those which are not. In this work, I reserve the variables $x...y$ for stable referential entities, whereas s is used for states (stable non-referential manifestations) and e for other eventualities (i.e. non-stable but possibly referential). I use ϵ to describe eventualities in general.

To reiterate, this indexical system of individuals, states and eventualities is a categorical abstraction over a gradient system: there are fine-grained differences between types of indices that the current system must be sensitive to. As already mentioned, one could if desired sort indices in a fine-grained ontology like the one developed by Asher (2011), or resort to various features to characterize the conceptual dimensions of the denoted concept. For example, primitives like [STABILTY±], [REFERENCE±], [DURATION±], [CONCRETENESS±], [ACTION±], etc. Crucially, the present system allows for the existence of words with mixed semantic properties like *war* or *happiness*. Because both words describe concepts that are stable and referential, they have nominal morphosyntactic features, and therefore a nominal distribution. I refer to these eventuality-turned-individual expressions using $x...y$ variables rather than e or s. Similarly, nouns like *claim* bear nominal morphosyntactic features because they are conceptualized as being individual-like manifestations, even though they share some conceptual properties with verbs. A claim is a monadic predicate that describes a type of message: a countable propositional entity brought about by the verbal action of claiming. As such, it can be predicated by truth-value expressions and be modified by adjectives as in *that last claim is true.* Also, like all count nouns, it must combine with a determiner. The same analysis applies to other nominals that share some conceptual properties with verbs, such as *action*, *event*, and *process.* Gerunds are a more extreme instance of this phenomenon of mixed nominal/verbal grammatical alignments. Although their root morphemes describe canonical eventualities, the gerundial form corresponds to a more individual-like region of conceptual space. Consequently, the distribution of the phrases they project overlaps with the distribution of more canonical nominal phrases.

A final assumption about semantics is that predicates impose semantic constraints on their arguments. For example, semantically, a verb like *leave* corresponds to [FRAMES $\langle \exists e\, leave(e, x, y), agent(x), area(y) \rangle$]. Basically, the verb requires that x is a volitional entity and that y is a spatial area. Hence, (17a) is well-formed, but (17b) is not.

(17) a. The cat exited the garage.
b.*The instant exited the shouting.

There is much independent motivation for the existence of semantic selection constraints. As already discussed in §1, certain complements can be of any category as long as they denote a location, such as (18).

(18) The magician emerged from [behind the curtain]/[the box].

The opposite situation is illustrated in (19), which shows that *speak* selects an extremely restricted class of complements.

(19) a.*Kim spoke a story/poem/joke (about Robin).
b. Kim spoke [something]/[a few words] about Robin.

Semantic selection constraints also explain the oddness of (20), which arises when the complement adds no new information to the constraints already imposed by the verb.

(20) a. Kim buttered the bread with ??(unsalted) butter.
b. Sue elbowed me with her ??(arthritic) elbow.
c. We danced a ??(traditional Indian) dance.

2.4 Nominal environments

In this theory there is no general notion of NP. What we have is a family of overlapping distributional classes which emerge from lexical and constructional constraints on semantic and morphosyntactic properties. Let us start by the simplest possible case. Dummy pronouns *there* and *it* are directly selected by certain verbs in certain constructions, without any effect on semantic interpretation. For illustration, I provide in full the lexical entry for dummy *it* in (21).

(21)
$$\begin{bmatrix} \textit{word} & \\ \text{PHON} & \langle \textit{it} \rangle \\ \text{SYN} & \begin{bmatrix} \text{CAT} & \begin{bmatrix} \text{AUX} & - \\ \text{INV} & - \\ \text{FORM} & \textit{none} \end{bmatrix} \\ \text{XARG} & \textit{none} \\ \text{VAL} & \langle\,\rangle \\ \text{SEL} & \textit{none} \\ \text{CRD} & - \end{bmatrix} \\ \text{SEM} & \begin{bmatrix} \text{INDEX} & \textit{it} \\ \text{FRAMES} & \langle\,\rangle \end{bmatrix} \end{bmatrix}$$

The lexical entry for the verb *rains* is given in (22). The features in SYN and SEM are typical of a verbal sign. Note, however, that this verb directly selects the dummy *it* subject, without appeal to any categorial constraints whatosoever. Drawing from Sag 2010, the specification $X{:}\phi$ means that X has at least the features described in ϕ.

(22)
$$\begin{bmatrix} \textit{word} & \\ \text{PHON} & \langle \textit{rains} \rangle \\ \text{SYN} & \begin{bmatrix} \text{CAT} & \begin{bmatrix} \text{AUX} & - \\ \text{INV} & - \\ \text{CASE} & \textit{none} \\ \text{FORM} & \textit{fin} \end{bmatrix} \\ \text{XARG} & X{:}\begin{bmatrix} \text{SEM} \mid \text{INDEX} \ \textit{it} \end{bmatrix} \\ \text{VAL} & \langle X \rangle \\ \text{SEL} & \textit{none} \\ \text{CRD} & - \end{bmatrix} \\ \text{SEM} & \begin{bmatrix} \text{INDEX} & e \\ \text{LABEL} & l_2 \\ \text{FRAMES} & \left\langle [l_1 : \exists e(l_1)], [l_2 : \textit{rain}(e)] \right\rangle \end{bmatrix} \end{bmatrix}$$

Drawing from Sag 2010, the constructional rule in (23) allows a subject phrase of any kind to combine with an eventuality-denoting predicate phrase. The specification $Y!\varphi$ means that the various occurrences of Y share all their features except those mentioned in φ.[8]

[8] For illustration, consider the descriptions in (i) and (ii), and assume that F1 and F2 are the only features appropriate for τ. The description (i) abbreviates (ii).

(i) $\begin{bmatrix} \text{G1} & X!\begin{bmatrix} \tau \\ \text{F2} \ \alpha \end{bmatrix} \\ \text{G2} & X \end{bmatrix}$ (ii) $\begin{bmatrix} \text{G1} & \begin{bmatrix} \tau & \\ \text{F1} & X \\ \text{F2} & \alpha \end{bmatrix} \\ \text{G2} & \begin{bmatrix} \tau & \\ \text{F1} & X \end{bmatrix} \end{bmatrix}$

(23) SUBJECT-PREDICATE CONSTRUCTION

$$
\textit{subj-pred-cxt} \Rightarrow \begin{bmatrix} \text{MTR} & \begin{bmatrix} \text{SYN} & Y!\begin{bmatrix}\text{VAL} & \langle\rangle\end{bmatrix} \\ \text{SEM} & \begin{bmatrix} \text{INDEX} & \epsilon \\ \text{LABEL} & l \end{bmatrix} \end{bmatrix} \\ \text{DTRS} & \left\langle X, \begin{bmatrix} \text{SYN} & Y : \begin{bmatrix} \text{CAT} & \begin{bmatrix}\text{FORM} & \neg none\end{bmatrix} \\ \text{XARG} & X \\ \text{VAL} & \langle X \rangle \end{bmatrix} \\ \text{SEM} & \begin{bmatrix} \text{INDEX} & \epsilon \\ \text{LABEL} & l \end{bmatrix} \end{bmatrix} \right\rangle \\ \text{CX-CONTENT} & \langle\rangle \end{bmatrix}
$$

I adopt the type hierarchy of Sag (2010). Hence, *subj-pred-cxt* is a sub-type of *head-cxt*, which in turn is a sub-type of *phrasal-cxt*.

The constructional rule in (24), drawn from Copestake et al. 2005, specifies how semantic composition takes place. The feature CX-CONTENT allows constructions to make a semantic contribution.

(24) PRINCIPLE OF COMPOSITIONALITY

$$
\textit{phrasal-cxt} \Rightarrow \begin{bmatrix} \text{MTR} & \begin{bmatrix}\text{SEM} & \begin{bmatrix}\text{FRAMES} & X_0 \oplus X_1 \oplus \ldots \oplus X_n\end{bmatrix}\end{bmatrix} \\ \text{DTRS} & \left\langle \begin{bmatrix}\text{SEM} & \begin{bmatrix}\text{FRAMES} & X_1\end{bmatrix}\end{bmatrix}, \ldots, \begin{bmatrix}\text{SEM} & \begin{bmatrix}\text{FRAMES} & X_n\end{bmatrix}\end{bmatrix} \right\rangle \\ \text{CX-CONTENT} & X_0 \end{bmatrix}
$$

The proposed grammar fragment licenses the construct in Figure 2. Following standard practice in construction grammar, the structures licensed by constructions are referred to as constructs. In this paper, I exclusively depict constructs in figures.

Let us now discuss non-expletive nominal phrases. For convenience, I use the abbreviation 'NP' to refer to a non-expletive and non-predicative nominal phrase. To be clear, this is nothing but a shorthand for the constraints in (25). This is reminiscent of Van Valin (2008), where 'RP' (reference phrase) replaces the 'NP' label.

$$\begin{bmatrix} \textit{phrase} & \\ \text{PHON} & \langle \textit{it}, \textit{rains} \rangle \\ \text{SYN} & \begin{bmatrix} \text{CAT} & \boxed{1}\begin{bmatrix} \text{AUX} & - \\ \text{INV} & - \\ \text{FORM} & \textit{fin} \\ \text{CASE} & \textit{none} \end{bmatrix} \\ \text{XARG} & \boxed{2} \\ \text{VAL} & \langle\, \rangle \\ \text{SEL} & \textit{none} \\ \text{CRD} & - \end{bmatrix} \\ \text{SEM} & \begin{bmatrix} \text{INDEX} & e \\ \text{LABEL} & l_1 \\ \text{FRAMES} & \langle \boxed{3}, \boxed{4} \rangle \end{bmatrix} \end{bmatrix}$$

$$\boxed{2}\begin{bmatrix} \textit{word} & \\ \text{PHON} & \langle \textit{it} \rangle \\ \text{SYN} & \begin{bmatrix} \text{CAT} & \begin{bmatrix} \text{AUX} & - \\ \text{INV} & - \\ \text{FORM} & \textit{none} \end{bmatrix} \\ \text{XARG} & \textit{none} \\ \text{VAL} & \langle\, \rangle \\ \text{SEL} & \textit{none} \\ \text{CRD} & - \end{bmatrix} \\ \text{SEM} & \begin{bmatrix} \text{INDEX} & \textit{it} \\ \text{LABEL} & \textit{none} \\ \text{FRAMES} & \langle\, \rangle \end{bmatrix} \end{bmatrix} \quad \begin{bmatrix} \textit{word} & \\ \text{PHON} & \langle \textit{rains} \rangle \\ \text{SYN} & \begin{bmatrix} \text{CAT} & \boxed{1} \\ \text{XARG} & \boxed{2} \\ \text{VAL} & \langle \boxed{2} \rangle \\ \text{SEL} & \textit{none} \\ \text{CRD} & - \end{bmatrix} \\ \text{SEM} & \begin{bmatrix} \text{INDEX} & e \\ \text{LABEL} & l_2 \\ \text{FRAMES} & \left\langle \boxed{3}[l_1 : \exists e(l_2)], \boxed{4}[l_2 : \textit{rain}(e)] \right\rangle \end{bmatrix} \end{bmatrix}$$

FIGURE 2 A Subject-Predicate construct

(25)

$$\text{NP}_x \quad \text{abbreviates} \quad \begin{bmatrix} \text{SYN} & \begin{bmatrix} \text{CAT} & \begin{bmatrix} \text{AUX} & - \\ \text{INV} & - \\ \text{CASE} & \neg\textit{none} \end{bmatrix} \\ \text{VAL} & \langle\, \rangle \\ \text{SEL} & \textit{none} \\ \text{CRD} & - \end{bmatrix} \\ \text{SEM} & \begin{bmatrix} \text{INDEX} & x \\ \text{LABEL} & l \\ \text{FRAMES} & \left\langle l : \left[Qx \right], \ldots \right\rangle \end{bmatrix} \end{bmatrix}$$

A nominal phrase is therefore a sign that bears noun-like morphosyntactic and semantic information. It is a referential phrase that is semantically 'determined' by some quantifier Q. I assume direct access to the relevant frame in FRAMES via the label, but this could also be modeled via the feature HOOK (Copestake et al. 2005) or LID (Sag 2012).

Also consistent with (25) are noun phrases with covert determiners such as bare plural and non-count nominal phrases. Proper names are assumed to contain a bound variable as well, along the lines of Kamp and Reyle (1993) (e.g. $\exists x\, kim(x)$).

Note that the presence of such a quantifier is not restricted to nominals. Verbs, adjectives, adverbs, and some prepositions are lexically specified as containing a quantified Neo-Davidsonian variable (i.e. existential closure). The result is that a wide range of phrases will be compatible with the constraints in (25), including gerundial, complementizer, infinitival, and (certain) prepositional and adjectival phrases.

The symbol 'N' is used to abbreviate a nominal phrase whose index is not quantificationally bound. For example, determiners select such a nominal host via the feature SEL, as (26) shows.

(26)
$$\begin{bmatrix} \textit{word} & \\ \text{PHON} & \langle \textit{each} \rangle \\ \text{SYN} & \begin{bmatrix} \text{CAT} & \begin{bmatrix} \text{AUX} & - \\ \text{INV} & - \\ \text{FORM} & \textit{none} \\ \text{CASE} & \textit{none} \end{bmatrix} \\ \text{VAL} & \langle\, \rangle \\ \text{XARG} & \textit{none} \\ \text{SEL} & \text{N}_x\begin{bmatrix} \text{LABEL} & l_2 \end{bmatrix} \\ \text{CRD} & - \end{bmatrix} \\ \text{SEM} & \begin{bmatrix} \text{INDEX} & x \\ \text{LABEL} & l_1 \\ \text{FRAMES} & \left\langle [l_1 : \forall x(l_2 \rightarrow l_3)] \right\rangle \end{bmatrix} \end{bmatrix}$$

The lexical entry for a singular common noun is shown in (27).

(27)
$$\begin{bmatrix} \textit{word} \\ \text{PHON } \langle \textit{cat} \rangle \\ \text{SYN} \begin{bmatrix} \text{CAT} \begin{bmatrix} \text{AUX} & - \\ \text{INV} & - \\ \text{FORM} & \textit{none} \end{bmatrix} \\ \text{VAL} \ \langle\, \rangle \\ \text{XARG} \ \textit{none} \\ \text{SEL} \ \textit{none} \\ \text{CRD} \ - \end{bmatrix} \\ \text{SEM} \begin{bmatrix} \text{INDEX} \ x \begin{bmatrix} \text{NUM} & \textit{sg} \\ \text{PER} & \textit{3rd} \\ \text{GEN} & \textit{neut} \end{bmatrix} \\ \text{LABEL} \ l_2 \\ \text{FRAMES} \left\langle [l_2 : \textit{cat}(x)] \right\rangle \end{bmatrix} \end{bmatrix}$$

The HEAD-FUNCTOR CONSTRUCTION in (28), taken from Sag 2012, allows determiners, modifiers, adpositions, and markers to select the head phrases that they combine with, via the feature SEL(ECT). In this work, I assume linearization is handled as in Kathol 2000.

(28) HEAD-FUNCTOR CONSTRUCTION

$$\textit{head-functor-cxt} \Rightarrow \begin{bmatrix} \text{MTR} \begin{bmatrix} \text{SYN } Y \\ \text{SEM} \begin{bmatrix} \text{INDEX } \alpha \\ \text{LABEL } l \end{bmatrix} \end{bmatrix} \\ \text{DTRS} \left\langle \begin{bmatrix} \text{SYN} \begin{bmatrix} \text{SEL } X \\ \text{VAL } \langle\rangle \end{bmatrix} \\ \text{SEM} \begin{bmatrix} \text{INDEX } \alpha \\ \text{LABEL } l \end{bmatrix} \end{bmatrix}, X{:}\begin{bmatrix} \text{SYN } Y \end{bmatrix} \right\rangle \\ \text{CX-CONTENT } \langle\rangle \end{bmatrix}$$

I use α to refer to referential indices of any kind, without specifying if they correspond to individuals or eventualities. We license constructs like *each cat* as shown in Figure 3. This is the result of combining the two signs in (26) via the *head-functor construction* in (23). The two daughters are omitted from Figure 3 due to space limitations.

Since (28) is a headed construction, it inherits all the constraints in (23) and (24). Verbs impose morphosyntactic and semantic constraints on valents as illustrated by the verb shown in (29).

$$\begin{bmatrix} \textit{phrase} \\ \text{PHON} \ \langle \textit{each}, \textit{cat} \rangle \\ \text{SYN} \begin{bmatrix} \text{CAT} \begin{bmatrix} \text{AUX} & - \\ \text{INV} & - \\ \text{FORM} & \textit{none} \end{bmatrix} \\ \text{VAL} \quad \langle\,\rangle \\ \text{XARG} \quad \textit{none} \\ \text{SEL} \quad \textit{none} \\ \text{CRD} \quad - \end{bmatrix} \\ \text{SEM} \begin{bmatrix} \text{INDEX } x \begin{bmatrix} \text{NUM} & \textit{sg} \\ \text{PER} & \textit{3rd} \\ \text{GEN} & \textit{neut} \end{bmatrix} \\ \text{LABEL } l_1 \\ \text{FRAMES} \left\langle [l_1 : \forall x(l_2 \rightarrow l_3)],\ [l_2 : \textit{cat}(x)] \right\rangle \end{bmatrix} \end{bmatrix}$$

FIGURE 3 A Noun Phrase construct (daughters omitted)

(29)
$$\begin{bmatrix} \textit{word} \\ \text{PHON} \ \langle \textit{yawns} \rangle \\ \text{SYN} \begin{bmatrix} \text{CAT} \begin{bmatrix} \text{AUX } - \\ \text{INV } - \\ \text{FORM } \textit{fin} \\ \text{CASE } \textit{none} \end{bmatrix} \\ \text{XARG } Y \\ \text{VAL} \quad \left\langle Y : \text{NP}_x \begin{bmatrix} \text{AGR} & \textit{3rd} \\ \text{NUM} & \textit{sg} \end{bmatrix} \right\rangle \\ \text{SEL} \quad \textit{none} \\ \text{CRD } - \end{bmatrix} \\ \text{SEM} \begin{bmatrix} \text{INDEX } e \\ \text{LABEL } l_2 \\ \text{FRAMES} \left\langle [l_1 : \exists e(l_2)], [l_2 : \textit{yawn}(e,x)], [l_2 : \textit{animate}(x)] \right\rangle \end{bmatrix} \end{bmatrix}$$

Let us now turn to prepositional phrases. As illustrated in (36a), so-called 'case marking' prepositions make a basic semantic case contribution, consisting of semantic role predicates such as $agent(x)$, $source(x)$, $patient(x)$, etc. (see, for example, Wechsler 1995 and Davis 2001).

(30)
$$
\begin{bmatrix}
\textit{word} & \\
\text{PHON} & \langle \textit{on} \rangle \\
\text{SYN} & \begin{bmatrix}
\text{CAT} & \begin{bmatrix} \text{AUX} & - \\ \text{INV} & - \\ \text{FORM} & \textit{none} \end{bmatrix} \\
\text{VAL} & \left\langle \begin{bmatrix}
\text{SYN} & \begin{bmatrix}
\text{CAT} & \begin{bmatrix} \text{AUX} & - \\ \text{INV} & - \\ \text{CASE} & \textit{none} \end{bmatrix} \\
\text{VAL} & \langle\, \rangle \\
\text{SEL} & \textit{none} \\
\text{CRD} & -
\end{bmatrix} \\
\text{SEM} & \begin{bmatrix} \text{INDEX} & x \\ \text{LABEL} & l \end{bmatrix}
\end{bmatrix} \right\rangle \\
\text{XARG} & \textit{none} \\
\text{SEL} & \textit{none} \\
\text{CRD} & -
\end{bmatrix} \\
\text{SEM} & \begin{bmatrix}
\text{INDEX} & x \\
\text{LABEL} & l \\
\text{FRAMES} & \left\langle [l : \textit{support}(x)] \right\rangle
\end{bmatrix}
\end{bmatrix}
$$

After combining with an NP, the resulting phrase is a suitable complement for a verb like *rely*, which selects a support-denoting individual.

The construction that allows heads to combine their complements is shown in (31), adapted from Sag 2012. This states that a lexical sign Z that selects a non-empty list of valents yields a phrase that is similar to X, except that its valence is saturated.[9]

[9] I assume that auxiliary verbs are [XARG *none*]. Consequently, this constructional rule can also license subject-inversion structures *Are you tired?* and *Am I tired!*

(31) SATURATIONAL HEAD-COMPLEMENT CONSTRUCTION

$$sat\text{-}head\text{-}comp\text{-}cxt \Rightarrow \begin{bmatrix} \text{MTR} & \begin{bmatrix} \text{SYN } X!\begin{bmatrix}\text{VAL } \langle\rangle\end{bmatrix} \\ \text{SEM}\begin{bmatrix}\text{INDEX } \alpha \\ \text{LABEL } l\end{bmatrix}\end{bmatrix} \\ \text{DTRS} & \left\langle \begin{bmatrix} word \\ \text{SYN } X{:}\begin{bmatrix}\text{VAL } \langle Y\rangle \oplus L \\ \text{XARG } \neg Y\end{bmatrix} \\ \text{SEM}\begin{bmatrix}\text{INDEX } \alpha \\ \text{LABEL } l\end{bmatrix}\end{bmatrix}, Y \right\rangle \oplus L \\ \text{CX-CONTENT} & \langle\rangle \end{bmatrix}$$

As (30) combines with its complement, the result is a *support*-denoting NP. For convenience, I abbreviate such phrases with the label $\text{PP}_x[C]$. This is an NP_x specified as [CASE *none*] that contains in FRAMES a semantic condition C on index x. The verb *rely* is given in (32).

(32)
$$\begin{bmatrix} word \\ \text{PHON } \langle rely\rangle \\ \text{SYN} & \begin{bmatrix} \text{CAT} & \begin{bmatrix} \text{AUX} & - \\ \text{INV} & - \\ \text{CASE} & none \\ \text{FORM} & fin \end{bmatrix} \\ \text{VAL} & \left\langle Y{:}\text{NP}_x\begin{bmatrix}\text{CASE } nom\end{bmatrix}, \text{PP}_y[support] \right\rangle \\ \text{XARG} & Y \\ \text{SEL} & none \\ \text{CRD} & - \end{bmatrix} \\ \text{SEM} & \begin{bmatrix} \text{INDEX} & e \\ \text{LABEL} & l_2 \\ \text{FRAMES} & \left\langle [l_1 : \exists e(l_2)], [l_2 : rely(e,x,y)], [l_2 : animate(x)] \right\rangle \end{bmatrix} \end{bmatrix}$$

Since the subject of *rely* is required to be animate, sentences like **Our future relies on sustainable energy sources* are deemed anomalous. Conversely, a verb like *depend* makes no such requirement and can therefore combine with a wider range of subjects, including actions, regions and abstract entities (e.g. *Our future depends on sustainable energy sources*).[10]

[10] A reviewer argues against this analysis given the acceptability of attested examples like *such calculations rely on two concepts from algebra.* But this is probably

There are still some constraints limits, however, since *depend* verb cannot apply to locatives as shown by **there depends on it* and by **near the door depends on it.*

There are many other uses for the preposition *on*. Consider the one shown in (33), for example. This preposition denotes the spatial location x where y is situated, and is therefore not a semantically empty preposition.

(33)
$$\begin{bmatrix} \textit{word} & \\ \text{PHON} & \langle \textit{on} \rangle \\ \text{SYN} & \begin{bmatrix} \text{CAT} & \begin{bmatrix} \text{AUX} & - \\ \text{INV} & - \\ \text{FORM} & \textit{none} \end{bmatrix} \\ \text{VAL} & \langle\ \text{NP}_y\ \rangle \\ \text{XARG} & \textit{none} \\ \text{SEL} & \textit{none} \\ \text{CRD} & - \end{bmatrix} \\ \text{SEM} & \begin{bmatrix} \text{INDEX} & x \\ \text{LABEL} & l_1 \\ \text{FRAMES} & \left\langle [l_1 : \exists x(l_2)], [l_2 : region(x),\ l_2 : on(x,y)] \right\rangle \end{bmatrix} \end{bmatrix}$$

The x referent is internal to the preposition in the same way that a relational noun like *owner* implies two different individuals: a possessor (the internal referent) and a possessed (which is external, and introduced by a subcategorized PP[*possessed*] complement).

Because prepositions like (33) are not specified for case and denote a stable (spatial or temporal) entity, they can occur in nominative and accusative NP environments as long as the verb does not impose conflicting semantic constraints, as in (34).

(34) a. [(On/Under) the table] became my favorite place to sleep.
b. The cat jumped from [(under) the table].
c. He considered [(under/in) the closet] a good place for the key.

---

a different, though related, use of the verb. In this example, the calculations are brought about by the algebraic operations, and there is no underlying purpose served by the relation between the calculations and the algebraic operations. Thus, purpose phrases are disallowed: **Such calculations rely on two algebraic operations to solve equations.* The meaning of this use of *rely* is essentially the same as that of *depend*, and any dynamic referential entity will serve as a subject. In the use of *rely* that (32) is intended to correspond to, the entity denoted by the subject is not brought about by the object That is, in *Tom relies on Sue* the existence of Tom is not bought about by Sue. Moreover, there is an implicit goal for the relation between the two individuals, which explains why purpose phrases are allowed, e.g. *Tom relies on Sue to paint the garage.*

d. [From/Between here to downtown] is a distance of thirty miles.
e. [(After/By/On) Christmas] is not considered to be too late.
f. [(By/Before) the end of the week] would suit me better.
g. The magician emerged [from [(behind/inside) the closet]].
h. The meeting lasted [two hours] / [much too long] / [until midnight].

There is also a double coordinator construction, illustrated in (35), that allows two such PPs to be combined. The result is a phrase that denotes a vector between the endpoints denoted by the daughters. In SBCG this double PP structure can be easily modeled by a construction that takes two such PPs and that adds the vector semantics via CX-CONTENT. The whole phrase is referential and therefore suitable for subject and complement environments.

(35) a. Tom searched from Boston to Providence.
b. From Boston to Providence is not far.
(Huddleston and Pullum 2002, 641)

The adnominal counterpart of (33) is given in (36). This word denotes the state of x being spatially located on y and projects a phrase that modifies NPs. This is achieved via the [SEL NP] specification, which allows the prepositional phrase to combine with a nominal host via the HEAD FUNCTOR CONSTRUCTION in (28). Note that the preposition must combine with the complement before it can adjoin to the nominal head, since (28) requires the functor to be specified as [VAL $\langle\,\rangle$].

(36)
$$\begin{bmatrix} \textit{word} & \\ \text{PHON} & \langle \textit{on} \rangle \\ \text{SYN} & \begin{bmatrix} \text{CAT} & \begin{bmatrix} \text{AUX} & - \\ \text{INV} & - \\ \text{CASE} & \textit{none} \\ \text{FORM} & \textit{none} \end{bmatrix} \\ \text{VAL} & \left\langle \text{NP}_y \right\rangle \\ \text{XARG} & \textit{none} \\ \text{SEL} & \text{NP}_x \\ \text{CRD} & - \end{bmatrix} \\ \text{SEM} & \begin{bmatrix} \text{INDEX} & e \\ \text{LABEL} & l_2 \\ \text{FRAMES} & \left\langle [l_1 : \exists s(l_2)],\ [l_2 : on(s,x,y)] \right\rangle \end{bmatrix} \end{bmatrix}$$

2.5 Predicative environments

A predicative phrase is an expression that assigns a thematic role to a referential phrase which is external to the projection. Sometimes this is mediated by a raising verb (*We are happy*) sometimes not (*This made us happy*). There are many constructions which involve predicative structures, including certain adnominal environments (e.g. *All rivers navigable are being controlled*), subject-oriented dangling modifiers (*Furious, Kim stormed out of the room*) and absolute constructions (*With Sue injured, the play could not continue*). What is common to all of these structures is that the predicative phrase imposes constraints on an external argument. In some cases, the external argument is not a valent. The feature XARG is ideal to capture this phenomenon, since it allows one distinguished sign to be visible outside its local domain. For example, Bender and Flickinger (1999) use XARG to model the fact that tag questions must access the syntactic subject of the preceding clause (cf. *Sarah read the book, didn't she/*it?* with *The book was read by Sarah, wasn't it/*she*), Sag (2012) uses it for 'copy-raising' (cf. *There looks like there's/*it's going to be a storm* with *It looks like it's/*there's going to rain*) and for certain idioms (e.g. *Bob*$_i$ *lost his*$_i$ *marbles*), and Chaves (2006) uses XARG to ensure that dangling modifiers can predicate the syntactic subject of the clause they adjoin to (cf. *Furious, Kim threw the TV out the window* with **Furious, the TV was thrown out the window*).

I therefore reject the purely descriptive feature PRED (Gazdar et al. 1985, 85) and attempt to characterize predicative environments via independently motivated features like XARG. In what follows, I focus on the constraints imposed on post-copular environments. The features common to all post-copular predicative expressions are in Figure 4.

$$\begin{bmatrix} \text{SYN} & \begin{bmatrix} \text{VAL} & \langle\rangle \\ \text{XARG} & \text{NP}_x \\ \text{SEL} & \textit{none} \\ \text{CRD} & - \end{bmatrix} \\ \text{SEM} & \mid \ \text{INDEX}\ \epsilon \end{bmatrix}$$

FIGURE 4 A post-copular predicative sign

A post-copular predicative phrase is therefore a non-modifier sign that denotes an eventuality ϵ of some kind, requires a nominal external argument, and has saturated valence. Such signs are selected as complements by linking verbs, as illustrated in (37).[11] The complement must have saturated valence, must have an external NP coindexed with the copula's subject, must not be a modifier, and must describe an eventuality of some kind. The index ϵ corresponds to any kind of eventuality, including states.

(37)
$$\begin{bmatrix} \textit{word} \\ \text{PHON} \ \langle \textit{is} \rangle \\ \text{SYN} \begin{bmatrix} \text{CAT} \begin{bmatrix}\text{CASE } \textit{none}\\ \text{FORM } \textit{fin}\end{bmatrix} \\ \text{VAL} \left\langle K:\text{NP}^{nom}{}_{x}\begin{bmatrix}\text{NUM } \textit{sg}\\ \text{PER } \textit{3rd}\end{bmatrix}, \begin{bmatrix}\text{SYN}\begin{bmatrix}\text{VAL} & \langle\rangle \\ \text{XARG} & \text{NP}_x\\ \text{SEL} & \textit{none} \\ \text{CRD} & - \end{bmatrix}\\ \text{SEM}\begin{bmatrix}\text{INDEX } \epsilon\\ \text{LABEL } l\end{bmatrix}\end{bmatrix}\right\rangle \\ \text{XARG} \ \ K \\ \text{SEL} \ \ \textit{none} \\ \text{CRD} \ \ - \end{bmatrix} \\ \text{SEM} \begin{bmatrix} \text{INDEX } \epsilon \\ \text{LABEL } l \\ \text{FRAMES} \ \ \langle [l : t(\epsilon) = t_{now}] \rangle \end{bmatrix} \end{bmatrix}$$

The index and label of the verb are the same as the complement so that VP adjuncts can access the predicate's semantics. The constraints imposed on the complement are minimal, which explains why so many different kinds of phrases can be used predicatively. This combinatorial flexibility is obtained without resorting to such part of speech labels.

Let us consider some examples. Predicative and attributive uses of the same adjective are distinguished by different lexical specifications. This is consistent with the fact that predicative adjectives that select objects cannot do so in their attributive pre-nominal use, as (38) shows. Whereas the attributive adjective in (38b) is as [SEL NP], [XARG *none*], and [VAL ⟨⟩], the predicative use in (38a) is specified as [SEL *none*], [XARG NP], and [VAL ⟨PP⟩]. Similarly, the only syntactic difference between attributive *drunken* and the predicative *drunk* is the SEL and XARG specifications.[12]

[11] The copula verb is underspecified for AUX and INV, so that it may occur in various (non)inverted (non)auxiliary environments (e.g. *Was I wrong? I wasn't wrong, was I? I was wrong. Boy, was I wrong!*).

[12] The complex adnominal adjunct in (38b) is acceptable if the entire expres-

(38) a. The team is proud (of the coach).
b. The proud (*of the coach) team.

A predicative adjective is shown in (39). It requires a physical entity x and denotes a state. This predicate is a suitable complement for (37).

(39)
$$\begin{bmatrix} \textit{word} & \\ \text{PHON} & \langle \textit{yellow} \rangle \\ \text{SYN} & \begin{bmatrix} \text{CAT} & \begin{bmatrix} \text{AUX} & - \\ \text{INV} & - \\ \text{FORM} & \textit{none} \\ \text{CASE} & \textit{none} \end{bmatrix} \\ \text{VAL} & \langle\, \rangle \\ \text{XARG} & \text{NP}_x \\ \text{SEL} & \textit{none} \\ \text{CRD} & - \end{bmatrix} \\ \text{SEM} & \begin{bmatrix} \text{INDEX} & s \\ \text{LABEL} & l_2 \\ \text{FRAMES} & \left\langle [l_1 : \exists s(l_2)], [l_2 : \textit{yellow}(s,x)] \right\rangle \end{bmatrix} \end{bmatrix}$$

The adnominal counterpart of the adjective is shown in (40). It selects a referential nominal index x which is not yet bound by a quantifier. Given the non-empty SEL value and the null value for XARG, it is clear that this adjective cannot occur in a predicative position.

(40)
$$\begin{bmatrix} \textit{word} & \\ \text{PHON} & \langle \textit{yellow} \rangle \\ \text{SYN} & \begin{bmatrix} \text{CAT} & \begin{bmatrix} \text{AUX} & - \\ \text{INV} & - \\ \text{FORM} & \textit{none} \\ \text{CASE} & \textit{none} \end{bmatrix} \\ \text{VAL} & \langle\, \rangle \\ \text{XARG} & \textit{none} \\ \text{SEL} & \text{N}_x[\text{LABEL } l_1] \\ \text{CRD} & - \end{bmatrix} \\ \text{SEM} & \begin{bmatrix} \text{INDEX} & s \\ \text{LABEL} & l_2 \\ \text{FRAMES} & \left\langle [l_1 : \exists s(l_2)], [l_2 : \textit{yellow}(s,x)] \right\rangle \end{bmatrix} \end{bmatrix}$$

sion *proud-of-the-coach* is taken to be a compound morphological unit. As Bresnan and Mchombo (1995, 194) note with examples like *an-I-told-you-so-attitude*, such phrasal material is quotational, and can even involve phrases from foreign languages such as *a certain je ne sais quoi quality*.

The two adjective uses need not be listed in the grammar as two distinct lexemes. One could be derived from the other, or each could be a subtype of a more general and abstract lexeme type, as in the analysis for alternations proposed by Sag (2012).

A predicative use of a preposition is given in (41). This preposition combines with an NP complement in the usual way and yields a PP that is a suitable complement for (37).

(41)
$$\begin{bmatrix} \textit{word} \\ \text{PHON } \langle \textit{on} \rangle \\ \text{SYN} \begin{bmatrix} \text{CAT} \begin{bmatrix} \text{CASE} & - \\ \text{AUX} & - \\ \text{INV} & - \\ \text{CASE} & \textit{none} \\ \text{FORM} & \textit{none} \end{bmatrix} \\ \text{VAL} \quad \left\langle \text{NP}_y \begin{bmatrix} \text{CASE } \textit{acc} \end{bmatrix} \right\rangle \\ \text{XARG} \quad \text{NP}_x \\ \text{SEL} \quad \textit{none} \\ \text{CRD} \quad - \end{bmatrix} \\ \text{SEM} \begin{bmatrix} \text{INDEX} & s \\ \text{LABEL} & l_2 \\ \text{FRAMES} & \left\langle [l_1 : \exists s(l_2)], [l_2 : on(s,x,y)] \right\rangle \end{bmatrix} \end{bmatrix}$$

Predicative NPs are obtained by a *pred-nom-cx* construction that takes any N_x sign (lexical or phrasal) and coerces it into a predicative nominal sign. This is essentially a semantic process. For example, a nominal predicate like *republican*(x) specified as [INDEX x] and [XARG *none*] then becomes *republican*(s, x) where [INDEX s] and [XARG NP_x]. The construction is shown in (42).

(42) Predicative Nominal Construction

pred-nom-cx $\Rightarrow$

$$\begin{bmatrix} \text{MTR} & \begin{bmatrix} \textit{phrase} \\ \text{PHON } P \\ \text{SYN } X!\begin{bmatrix}\text{XARG NP}_{x_1}\end{bmatrix} \\ \text{SEM} \begin{bmatrix} \text{INDEX } s \\ \text{LABEL } l \\ \text{FRAMES } L_1 \oplus \langle [l : R(s, x_1, ..., x_n)] \rangle \oplus L_2 \end{bmatrix} \end{bmatrix} \\ \text{DTRS} & \left\langle \begin{bmatrix} \text{PHON } P \\ \text{SYN } X{:}\begin{bmatrix} \text{VAL} & \langle\,\rangle \\ \text{XARG} & \textit{none} \end{bmatrix} \\ \text{SEM} \begin{bmatrix} \text{INDEX } x_1 \\ \text{LABEL } l \\ \text{FRAMES } L_1 \oplus \langle [l : R(x_1, ..., x_n)] \rangle \oplus L_2 \end{bmatrix} \end{bmatrix} \right\rangle \\ \text{CX-CONTENT} & \langle\rangle \end{bmatrix}$$

It is important that this process can apply to phrases as well as words. This way, adnominal phrases like adjectives can combine and modify the nominal index of the N before the coercion changes the value of INDEX from x to s. Thus, (42) can apply to complex non-predicative nominal expressions like *a [great and wonderful woman who put her heart and soul into creating a better world]* and create a predicative counterpart. For illustration, the derivation of the predicative counterpart of the noun *genius* is shown in Figure 5.

This case is fairly simple, but (42) can handle cases where the noun is relational and cases where the nominal expression is not lexical. Since the index s of the predicative nominal expression is not bound, this phrase must combine with a determiner before it can function as an NP. However, because it denotes a (stative) eventuality and has a nominal external argument NP_x, it can only occur in predicative environments, such as the complement of a copula.

$$
\begin{bmatrix}
\textit{phrase} & \\
\text{PHON} & \boxed{1}\langle \textit{genius} \rangle \\
\text{SYN} & \begin{bmatrix}
\text{CAT} & \boxed{2}\begin{bmatrix}\text{AUX} & - \\ \text{INV} & - \\ \text{FORM} & \textit{none}\end{bmatrix} \\
\text{VAL} & \boxed{3}\langle\,\rangle \\
\text{XARG} & \text{NP}_x \\
\text{SEL} & \boxed{4}\textit{none}
\end{bmatrix} \\
\text{SEM} & \begin{bmatrix}
\text{INDEX} & s \\
\text{LABEL} & l \\
\text{FRAMES} & \left\langle [l : \textit{genius}(s,x)] \right\rangle
\end{bmatrix}
\end{bmatrix}
$$

$$
|
$$

$$
\begin{bmatrix}
\textit{word} & \\
\text{PHON} & \boxed{1} \\
\text{SYN} & \begin{bmatrix}
\text{CAT} & \boxed{2} \\
\text{VAL} & \boxed{3} \\
\text{XARG} & \textit{none} \\
\text{SEL} & \boxed{4}
\end{bmatrix} \\
\text{SEM} & \begin{bmatrix}
\text{INDEX} & x \\
\text{LABEL} & l \\
\text{FRAMES} & \left\langle [l : \textit{genius}(x)] \right\rangle
\end{bmatrix}
\end{bmatrix}
$$

FIGURE 5 A predicative lexical construct licensed by (42)

Passive verbs can be obtained via the familiar lexical construction in (43). Note that this construction suppresses the passive subject Y from VAL, although it is still recorded in XARG. As a consequence, passive phrases never combine with their syntactic subjects. The function f_{pass} computes the phonological form of the passive.[13]

[13]This construction is part of a family of related constructions. For example, a variant of (43) licenses passive verb forms that are specified as SEL NP_x. This allows such verbs to project adnominal modifier phrases, as in [[*the squirrel and the chipmunk*] *chased by the dog*] *are still on the tree*. Yet another construction models prepositional passives, like *this bed was slept on by George Washington*.

(43) Passive Lexical Construction

$$
\textit{pass-lcx} \Rightarrow \begin{bmatrix} \text{MTR} & \begin{bmatrix} \textit{lexeme} \\ \text{PHON}\ \langle f_{pass}(F) \rangle \\ \text{SYN}\ X! \begin{bmatrix} \text{CAT} \begin{bmatrix} \text{FORM} & \textit{pass} \end{bmatrix} \\ \text{VAL}\ L \oplus \left\langle (\text{PP}_x[\textit{by}]) \right\rangle \\ \text{XARG}\ Y \end{bmatrix} \\ \text{SEM}\ Z \end{bmatrix} \\ \text{DTRS} & \left\langle \begin{bmatrix} \textit{lexeme} \\ \text{PHON}\ \langle F \rangle \\ \text{SYN}\ X{:} \begin{bmatrix} \text{CAT} \begin{bmatrix} \text{AUX} & - \\ \text{INV} & - \\ \text{FORM} & \textit{base} \\ \text{CASE} & \textit{none} \end{bmatrix} \\ \text{VAL} \left\langle \text{NP}_x, Y \right\rangle \oplus L \end{bmatrix} \\ \text{SEM}\ Z \end{bmatrix} \right\rangle \end{bmatrix}
$$

Passive verb phrases are suitable copula complements because they satisfy all the constraints in (37). Verbs like *remain* are essentially like *be*, but other linking verbs like *become*, *grow*, and *seem* impose additional semantic constraints on their complements. For example, *become* selects complements that denote states, which excludes action-denoting or location-denoting expressions, as in (44).

(44) a. Robin [became/remained] [wealthy/wealthier/a priest].
b.*Robin became [in bed/standing/loved by everyone].
c. Robin remained [in bed/standing /loved by everyone].

The verb *seem* has a similar distribution, with some idiosyncratic exceptions perhaps best seen as conventionalized structures (e.g. *At this point he seems *[in the water]/*[in panic]/ [in pain]/[in good spirits]*). Conversely, *grow* requires a complement that denotes a scalar property, as the data in (45) indicate.

(45) a. Robin grew [wealthy/wealthier].
b.*Robin grew [dead/a Republican/smoking/in bed/loved by everyone].

Of course, the denotation of the complement must be compatible with the subject's. For example, the oddness of **Kim grew a temperature* ('Kim gradually changed into being a temperature') follows from the fact that the scalar property denoted by the predicative NP *a temperature* is not compatible with the subject's denotation. Whereas the subject *Kim* denotes a concrete animate entity, the predicate requires an abstract numerical value that can be changed into a temperature value. The same goes for **Kim is orthogonal* or **Robin became null.*

A reviewer claims that this cannot be right, given uses like *Juno of Rome grew pregnant at the touch of a flower* or *our choices grew infinite.* In these examples the meaning of *grow* is essentially the same as *become.* However, corpora evidence indicates that such uses are non-standard: they are non-existent in the Switchboard, Brown, and Wall Street Journal, and are mostly restricted to religious and poetic writing according to COCA (http://corpus.byu.edu/coca/) and Google Books (http://googlebooks.byu.edu/). This rare and stylistically restricted use of *grow* can indeed combine with predicative NPs as shown in (46).

(46) a. She very soon grew a woman of note.
[www.archives.nd.edu/Scholastic/VOL_0005/VOL_0005_ISSUE_0009.pdf]

b. The place I grew a man was the farm of Brendan and Mary Whelan.
[www.smashwords.com/extreader/read/84752/8/the-bleeding-hills]

Other predicative environments are even more constrained. Resultatives like (47) select objects denoting a gradable physical state (see Wechsler 2001).

(47) I cut the bread [thin/into slices/*tasty/*twenty slices].

2.6 Gerunds

The *-ing* suffix is assumed to take a verb stem and to coerce it to something more nominal – both semantically and morphosyntactically. The result is an alignment of semantic and morphosyntactic constraints that has mixed properties. In this work, four types of gerund are distinguished (verbal, predicative, nominal, and noun-gerund), and modeled as a family of lexical constructions, shown in Figure 6.

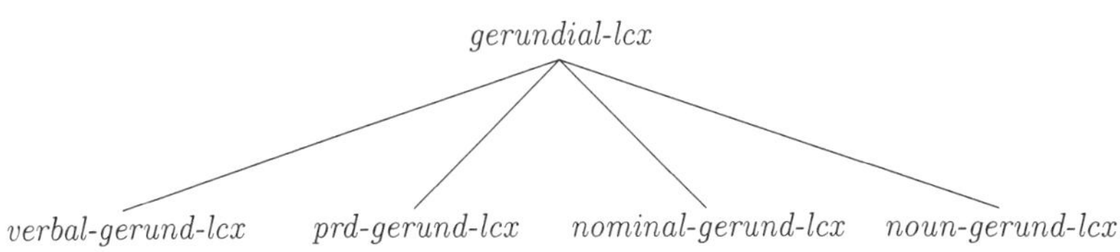

FIGURE 6 Type hierarchy of gerundial constructions

The various types of gerundial formation share a number of properties, which are captured by the construction in (48). All types of gerund inherit these constraints. Note that lexical constructions are not subtypes of *phrasal-cxt* and therefore not subject to rules like (23) and (24).

(48)

$$gerundial\text{-}lcx \Rightarrow \begin{bmatrix} \text{MTR} & \begin{bmatrix} word \\ \text{PHON} \ \langle F, ing \rangle \\ \text{SYN} \ \begin{bmatrix} \text{CAT } X! \begin{bmatrix} \text{FORM} & prp \\ \text{CASE} & case \end{bmatrix} \end{bmatrix} \\ \text{SEM} \ \begin{bmatrix} \text{INDEX } y \begin{bmatrix} \text{PER} & 3rd \\ \text{NUM} & sg \\ \text{GEN} & neut \end{bmatrix} \end{bmatrix} \end{bmatrix} \\ \text{DTRS} & \left\langle \begin{bmatrix} lexeme \\ \text{PHON} \ \langle F \rangle \\ \text{SYN} \ \begin{bmatrix} \text{CAT } X : \begin{bmatrix} \text{AUX} & - \\ \text{INV} & - \\ \text{FORM} & base \\ \text{CASE} & none \end{bmatrix} \\ \text{VAL} \left\langle \text{NP}_x \begin{bmatrix} \text{CASE } nom \end{bmatrix}, \ldots \right\rangle \end{bmatrix} \end{bmatrix} \right\rangle \end{bmatrix}$$

Let us first consider the verbal gerund type (*verbal-gerund-lcx*), illustrated in (49). These are verbal gerunds because they allow adverbial modifiers, disallow adjectival modifiers, select an NP complement, and take a subject. Semantically, verbal gerunds correspond to concepts with spatiotemporal properties and as such can be modified by spatiotemporal adverbials as (49c,d) illustrate.

(49) a. I remember [(his/him) constantly questioning Tom's motives].

b. [His/Him quickly proving the theorem] astonished everyone.

c. Tom proving the theorem [in class]/[in under 10 seconds] was amazing.

d. [(Madonna) singing that song [for half an hour]/[in London]] was amazing.

Gerunds retain some of the eventuality-like properties of their stems, and therefore behave like a mixed category because they describe regions of the conceptual space that have both nominal- and verb-like properties. Lees (1960, 65) argues verbal gerunds denote facts, as suggested by the paraphrase in (50). I further conjecture that the nominal-like properties of gerunds follow if facts are conceptualized as stable and referential entities.

(50) Kim's drawing Sue surprised me.
(the fact that he drew Sue surprised me)

In order to model verbal gerundial formation, I assume the lexical construction in (51). The first non-nominal NP valent is the subject, and it is licensed in the usual way, via the SUBJECT-PREDICATE CONSTRUCTION in (23). Note that the verbal gerund has no external argument, as there is no need for one (e.g. verbal gerunds do not allow tag questions). Any other valents in L remain complements, as in the verb stem.

(51) VERBAL GERUND LEXICAL CONSTRUCTION
verbal-gerund-cx $\Rightarrow$

$$
\left[\begin{array}{ll}
\text{MTR} & \left[\begin{array}{ll} \text{SYN} & \left[\begin{array}{l} \text{VAL} \left\langle \text{NP}_x\left[\text{CASE } acc \vee gen\right] \right\rangle \oplus L \\ \text{XARG } none \end{array}\right] \\ \text{SEM} & \left[\begin{array}{l} \text{INDEX } y \\ \text{LABEL } l_1 \\ \text{FRAMES } \langle : [l_1 : \exists y(l_2)],\ [l_2 : fact(y, l_3)]\rangle \oplus Y \end{array}\right] \end{array}\right] \\
\text{DTRS} & \left\langle \left[\begin{array}{ll} \text{SYN} & \left[\text{VAL } \left\langle \text{NP}_x \right\rangle \oplus L\right] \\ \text{SEM} & \left[\begin{array}{l}\text{LABEL } l_3 \\ \text{FRAMES } Y\end{array}\right]\end{array}\right]\right\rangle
\end{array}\right]
$$

The predicate $fact(y, l_3)$ embeds the semantics of the verb stem, labeled as l_3. Although y describes something that is stable, referential, and spatially located, it also has certain semantic properties that are typical of eventualities, such as being temporally located (Lees 1960). This is what enables verbal gerunds to be selected by adverbials rather than by adjectives. This follows from the particular semantic constraints imposed by such modifiers. On the other hand, verbal gerunds can have structural case, and their referents are quantificationally bound. As a consequence, a verbal gerund phrase is compatible with the abbreviation 'NP' in (25) in §2.4. This explains why their distribution overlaps with the distribution of more canonical NPs. For example, verbs like *remember* and *astonish* impose few semantic constraints on their subjects (perhaps simply requiring that they denote stable and referential manifestations) and gerundial phrases are suitable subjects, as well as more canonical nominal subjects. The result of the hybrid grammatical alignment that gerunds have is that the phrases they project are verbal to modifiers and nominal to verbs.

There is a related use of verbal gerunds which is restricted to predicative environments, as in (52).[14]

(52) Tom was singing a song.

Such predicative gerunds can be modeled with the rule in (53).

(53) Predicative gerund lexical construction
predicative-gerund-cx ⇒

$$
\left[\begin{array}{ll}
\text{MTR} & \left[\begin{array}{ll} \text{SYN} & \left[\begin{array}{ll}\text{VAL} & L\\ \text{XARG} & X\end{array}\right] \\ \text{SEM} & \left[\begin{array}{ll}\text{INDEX} & y \\ \text{LABEL} & l_1 \\ \text{FRAMES} & \langle\ [l_1 : \exists y(l_2)],\ [l_2 : \textit{fact}(y, l_3)]\rangle \oplus Y\end{array}\right]\end{array}\right]\\
\text{DTRS} & \left\langle \left[\begin{array}{ll}\text{SYN} & \left[\text{VAL}\ \left\langle X{:}\text{NP}_x\right\rangle \oplus L\right]\\ \text{SEM} & \left[\begin{array}{ll}\text{LABEL} & l_3\\ \text{FRAMES} & Y\end{array}\right]\end{array}\right]\right\rangle
\end{array}\right]
$$

A derivation of a predicative gerund is shown in Figure 7, licensed by (53) and (48). Note that XARG corresponds to the subject, and INDEX is a existentially quantified index that has both eventuality-like and individual-like properties. The result is a verbal gerund that can combine with its complements and project a phrase suitable for the post-copular environment, as specified in (37). This SYN specification makes this type of gerund unsuitable for non-predicative nominal environments (cf. with in (25) in §2.4).

In (54), we see a nominal gerund use. It allows adjectival modifiers, prohibits adverbial modifiers, selects an oblique complement, and exhibits number inflection.

(54) a. [His quick/*quickly proving of the theorem] astonished everyone.
b. I resented [his constant/*constantly questioning of my motives].
c. [Tom's proving of the theorem] was in class/took twenty minutes.

[14]There are various other verbal gerund uses. For example, in *I remember constantly questioning Tom's motives*, the unexpressed subject of the gerund must be understood as the matrix subject. In this case, the verb *remember* must link its subject to the subject of the VP. Other uses are *No playing loud music!* and *There's no mistaking that voice.* Here, *no* combines with a verbal gerund with an understood subject, and yields a main-clause prohibition structure (Jørgensen 1981; Quirk et al. 1985).

$$
\begin{bmatrix}
\text{PHON} & \langle \textit{swim, ing} \rangle \\
\text{SYN} & \begin{bmatrix}
\text{CAT} & \begin{bmatrix} \text{AUX} & \boxed{2} \\ \text{INV} & \boxed{3} \\ \text{FORM} & \textit{prp} \end{bmatrix} \\
\text{VAL} & \langle\rangle \\
\text{XARG} & \boxed{4} \\
\text{SEL} & \textit{none} \\
\text{CRD} & -
\end{bmatrix} \\
\text{SEM} & \begin{bmatrix}
\text{INDEX } y & \begin{bmatrix} \text{PER} & \textit{3rd} \\ \text{NUM} & \textit{sg} \\ \text{GEN} & \textit{neut} \end{bmatrix} \\
\text{LABEL } l_1 & \\
\text{FRAMES} & \left\langle [l_1 : \exists y(l_2)],\ [l_2 : fact(y, l_3)],\ [l_3 : \exists e(l_4)],\ [l_4 : swim(e, x)] \right\rangle
\end{bmatrix}
\end{bmatrix}
$$

$$|$$

$$
\begin{bmatrix}
\text{PHON} & \langle \textit{swim} \rangle \\
\text{SYN} & \begin{bmatrix}
\text{CAT} & \begin{bmatrix} \text{AUX} & \boxed{2}- \\ \text{INV} & \boxed{3}- \\ \text{FORM} & \textit{base} \\ \text{CASE} & \textit{none} \end{bmatrix} \\
\text{VAL} & \langle \boxed{4}\text{NP}_x[\text{CASE } \textit{nom}] \rangle \\
\text{XARG} & \boxed{4} \\
\text{SEL} & \textit{none} \\
\text{CRD} & -
\end{bmatrix} \\
\text{SEM} & \begin{bmatrix}
\text{INDEX } e \\
\text{LABEL } l_2 \\
\text{FRAMES} \left\langle [l_1 : \exists e(l_2)],\ [l_2 : swim(e, x)] \right\rangle
\end{bmatrix}
\end{bmatrix}
$$

FIGURE 7 Derivation of a nominal gerund construct

d. [Tom's sightings of UFOs] make me nervous.

Lees (1960, 65–66) argues that nominal gerunds contrast with verbal gerunds in that the former denote actions. This is illustrated in (55).

(55) Kim's drawing of Sue fascinated me.
(the way he drew Sue fascinated me)

Only action-verbs can be converted to nominal gerunds (compare **his believing of it* and **his admiring of her* with *his having a hat* and *his admiring her*). I therefore assume that nominal gerunds denote actions and that actions are nominal-like in that they correspond to stable and referential denotata. They retain very few verb-like properties from the verb stem. Nominal gerund formation is modeled by the construction in (56).

(56) Nominal gerund lexical construction
nominal-gerund-cx ⇒

$$\begin{bmatrix} \text{MTR} & \begin{bmatrix} \text{SYN} & \begin{bmatrix} \text{VAL} \left\langle (\text{PP}_y[\textit{of}]) \right\rangle \oplus L \\ \text{XARG } \textit{none} \end{bmatrix} \\ \text{SEM} & \begin{bmatrix} \text{INDEX } w \\ \text{LABEL } l_1 \\ \text{FRAMES } \langle [l_1 : \textit{action}(w, l_2)] \rangle \oplus Y \end{bmatrix} \end{bmatrix} \\ \text{DTRS} & \left\langle \begin{bmatrix} \text{SYN} & \begin{bmatrix} \text{VAL} \left\langle \text{NP}_x \; (,\text{NP}_y) \right\rangle \oplus L \end{bmatrix} \\ \text{SEM} & \begin{bmatrix} \text{LABEL } l_2 \\ \text{FRAMES } Y \end{bmatrix} \end{bmatrix} \right\rangle \end{bmatrix}$$

The NP_x subject is dropped from the valence list, and the resulting sign is not quantificationally determined. Hence, the nominal gerund cannot yet function as an NP; it must first combine with a determiner phrase via the HEAD-FUNCTOR CONSTRUCTION in (67) so that the index is quantificationally bound. The condition $action(x, l)$ ensures both that the stem predication l is an action-verb and that the gerund denotes an action. I conjecture that actions are more individual-like entities than facts, conceptually. Hence, number inflection is possible and adjectival modifiers are allowed.

A final type of nominal gerund is shown in (57). Here, the logical subject is realized as an oblique complement, and non-possessive determiners like *the* and *each* are allowed.

(57) a. I recall [the constant questioning (by John) (about the movie)].
b. [The quick proving of the theorem (by John)] astonished everyone.

I capture this kind of gerund with (58). Since there is no external argument, none of the valents is realized in subject position, as ensured by the *sat-head-comp-cxt* in (31). This use of the nominal gerund is different from the above in that the x variable is not quantified. This means that this kind of gerund must combine with a determiner to project an NP. Of course, any number of adnominal phrases are allowed in between.

(58) NOUN GERUND LEXICAL CONSTRUCTION
noun-gerund-cx ⇒

$$\left[\begin{array}{ll}\text{MTR} & \left[\begin{array}{ll}\text{SYN} & \left[\begin{array}{l}\text{VAL}\ \left\langle(\text{PP}_y[of])\right\rangle \oplus L \oplus \left\langle(\text{PP}_x[by]\right\rangle \\ \text{XARG}\ none\end{array}\right] \\ \text{SEM} & \left[\begin{array}{l}\text{INDEX}\ y \\ \text{LABEL}\ l_1 \\ \text{FRAMES}\ \langle Z : [l_1 : action(y, l_2)]\rangle \oplus Y\end{array}\right]\end{array}\right] \\ \text{DTRS} & \left\langle\left[\begin{array}{ll}\text{SYN} & \left[\text{VAL}\ \left\langle \text{NP}_x\ (,\text{NP}_y)\right\rangle \oplus L\right] \\ \text{SEM} & \left[\text{LABEL}\ l_2\right]\end{array}\right]\right\rangle\end{array}\right]$$

2.7 Complementizers

Kim and Sag (2005) assume that complementizers correspond to a mixed formal category located somewhere between nominal and verbal. Since the present work rejects the existence of part of speech labels, their distribution must instead reflect independently motivated semantic and morphosyntactic properties.

Ginzburg and Sag (2000) argue that clauses and complementizer phrases oscillate between various ontological (*austinian*) entities. As usual, different verbs impose different semantic constraints on the objects they combine with. Verbs like *ask*, *wonder* and *investigate* only combine with question-denoting objects, verbs like *believe*, *deny* and *prove* combine with proposition-denoting objects, verbs *know*, *discover* and *forget* require fact-denoting objects, and *demand*, *require* and *want* select outcome-denoting objects. But since propositions can be realized as S or as CP, there is no obvious way to prevent S subjects and allow CP subjects. Observe the data in (59), from Webelhuth (2012, 210). The fact that S is not a suitable subject, but CP and the pronoun *that* are, indicates that CPs and pronominal *that* have a different meaning from S.

(59) a. [That Sandy tried to cheat] is true.
b.*[Sandy tried to cheat] is true.
c. A: [Sandy tried to cheat].
B: [That] / [That claim] is true.

In this work, I assume a finer-grained multi-inheritance ontology of *austinian* entities than Ginzburg and Sag (2000), so that the complementizer *that* introduces a certain kind of propositional content that is compatible with various *austinian* entities, but is not exactly the same as the propositional content of an S clause (see Ginzburg and Sag (2000, 121) for related discussion). I propose that the semantic contribution of *that* is conceptualized as a semantic relation $fact(x, l)$, which is different from what Ginzburg and Sag (2000) view as a 'fact'. I take this denotation to correspond to a stable, non-concrete, non-temporal, non-scalar propositional entity. Because this meaning has individual-like semantic features, CPs occur in some environments typical of NPs, as shown in (60).

$$\text{(60)}\quad \left\{\begin{array}{c}\text{The fact that he proved the theorem}\\ \text{That he proved the theorem}\end{array}\right\} \left\{\begin{array}{c}\text{was surprising}\\ \text{*lasted a long time}\\ \text{*took place in class}\end{array}\right\}$$

Spatiotemporal modifiers are disallowed because $fact(x, l)$ denotes a concept without spatiotemporal properties. Adnominal modifiers, such as adjectives and prepositional phrases, cannot combine with CPs, either, because of similar semantic conditions. Although $fact(x, l)$ describes an individual-like stable and referential denotation, it also has other semantic properties which are not consistent with prototypical individuals.

The lexical entry for *that* is given in (61), based on Ginzburg and Sag's (2000, 46, 50) entry. The fact that finite CPs can have case and denote individual-like properties allows them to occur in nominal environments that do not impose very restrictive semantic constraints.

$$\text{(61)}\quad \begin{bmatrix} \textit{word} & \\ \text{PHON} & \langle \textit{that} \rangle \\ \text{SYN} & \begin{bmatrix} \text{CAT} & \begin{bmatrix} \text{AUX} & - \\ \text{INV} & - \\ \text{FORM} & \textit{fin} \end{bmatrix} \\ \text{VAL} & \langle\ \rangle \\ \text{XARG} & \textit{none} \\ \text{SEL} & \text{S}\begin{bmatrix} \text{SYN} & \begin{bmatrix} \text{CAT} & \begin{bmatrix} \text{INV} & - \\ \text{FORM} & \textit{fin} \\ \text{CASE} & \textit{none} \end{bmatrix} \end{bmatrix} \\ \text{SEM} & \begin{bmatrix} \text{LABEL} & l_3 \end{bmatrix} \end{bmatrix} \end{bmatrix} \\ \text{SEM} & \begin{bmatrix} \text{INDEX} & x \\ \text{LABEL} & l_1 \\ \text{FRAMES} & \left\langle [l_1 : \exists x(l_2)],\ [l_2 : fact(x, l_3)] \right\rangle \end{bmatrix} \end{bmatrix}$$

This allows some control over the distribution of CPs. For example, certain predicates verbs are well-known to be compatible with CP complements, but not with S or NP complements, as in (62). Hence, *alleged, confident* and *insistent* must impose restrictive semantic constraints on their objects, requiring *message*-denoting propositions with some verbal properties (e.g. bearing finite tense).

(62) a. Robin marveled *(that) Kim was now ten years old.
b.*Robin marveled it/that claim.
c. Sue objected *(that) it was too cold outside.
d.*Sue objected it/that claim.
e. Kim alleged *(that) Tom proved the theorem.
f.*Kim alleged it/that claim.

Other predicates like *confident, sure* and *certain* can combine with S and CP, but not with NP. This is shown in (63). One possibility is that these adjectives require a finite proposition-denoting complement with saturated valence.[15]

(63) a. Bob is confident (that) Kim is now ten years old.
b.*Bob is confident it/that claim.

Finally, verbs like *remember* are much less restricted and therefore compatible with a wide range of complements, as shown in (64). As long as the complement denotes stable individual-like properties, it can function as an object.

(64) a. I remember (that) [he used to play that song for me].
b. I remember [(him) playing me that song]/[the building of the airport].
c. I remember [the day that we met]/[the prediction that the world would end].

The same account may be used for non-finite complementizers. For example, assuming that *for* also corresponds to some outcome-based propositional content that individuates both nominal and verbal properties, then the nominal-like distribution of infinitival CPs emerges as a consequence, as in (65).

(65) a. [For us to win] would be amazing.
b. Robin asked [for us to be fired].

Because the complementizer has individual- and verbal-like semantic properties, the result is an infinitival clause that can occur in some

[15] A related use of *confident* requires PP[*of*] complements denoting a proposition.

environments.[16] Similarly, I assume that infinitivals, like that in (66), can also have a use in which they are associated with mixed semantic content.

(66) a. [To do otherwise] would be a mistake.
b. Robin said [to do otherwise].

In Ginzburg and Sag 2000, such infinitival phrases can have a variety of different types of austinian properties. I propose that a unary branching rule takes infinitival *to*-phrases and embeds their semantics under a suitable propositional meaning like $\exists x(statement(x, l))$. Such a rule would make sure that the unexpressed subject is generically quantified, and that both AUX and CASE are underspecified. This analysis would enable the infinitival to occur in (non)auxiliary verbal environments as well as in certain nominal environments.

3 Coordination

Let us now consider how the theory sketched above can handle the categorial flexibility observed in coordinate structures, discussed in §1.1. The coordination of unlikes phenomena will emerge from the morphosyntactic and semantic constraints that are required of the coordinate phrase by a functor external to the coordination. In this account, any semantic constraints imposed on the coordination structure distribute to each conjunct without further stipulations.

I start by assuming that words like *and*, *or* and *but* are markers, and as such do not subcategorize any valents. Instead, they select their hosts via SEL and therefore combine with them via the HEAD-FUNCTOR CONSTRUCTION from §2.4. The conjunction *and* is shown in (67).

[16]Since the for-CP clause has verbal morphosyntactic properties (saturated valence and an infinitival FORM) it can be selected as a verbal complement of *though*-movement predicates (e.g. *Robin is easy* [(*for us*) *to please*]). Following Levine (2001), I assume that *for* selects an infinitival S and projects an infinitival CP. The feature XARG allows *easy* to access the subject of the CP.

(67)
$$\begin{bmatrix} \textit{word} \\ \text{PHON} \ \langle \ \textit{and} \ \rangle \\ \text{SYN} \begin{bmatrix} \text{CAT} & \begin{bmatrix} \text{AUX} & - \\ \text{INV} & - \\ \text{FORM} & \textit{none} \\ \text{CASE} & \textit{none} \end{bmatrix} \\ \text{VAL} & \langle\rangle \\ \text{XARG} & \textit{none} \\ \text{SEL} & \begin{bmatrix} \text{SYN} \begin{bmatrix} \text{CRD} \ - \end{bmatrix} \\ \text{SEM} \begin{bmatrix} \text{INDEX} \ \beta \end{bmatrix} \end{bmatrix} \\ \text{CRD} \ + & \end{bmatrix} \\ \text{SEM} \begin{bmatrix} \text{INDEX} & \beta \\ \text{FRAMES} & \langle\rangle \end{bmatrix} \end{bmatrix}$$

The feature CRD can take various values, according to the coordinator type. Thus, [CRD +] corresponds to a Non-Boolean Linkean sum conjunction and [CRD $\vee$] corresponds to disjunction.

The coordination construction is essentially a phrase structure rule of the form $X \rightarrow X_0 ... X_n$, implemented as seen in (68). The conjuncts and the mother must have the same SYN information, modulus the CRD marking value. Only the last conjunct is marked by a coordinator.[17]

(68) COORDINATION CONSTRUCTION

coord-cxt $\Rightarrow$

$$\begin{bmatrix} \text{MTR} & \begin{bmatrix} \text{SYN} \ X! \begin{bmatrix} \text{CRD} \ - \end{bmatrix} \\ \text{SEM} \begin{bmatrix} \text{INDEX} \ \alpha \\ \text{LABEL} \ l \end{bmatrix} \end{bmatrix} \\ \text{DTRS} & \left\langle \begin{bmatrix} \text{SYN} \ X! \begin{bmatrix} \text{CRD} \ - \end{bmatrix} \\ \text{SEM} \begin{bmatrix} \text{INDEX} \ \beta_0 \end{bmatrix} \end{bmatrix}, ..., \begin{bmatrix} \text{SYN} \ X! \begin{bmatrix} \text{CRD} \ - \end{bmatrix} \\ \text{SEM} \begin{bmatrix} \text{INDEX} \ \beta_{n-1} \end{bmatrix} \end{bmatrix}, \begin{bmatrix} \text{SYN} \ X! \begin{bmatrix} \text{CRD} \ R \end{bmatrix} \\ \text{SEM} \begin{bmatrix} \text{INDEX} \ \beta_n \end{bmatrix} \end{bmatrix} \right\rangle \\ \text{CX-CONTENT} & \left\langle Y : \begin{bmatrix} \text{LABEL} & l \\ \text{RELN} & R \\ \text{INDEX} & \alpha \\ \text{ARGS} & \langle \beta_0, ..., \beta_{n-1}, \beta_n \rangle \end{bmatrix} \right\rangle \end{bmatrix}$$

Semantically, the coordination construction adds the semantics $R(\beta_0, ..., \beta_{n-1}, \beta_n)$ via CX-CONTENT, where β_n ($n \geq 1$) is the index of the each conjunct. If the value of the last conjunct's CRD is an i-sum

[17] I assume that polysyndetic coordinations like *Tom and Sue and Fred* obtain trough multiple applications of the construction in (68).

'+', then α is a plurality formed with $\beta_0, ..., \beta_{n-1}, \beta_n$ as shown in (69a). If the value of CRD is a disjunction (i.e. '$\vee$'), then α is identical to one of the β indices, as in (69b).

(69) a. $\begin{bmatrix} \text{RELN} & + \\ \text{INDEX} & \alpha \\ \text{ARGS} & \langle \beta_1, \beta_2 \rangle \end{bmatrix} \equiv \alpha = (\beta_1 + \beta_2)$

b. $\begin{bmatrix} \text{RELN} & \vee \\ \text{INDEX} & \alpha \\ \text{ARGS} & \langle \beta_1, \beta_2 \rangle \end{bmatrix} \equiv (\alpha = \beta_1) \vee (\alpha = \beta_2)$

The effect of the coordination construction is shown in Figure 8. If the conjunct's indices are nominal, then it follows that the plurality that they form via the *i*-sum $z = x+y$ is also nominal. Similarly, if the conjuncts are eventualities, then the plurality they form is also an eventuality. For example, the coordination of predicative NPs is essentially identical to the coordination of non-predicative NPs. The main syntactic difference is that the conjuncts and the mother node are specified [XARG NP_y] instead of [XARG *none*]. For more discussion on non-nominal pluralities, see Bach (1986, 9), Link (1998a, 240), Carlson (1987, 540–542), Lasersohn (1995, 273) and Eckardt (1995). Evidence that conjunction can form non-nominal pluralities appears in (70).

(70) a. John is alternately [hot and cold].
b. They meet alternately [in Berlin and in Italy].
c. Robin is both [a physician and a dentist].
d. You can't simultaneously [drive a car and talk on the phone].
e. [Sue drank a beer and Robin ate a burger] in exactly twenty seconds.

Any coordination is possible as long as the value of the mother's SYN can be unified with the SYN values of the daughters, modulus CRD. This is illustrated by (71), where '$\bot$' indicates unification failure. Only the conflicting features are shown, for perspicuity.

(71) a. *Sue [[drank a soda]$_{[\text{VAL } \langle \text{NP}^{nom} \rangle]}$ and [devoured]$_{[\text{VAL } \langle \text{NP}^{nom}, \text{ NP}^{acc} \rangle]}$]$_{[\text{VAL } \bot]}$.
(cf. with 'Sue [drank a soda] / *[devoured]')
b. *Fred is [[happy]$_{[\text{XARG NP}]}$ and [drunken]$_{[\text{XARG } none]}$]$_{[\text{XARG } \bot]}$.
(cf. with 'Feed is happy / *drunken')

In Sag 2012, the AUX feature provides information about the environment of the sign rather than about the sign itself. Hence, non-auxiliary verbs are [AUX–], and auxiliary verbs are underspecified as [AUX *bool*]. Here, I assume instead that AUX provides information about the verbal

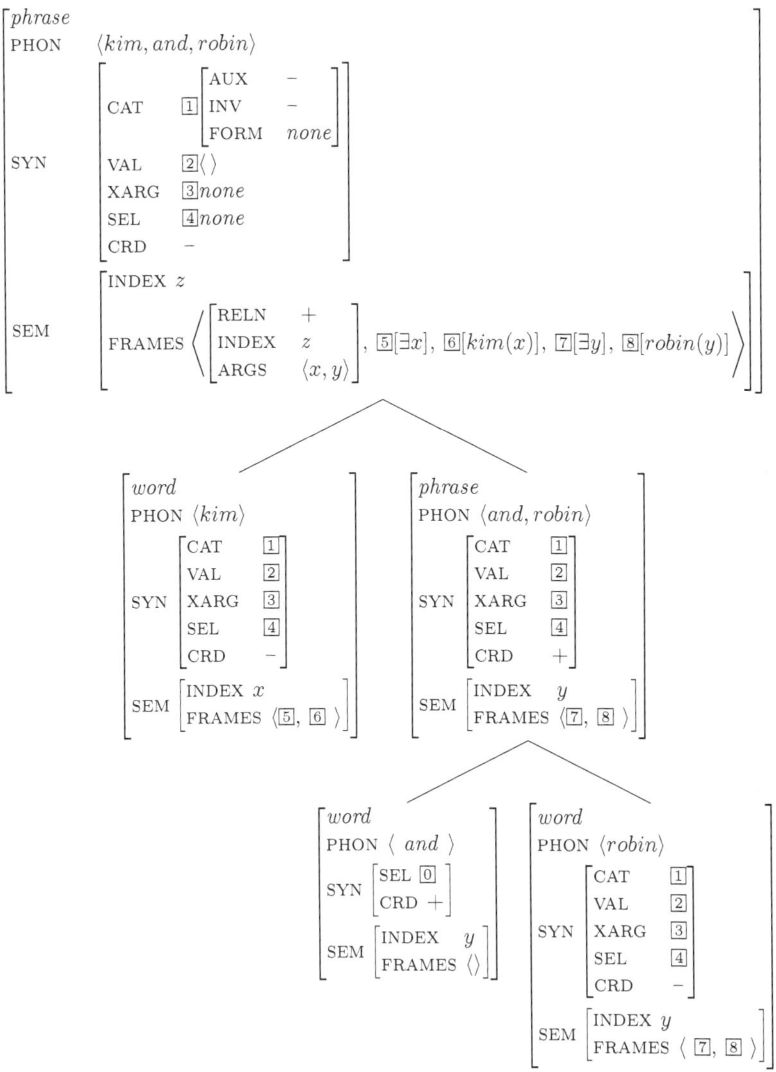

FIGURE 8 NP coordination construct (semantic relation labels omitted)

lexical sign that feeds auxiliary lexical constructions. More specifically, all auxiliary constructions take a verb that can be unified with [AUX+] and yield a counterpart that is [AUX *bool*]. Hence, the mother node of constructions that require the verb daughter to be compatible with AUX+ will be underspecified for AUX values. For example, the rule that handles auxiliary negation in Sag 2012 takes an [AUX+] verb and yields a negative counterpart [AUX–]. In my approach, the auxiliary negation rule just described above will take a non-negative [AUX+] verb and yield a negative counterpart specified as [AUX *bool*]. Similarly, the *auxiliary initial construction* which handles subject auxiliary inversion constructions requires the daughter verb to be [AUX+] and [INV–]. The mother is required to be [AUX *bool*] and [INV+]. Hence, coordinations like (72) are unproblematic, because there is no inconsistent AUX information. The conjuncts and the mother node can resolve as [AUX–] and [INV–].

(72) Kim ate a burger and Robin did, too.

Such coordination data suggest that lexical AUX information should not be made available non-locally, across different constructions. This is achieved by the analysis just proposed, by assuming AUX to be underspecified in the mother node of auxiliary verb constructions.

The present account readily predicts a wide range of coordination of categories that are traditionally viewed as fundamentally different. Such coordinations are unremarkable because the conjuncts have identical SYN information. For example, Figure 9 shows the result of coordinating phrases with mutually compatible predicative SYN specifications.

$$\begin{bmatrix} \textit{phrase} & \\ \text{PHON} & \langle \textit{wealthy, a, republican, and, from, Texas} \rangle \\ \text{SYN} & \begin{bmatrix} \text{CAT} & \begin{bmatrix} \text{AUX} & - \\ \text{INV} & - \\ \text{FORM} & \textit{none} \\ \text{CASE} & \textit{none} \end{bmatrix} \\ \text{VAL} & \langle\,\rangle \\ \text{XARG} & \text{NP}^{x} \\ \text{SEL} & \textit{none} \\ \text{CRD} & - \end{bmatrix} \end{bmatrix}$$

FIGURE 9 A predicative coordinate construct (daughters omitted)

Analogously, the phrase in Figure 10 is the result of conjoining two phrases that modify VPs. Many other unlike conjuncts are licensed in the same way, including gerunds, infinitival *to*-phrases, and complementizer phrases.

Although the coordination in (73) is well-formed, the resulting phrase is an unsuitable subject for the matrix verb *entered.* Syntactically, this verb requires the subject to be [XARG *none*] and [CASE *nom*]. Semantically, the subject is also required to correspond to an

$$\begin{bmatrix} \textit{phrase} & \\ \text{PHON} & \langle \textit{frequently, and, with, increasing, ferocity} \rangle \\ \text{SYN} & \begin{bmatrix} \text{CAT} & \begin{bmatrix} \text{AUX} & - \\ \text{INV} & - \\ \text{FORM} & \textit{none} \\ \text{CASE} & \textit{none} \end{bmatrix} \\ \text{VAL} & \langle\,\rangle \\ \text{XARG} & \textit{none} \\ \text{SEL} & \text{VP} \\ \text{CRD} & - \end{bmatrix} \end{bmatrix}$$

FIGURE 10 A coordinate adverbial construct (daughters omitted)

animate entity. The coordinate subject fails on both accounts. Predicative phrases denote states rather than individuals and are specified as [XARG NP] and [CASE *none*].

(73) *[A Republican and proud of it] entered the room.

In other cases, the incompatibility is semantic. Consider, for example, (74). As discussed above, the verb *become* selects complements that are not action-denoting. As the verb combines with the plural eventuality denoted by the coordinate phrase, the semantic selection constraints distribute over to the members of the plurality and infelicity arises because of the second conjunct.

(74) *Kim became [happier and laughing].

The contrast in (75a,b) is also due to semantic restrictions rather than syntax. As discussed above, *grew* selects complements that denote scalar concepts, but *remain* imposes no such constraint. The sentence in (75a) is ruled out because one of the conjuncts does not denote a scalar concept as required by the verb *grew*.[18]

(75) a. Kim remained wealthy/a Republican.
b. Kim grew wealthy/ *a Republican.
c. Kim remained/*grew wealthy and a Republican.

When two functors are coordinated, the COORDINATION CONSTRUCTION in (68) causes any semantic conditions imposed on the shared valents to be compounded. If one verbal conjunct imposes the constraints [FRAMES $\langle l_1{:}P(e_1, x), l_1{:}P'(x)\rangle$] and the other conjunct imposes

[18]But see §2.5 for other uses of this verb.

[FRAMES $\langle l_1{:}Q(e_2,x), l_1{:}Q'(x)\rangle$], then coordinate mother's FRAMES value is (76).[19]

(76) $\langle l{:}\exists z(l_1,l_2), l_1{:}P(e_1,x), l_1{:}P'(x), l_1{:}Q(e_2,x), l_1{:}Q'(x), l_1{:}z{=}e_1{+}e_2\rangle$

In other words, the shared dependent x must satisfy all the constraints imposed by both coordinate functors. This accounts for the contrasts in (77). Example (77a) is acceptable because the object adjective phrase satisfies all the syntactic and semantic constraints imposed by both verbs, whereas (77b,c) are not acceptable because one of the predicative conjuncts is incompatible with the semantic constraints imposed by the verbs. Namely, *grew* requires that the complement denotes a scalar concept, but the predicative NP *a Republican* denotes a state that is not intrinsically scalar.

(77) a. Kim grew and remained wealthy.
b.*Kim grew and remained a Republican.
c.*Kim grew and remained wealthy and a Republican.

Certain predicative adjectives, like *impressive* and *surprising*, impose no semantic constraints on their external arguments other than that they must be NP_x. This allows them to combine with a wide range of referential external arguments, including some CPs, gerundial phrases and infinitivals. This is also true for some verbs, as is the case of *mention*, as (78) shows. The bracketed argument need only refer to an individual-like entity. Hence, such functors can combine with a wide range of phrases, without appeal to enumerative disjunctive selection constraints.

(78) a. [The fusebox's hissing, the danger involved, and that the wiring had to be replaced] were clearly mentioned in the electrician's technical report.
b. The electrician's technical report clearly mentioned three problems: the fusebox's hissing, the danger involved, and that the wiring had to be replaced.

The oddness of (79) follows from the fact that the two case-marking prepositions introduce different role predicates (*source*(x) and *topic*(x), respectively), but the verb is incompatible with the latter. Hence, the PP[*on*] conjunct causes the VP to be odd.

[19] As in Reyle 1996, any predications with the same label are interpreted as being conjoined. Thus, the representation obtained above is equivalent to $\lambda z.\exists z(P(e_1,x) \wedge P'(x) \wedge Q(e_2,x) \wedge Q'(x) \wedge z{=}e_1 + e_2 \wedge \phi(z))$. See Copestake et al. (2005) for more discussion. I take such labeled predications to be interpreted as underspecified Dynamic Predicate Logic, as in Bos 1996.

(79) *Kim relies [on Sue]$_{PP[on]}$ [and of Fred]$_{PP[of]}$
(cf. with 'Kim relies on/*by Fred')

But if the verb is compatible with both case-marked PP arguments, or if the PPs are adjuncts instead, then such structures are legal.

There are also cases that seem to involve the apparent coordination of co-valents, as in (80). Here, each valent seems to satisfy a different valence constraint by the verb.

(80) a. We all heard the way she talked (both) to him and about him.
b. Every chapter of his book was written (both) by students and for students.

Note that (80a) is not equivalent to *we all heard the way she talked to him about him.* Rather, the corresponding paraphrase is *we all heard the way she talked to him and talked about him.* This suggests that (80) are best analyzed as involving VP coordinations where the second V is deleted and *both* floats to the right. This is independently motivated by data like (81) from Huddleston et al. (2002a, 1807).

(81) This was made clear both to the men and their employers.

For an account of the variable linear position of correlative coordination markers like *either*, see Hofmeister (2010). I leave the proper analysis of *both* and (80) for future research.

4 Conclusion

This speculative paper suggests that constraint-based grammar frameworks like Pollard and Sag 1994 are ideally suited to model phrasal distributional classes without resorting to part of speech labels. Such labels are artificial and have never been well-defined, arguably because the linguistic entities that they are meant to classify are not categorical at all, but rather, part of a continuum with different kinds of idiosyncrasy. However, if signs are viewed as fine-grained sets of features, containing different alignments of morphological, syntactic, and semantic information, it should be in principle possible to characterize the traditional part of speech classes in an emergent and well-motivated way. This work goes on to show how distributional overlap in a wide range of environments can in principle be modeled in Sign-based Construction Grammar (Sag 2012), as independently motivated fine-grained morphosyntactic and semantic constraints. Syntactic categories with flexible distributional environments emerge as a natural consequence of the small number of coarse-grained constraints that are imposed, whereas highly restricted environments result from the imposition of fine-grained constraints. The theory sketched in this paper also offers a straightforward account of so-called coordination of unlike categories, building on key aspects of the feature geometry in Sag 2012. Unlike previous accounts of coordination of unlikes, the grammar does not need to enumerate the parts of speech that each coordination environment tolerates. Rather, the phenomena follow from the interaction between coordination and the information contained in each sign.

References

Aarts, Bas. 2007. *Syntactic Gradience: The Nature of Grammatical Indeterminacy*. Oxford: Oxford University Press.

Adger, David, Daniel Harbour, and Laurel J. Watkins. 2009. *Mirrors and Microparameters - Phrase Structure Beyond Free Word Order*. Cambridge: Cambridge University Press.

Andersen, Lloyd B. 1974. Distinct sources of fuzzy data: ways of integrating relatively discrete and gradient types of language, and explaining grammar on the basis of semantic fields. In R. W. Shuy and C. N. Baley, eds., *Towards Tomorrow's Linguistics*, pages 50–64. Washington D.C.: Georgetown University Press.

Asher, Nicholas. 2011. *A Web of Words: Lexical Meaning in Context*. Cambridge: Cambridge University Press.

Bach, Emmon. 1986. The algebra of events. *Linguistics and Philosophy* 9:5–16.

Bayer, Samuel. 1996. The coordination of unlike categories. *Language* 72:579–616.

Beavers, John. 2003. More heads and less categories: A new look at noun phrase structure. In S. Müller, ed., *Proceedings of the 10th International Conference on Head-driven Phrase Structure Grammar*, pages 47–67. Stanford, CA: CSLI Publications.

Beavers, John and Ivan A. Sag. 2004. Ellipsis and apparent non-constituent coordination. In S. Müller, ed., *Proceedings of the 11th International Conference on Head-driven Phrase Structure Grammar*, pages 48–69. Stanford, CA: CSLI Publications.

Bender, Emily and Dan Flickinger. 1999. Peripheral constructions and core phenomena. In G. Webelhuth, A. Kathol, and J. Koenig, eds., *Lexical and Constructional Aspects of Linguistic Explanation*. Stanford, CA: CSLI Publications.

Bos, Johan. 1996. Predicate Logic Unplugged. In *Proceedings of the 10th Amsterdam Colloquium*, pages 133–143. Amsterdam: University of Amsterdam Press.

Bresnan, Joan and Sam A. Mchombo. 1995. The Lexical Integrity Principle: Evidence from Bantu. *Natural Language & Linguistic Theory* 13:181–252.

Carlson, Greg N. 1987. Same and different: Some consequences for syntax and semantics. *Linguistics and Philosophy* 10:531–565.

Chaves, Rui P. 2006. Coordination of unlikes without unlike categories. In S. Müller, ed., *Proceedings of the the 13th International Conference on Head-driven Phrase Structure Grammar*, pages 102–122. Stanford, CA: CSLI Publications.

Chaves, Rui P. 2007. *Coordinate Structures – Constraint-based Syntax-Semantics Processing*. Doctoral dissertation, University of Lisbon.

Chaves, Rui P. 2012. On the grammar of extraction and coordination. *Natural Language and Linguistic Theory* 30(2):465–512.

Collins, Allan M. and Ross M. Quillian. 1972. Experiments on semantic memory and language comprehension. In L. W. Gregg, ed., *Cognition in Learning and Memory*, pages 117–137. New York: Wiley.

Copestake, Ann, Daniel Flickinger, Ivan A. Sag, and Carl Pollard. 2005. Minimal recursion semantics: An introduction. *Journal Research on Language & Computation* 3(4):281–332.

Cree, George S. and Ken McRae. 2003. Analyzing the factors underlying the structure and computation of the meaning of chipmunk, cherry, chisel, cheese, and cello (and many other such concrete nouns). *Journal of Experimental Psychology: General* 132:163–201.

Croft, William. 1984. Semantic and pragmatic correlates to syntactic categories. In D. Testen, V. Mishra, and J. Drogo, eds., *Papers from the Parasession on Lexical Semantics, Twentieth Regional Meeting of the Chicago Linguistic Society*, pages 53–71.

Croft, William. 2001. *Radical Construction Grammar – Syntactic Theory in Typological Perspective*. Oxford: Oxford University Press.

Cruse, Alan. 2004. *Meaning in Language: An Introduction to Semantics and Pragmatics, 2nd Edition*. Oxford: Oxford University Press.

Crysmann, Berthold. 2000. Clitics and coordination in linear structure. In B. Gerlach and J. Grijzenhout, eds., *Clitics in Phonology, Morphology and Syntax*, vol. 36, pages 121–159. Amsterdam: John Benjamins.

Crystal, David. 1967. English. *Lingua* 17:24–56.

Daniels, Michael W. 2002. On a type-based analysis of feature neutrality and the coordination of unlikes. In F. V. Eynde, L. Hellan, and D. Beermann, eds., *Proceedings of the 8th International Conference on Head-driven Phrase Structure Grammar*, pages 137–147. Stanford, CA: CSLI Publications.

Davis, Anthony. 2001. *Linking by Types in the Hierarchical Lexicon*. Stanford, CA: CSLI Publications.

Eckardt, Regina. 1995. Does information flow in event structures? In G. Groenendijk, ed., *Ellipsis, Underspecification, Events and More in Dynamic Semantics*, pages 49–72. Institute for Logic, Language and Computation/Department of Philosophy, University of Amsterdam.

Elman, Jeffrey L. 2009. On the meaning of words and dinosaur bones: Lexical knowledge without a lexicon. *Cognitive Science* 33:1–36.

Elman, Jeffrey L. 2011. Lexical knowledge without a mental lexicon? *The Mental Lexicon* 60:1–33.

Engdahl, Elisabet and Enric Vallduví. 1994. Information packaging and grammar architecture: A constraint-based approach. In E. Engdahl, ed., *Integrating Information Structure into Constraint-based and Categorial Approaches*, pages 39–79. Amsterdam: Institute for Logic, Language and Computation.

Fillmore, Charles. 1999. Inversion and constructional inheritance. In G. Webelhuth, J. Koenig, and A. Kathol, eds., *Lexical and Constructional Aspects of Linguistic Explanation*, pages 113–128. Stanford, CA: CSLI Publications.

Fillmore, Charles J., Christopher R. Johnson, and Miriam R.L. Petruck. 2003. Background to Framenet. *International Journal of Lexicography* 16(3):235–250.

Gärdenfors, Peter. 2001. *Conceptual Spaces: The Geometry of Thought*. Cambridge, MA: MIT Press.

Gazdar, Gerald, Ewan Klein, Geoffrey K. Pullum, and Ivan A. Sag. 1985. *Generalized Phrase Structure Grammar*. Oxford: Blackwell and Cambridge, MA: Harvard University Press.

Ginzburg, Jonathan and Ivan A. Sag. 2000. *Interrogative Investigations: The Form, Meaning and Use of English Interrogative Constructions*. Stanford, CA: CSLI Publications.

Givón, Thomas. 1984. *Syntax: A Functional-Typological Introduction*. Amsterdam: John Benjamins Publishing Company.

Gundel, Jeanette. 2003. Information structure and referential givenness/newness: How much belongs in the grammar? In S. Müller, ed., *Proceedings of the 10th International Conference on Head-driven Phrase Structure Grammar*, pages 122–142. Stanford, CA: CSLI Publications.

Haji-Abdolhosseini, Mohammad. 2003. A constraint-based approach to information structure and prosody correspondence. In S. Müller, ed., *Proceedings of the 10th International Conference on Head-driven Phrase Structure Grammar*, pages 143–162. Stanford, CA: CSLI Publications.

Harm, Michael W. and Mark S. Seidenberg. 2004. Computing the meanings of words in reading: Cooperative division of labor between visual and phonological processes. *Psychological Review* 111:662–720.

Hinton, George E. and Tim Shallice. 1991. Lesioning an attractor network: Investigations of acquired dyslexia. *Psychological Review* 98:74–95.

Hintzman, Douglas L. 1986. 'Schema abstraction' in a multiple-trace memory model. *Psychological Review* 93:411–428.

Hjelmslev, Louis. 1975. *Résumé of a Theory of Language*. Madison: University of Wisconsin Press.

Hofmeister, Philip. 2010. A linearization account of *either ... or* constructions. *Natural Language and Linguistic Theory* 28(2):275–314.

Huddleston, Rodney D., John Payne, and Peter Peterson. 2002a. *Coordination and supplementation*, chap. 15, pages 1273–1362. Cambridge: Cambridge University Press.

Huddleston, Rodney D., John Payne, and Peter Peterson. 2002b. Nouns and noun phrases. In R. D. Huddleston and G. K. Pullum, eds., *The Cambridge Grammar of the English Language*, chap. 5, pages 323–522. Cambridge University Press.

Huddleston, Rodney D. and Geoffrey K. Pullum. 2002. *The Cambridge Grammar of the English Language*. Cambridge: Cambridge University Press.

Hudson, Richard. 1984. *Word Grammar*. Oxford: Blackwell.

Jackendoff, Ray. 1971. Gapping and related rules. *Linguistic Inquiry* 2:21–35.

Jackendoff, Ray. 1985. Multiple subcategorization and the θ-criterion: the case of *climb*. *Natural Language and Linguistic Theory* 3:271–295.

Jacobson, Pauline. 1987. Review of Gerald Gazdar, Ewan Klein, Geoffrey K. Pullum, and Ivan A. Sag, 1985: *Generalized Phrase Structure Grammar*. *Linguistics and Philosophy* 10:389–426.

Jørgensen, Eric. 1981. Gerund and *to*-infinitives after 'it is (of) no use', 'it is no good', and 'it is useless'. *English Studies* 62:156–163.

Kamp, Hans and Uwe Reyle. 1993. *From Discourse to Logic: An Introduction to Model Theoretic Semantics of Natural Language, Formal Logic and Discourse Representation Theory*. Dordrecht: Kluwer Academic Publishers.

Kathol, Andreas. 2000. *Linear Syntax*. Oxford: Oxford University Press.

Katz, Jerrold J. and Jerry A. Fodor. 1963. The structure of a semantic theory. *Language* 39(2):170–210.

Keenan, Edward L. and Leonard M. Faltz. 1985. *Boolean Semantics for Natural Language*. Dordrecht: D. Reidel.

Kim, Jong-Bok and Ivan A. Sag. 2005. English object extraposition: A constraint-based approach. In S. Müller, ed., *Proceedings of the 12th International Conference on Head-Driven Phrase Structure Grammar*, pages 192–212. Stanford, CA: CSLI Publications.

Klein, Ewan. 2000. Prosodic constituency in HPSG. In R. Cann, C. Grover, and P. Miller, eds., *Grammatical Interfaces in HPSG*, pages 169–200. Stanford, CA: CSLI Publications.

Koenig, Jean-Pierre. 1999. *Lexical Relations*. Stanford, CA: CSLI Publications.

Kuhn, Jonas. 1996. An underspecified HPSG representation for information structure. In J. Tsuji, ed., *Proceedings of Coling-96. 16th International Conference on Computational Linguistics (COLING96). Copenhagen, Denmark, August 5–9, 1996*, pages 670–675. Somerset, New Jersey: Association for Computational Linguistics.

Langacker, Ronald W. 1987. *Foundations of Cognitive Grammar, Volume 1: Theoretical Prerequisites*. Stanford CA: Stanford University Press.

Lasersohn, Peter. 1995. *Plurality, Conjunction and Events*. Dordrecht: Kluwer Academic Publishers.

Lees, Robert B. 1960. *The Grammar of English Nominalizations*. Ph.D. thesis, MIT.

Levine, Robert D. 2001. Tough complementation and the extraclausal propagation of argument descriptions. In D. Flickinger and A. Kathol, eds., *Proceedings of the 7th International Conference on Head-Driven Phrase Structure Grammar*, pages 325–344. Stanford, CA: CSLI Publications.

Levine, Robert D. 2011. Linearization and its discontents. In S. Müller, ed., *Proceedings of the 18th International Conference on Head-driven Phrase Structure Grammar*, pages 126–146. Stanford, CA: CSLI Publications.

Levine, Robert D. and Thomas E. Hukari. 2006. *The Unity of Unbounded Dependency Constructions*. Stanford, CA: CSLI Publications.

Levine, Robert D., Thomas E. Hukari, and Michael Calcagno. 2001. Parasitic gaps in English: Some overlooked cases and their theoretical implications. In P. Culicover and P. M. Postal, eds., *Parasitic Gaps*, pages 181–222. Cambridge, MA: MIT Press.

Link, Godehard. 1998a. *Algebraic Semantics in Language and Philosophy*. Stanford, CA: CSLI Publications.

Link, Godehard. 1998b. The ontology of individuals and events. In *Algebraic Semantics in Language and Philosophy*, pages 269–310. Stanford, CA: CSLI Publications.

Matilal, Bimal Krishna. 1990. *The word and the world: India's contribution to the study of language*. Oxford.

McCawley, James D. 1968. The role of semantics in a grammar. In E. Bach and R. T. Harms, eds., *Universals of Linguistic Theory*, pages 124–169. New York: Holt, Reinhart, and Winston.

McRae, Ken, George S. Cree, Mi Jin Cho, and Chris McNorgan. 2003. Distinguishing knowledge of living and nonliving things is computed quickly from concept names, and vice versa. Poster presented at the *Thirteenth Conference of the European Society for Cognitive Psychology*, Granada, Spain.

McRae, Ken, George S. Cree, Mark S. Seindenberg, and Chris McNorgan. 2005. Semantic feature production norms for a large set of living and nonliving things. *Behavior Research Methods, Instruments & Computers* 37(4):547–559.

McRae, Ken, Virginia R. de Sa, and Mark S. Seidenberg. 1997. On the nature and scope of featural representations of word meaning. *Journal of Experimental Psychology: General* 126:99–130.

Medin, Douglas L. 1989. Concepts and conceptual structure. *American Psychologist* 44:1469–1481.

Meurers, Detmar W. 1999. Raising spirits (and assigning them case). *Groninger Arbeiten zur Germanistischen Linguistik* 43:173–226.

Minsky, Marvin. 1975. A framework for representing knowledge. In P. H. Winston, ed., *The Psychology of Computer Vision*, pages 211–277. New York: McGraw-Hill.

Morrill, Glynn. 1990. Grammar and logical types. In M. Stokhof and L. Torenvliet, eds., *Proceedings of the Seventh Amsterdam Colloquium*. Amsterdam: Institute for Logic, Language and Information.

Morrill, Glynn. 1994. *Type Logical Grammar*. Dordrecht: Kluwer.

Murdock, B. B. 1982. A theory for the storage and retrieval of item and associative information. *Psychological Review* 89:609–626.

Norman, Donald A. and David E. Rumelhart. 1975. *Explorations in Cognition*. San Francisco: Freeman.

Orgun, Cemil Orhan. 2000. Sign-based morphology: A declarative theory of phonology-morphology interleaving. In B. Hermans and M. van Oostendorp, eds., *The Derivational Residue in Phonological Optimality Theory*, pages 247–267. Amsterdam: John Benjamin.

Plaut, David C. 2002. Graded modality-specific specialization in semantics: A computational account of optic aphasia. *Cognitive Neuropsychology* 19:603–639.

Plaut, David C. and Tim Shallice. 1993. Deep dyslexia: A case study of connectionist neuropsychology. *Cognitive Neuropsychology* 10:377–500.

Pollard, Carl and Ivan A. Sag. 1994. *Head-driven Phrase Structure Grammar*. Chicago: University of Chicago Press and Stanford, CA: CSLI Publications.

Quirk, Randolph, S. Greenbaum, G. Leech, and J. Svartvik. 1985. *A Comprehensive Grammar of the English Language*. Longman, Harcourt.

Reyle, Uwe. 1996. Co-indexing labelled DRSs to represent and reason with ambiguities. In S. Peters and K. van Deemter, eds., *Semantic Ambiguity and Underspecification*, pages 239–268. Stanford, CA: CSLI Publications.

Rosch, Eleanor. 1973. Natural categories. *Cognitive Psychology* 4:328–350.

Rosch, Eleanor and Carolyn B. Mervis. 1975. Family resemblances: Studies in the internal structure of categories. *Cognitive Psychology* 7:573–605.

Ross, John R. 1972. The category squish: Endstation hauptwort. In *Papers from the Eighth Regional Meeting of the Chicago Linguistics Society*, pages 316–328. Chicago: Chicago Linguistics Society.

Ross, John R. 1973. Nouniness. In O. Fujimura, ed., *Three Dimensions of Linguistic Theory*, pages 137–257. Tokyo: TEC Compnay.

Sag, Ivan A. 2002. Coordination and underspecification. In J.-B. Kim and S. Wechsler, eds., *Proceedings of the 9th International Conference on Head-Driven Phrase Structure Grammar*, pages 267–291. Stanford, CA: CSLI Publications.

Sag, Ivan A. 2005. Rules and exceptions in the English auxiliary system. Ms., Stanford University.

Sag, Ivan A. 2010. English filler-gap constructions. *Language* 86(3):486–545.

Sag, Ivan A. 2012. Sign-based construction grammar: An informal synopsis. In H. Boas and I. A. Sag, eds., *Sign-Based Construction Grammar*, pages 69–202. Stanford, CA: CSLI Publications.

Sag, Ivan A. and Carl Pollard. 1991. An integrated theory of complement control. *Language* 67(1):63–113.

Smith, E. E. and D. L. Medin. 1981. *Categories and Concepts*. Cambridge, MA: Harvard University Press.

Van Valin, Robert D. Jr. 2008. RPs and the nature of lexical and syntactic categories in role and reference grammar. In R. Van Valin, Jr., ed., *Investigations of the Syntax-Semantics-Pragmatics Interface*, pages 161–178. Amsterdam: John Benjamins Publishing Company.

Webelhuth, Gert. 2012. The distribution of *that*-clauses in English: An SBCG account. In H. Boas and I. A. Sag, eds., *Sign-based Construction Grammar*. Stanford, CA: CSLI Publications.

Wechsler, Stephen. 1995. Preposition selection outside the lexicon. In R. Aranovich, W. Byrne, S. Preuss, and M. Senturia, eds., *Proceedings of the Thirteenth West Coast Conference on Formal Linguistics*, pages 416–431. Stanford, CA: CSLI Publications.

Wechsler, Stephen. 2001. An analysis of English resultatives under the event-argument homomorphism model of telicity. In *Proceedings of the 3rd Workshop on Text Structure, University of Texas, Austin*, pages 1–15.

Wierzbicka, Anna. 1972. *Semantic Primitives*. Frankfurt: Athenäum.

Wierzbicka, Anna. 1996. *Semantics, Primes and Universals*. Oxford: Oxford University Press.

Wierzbicka, Anna. 2006. *English: Meaning and Culture*. Oxford: Oxford University Press.

Wilcock, Graham. 2005. Information structure and minimal recursion semantics. In A. Arppe, L. Carlson, K. Lindén, J. Piitulainen, M. Suominen, M. Vainio, H. Westerlund, and A. Yli-Jyrä, eds., *Inquiries into Words, Constraints and Contexts: Festschrift for Kimmo Koskenniemi on his 60th Birthday*, pages 268–277. Stanford, CA: CSLI Publications.

Williams, Edwin. 1980. Predication. *Linguistic Inquiry* 11:203–238.

Yatabe, Shûichi. 2002. A linearization-based theory of summative agreement in peripheral node-raising constructions. In J.-B. Kim and S. Wechsler, eds., *Proceedings of the 9th International Conference on Head-driven Phrase Structure Grammar*, pages 391–411. Stanford, CA: CSLI Publications.

Yatabe, Shûichi. 2004. A comprehensive theory of coordination of unlikes. In S. Müller, ed., *Proceedings of the 11 International Conference on Head-driven Phrase Structure Grammar*, pages 335–355. Stanford, CSLI Publications.

Yatabe, Shûichi. 2012. Comparison of the ellipsis-based theory of non-constituent coordination with its alternatives. In S. Müller, ed., *Proceedings of the 19th International Conference on Head-driven Phrase Structure Grammar*, pages 454–474. Stanford, CA: CSLI Publications.

≈ 3 ≈

Down the Rabbit Hole

LAURA STAUM CASASANTO

It might seem like an odd choice: Why meet with one of the most influential formal syntacticians in the world to talk about why grammar might have nothing to do with something? But if that syntactician is Ivan Sag, then you've come to the right place.

I first met with Ivan to discuss a phenomenon I had stumbled across in both speech and writing that seemed to exist in some kind of netherworld between grammaticality and ungrammaticality. People were producing complement clauses with more than one complementizer. And these constructions didn't sound quite right, but they didn't sound quite wrong. A standard syntactic approach to analyzing something like this might be to try to determine whether this phenomenon should be accounted for by grammar or not, and then either build a grammar that allows them or one that doesn't – essentially, asking the question, How does it work? But instead, we asked a different question, one which I now see, after several years of working with Ivan on this and related phenomena, is a precursor to asking how something works: Why does it happen?

The pursuit of the answer to that question has led Ivan and many of his students and collaborators down a rabbit hole that, so far, does not seem to have an end. Ivan's investigations into the interaction between grammar and processing have brought home why it is that a syntactician should care about processing difficulty: because grammatical theories are built on the basis of distinctions in things like accept-

The Core and the Periphery.
Philip Hofmeister and Elisabeth Norcliffe (eds.).

ability judgments and attestations, and these are influenced not just by formal constraints but also by functional ones. To answer questions about grammar, we first need to answer questions about what is in the purview of grammar, and what types of information constitute evidence about grammar. Ivan's work on these questions falls into three major categories: 1) finding functional explanations for phenomena that have previously been analyzed as the result of formal constraints; 2) identifying contributions of grammar and processing in phenomena that depend critically on both; and 3) finding ways to distinguish the effects of formal and functional constraints in either of these types of phenomena.

The first type of work has involved Ivan in a number of debates that continue to this day and may take quite some time to resolve. The third type of work is an attempt to provide further leverage on the debates raised in the first and the second types. The second type is exemplified by this chapter by Philip Hofmeister and Elisabeth Norcliffe, which demonstrates some of the theoretical implications of asking and answering questions in this tradition. The chapter addresses a specific example of the question, if something is ungrammatical, why do people persist in doing it?

Hofmeister and Norcliffe point out the difficulties of explaining the facts about resumption in English from a purely syntactic perspective. If one makes the assumption that when resumption occurs it is licensed by the grammar, one is doomed to creating categorical grammatical constraints to explain behavior that is fundamentally analog – the effects of difficulty on judgments of sentences with resumptives. If one makes the assumption that resumption is always ungrammatical, but adds no functional considerations, one has no way of explaining the facts at all. Hofmeister and Norcliffe do an admirable job of addressing how formal and functional constraints could combine to account for the observed behavior, but they do not stop with the hard questions there.

In its discussion, this chapter addresses one of the most difficult puzzles raised by the mere existence of what Langendoen and Bever (1973) originally christened Acceptable Ungrammatical constructions: Why do we have grammatical constraints that rule out things that make processing easier? The authors raise an interesting possibility: perhaps such scenarios arise when there are conflicts between the processing pressures experienced in production and comprehension. This unanswered question sets an agenda for a next phase in the research lives of those who join Ivan Sag in investigating the interaction between processing and grammar. I very much look forward to seeing the progress that is to come.

References

Langendoen, D.T. and T.G. Bever. 1973. Can a not unhappy man be called a not sad one? In S. Anderson and P. Kiparsky, eds., *A Festschrift for Morris Halle*, pages 392–409. New York: Holt, Rinehart and Winston, Inc.

7

Does Resumption Facilitate Sentence Comprehension?

PHILIP HOFMEISTER AND ELISABETH NORCLIFFE

While filler-gap dependencies (FGDs) in English typically have an omitted constituent (a 'gap') at the end of the dependency, pronominals can also appear in this position under certain circumstances:

(1) There was one prisoner that we heard that the guard taunted (___/him) mercilessly.

As opposed to languages such as Hebrew or Irish, where such resumptive pronominals are in free variation with gaps and are grammatically unmarked (Sells 1987; Sharvit 1999; McCloskey 2002), English resumptives lie at the margins of grammar. Referred to as 'intrusive' resumptive pronouns, they are often regarded as a 'last resort' device to preserve the grammaticality of the dependency (Ross 1967; Sells 1984). In particular, intrusive resumptive pronouns have famously been claimed to amnesty syntactic island violations, such as in the *wh*-island violation below (Ross 1967; Kroch 1981; Erteschik-Shir 1992; Haegeman 1994):

(2) This is the man whom$_i$ Emsworth told me when we will invite him$_i$.

The resumptive pronoun here purportedly 'saves' the island violation, and the result of this assumption has been a number of syntactic analyses explaining why islands are not violated in such circumstances.

As Alexopoulou and Keller (2007) (hereafter, AK) point out, the conclusion that resumptive pronouns save island violations was reached

The Core and the Periphery.
Philip Hofmeister and Elisabeth Norcliffe (eds.).

without precise measurements of acceptability, relying instead on researchers' intuitions. AK thus experimentally investigated judgments for island-violating sentences in English with and without intrusive resumptives. They found that island-violating sentences with resumptives were no more acceptable than minimally different gapped sentences. Depth of embedding, however, did influence the acceptability of resumptive items. Specifically, sentences with resumptives in English were judged more acceptable the more embedded the pronouns are, e.g.

(3) a. Who_i will we fire him_i?
    b. Who_i does Mary claim we will fire him_i?
    c. Who_i does Jane think Mary claims we will fire him_i?

These findings were replicated and expanded upon by Heestand et al. 2011. Given that resumptive pronouns never make sentences better than their gapped counterparts, they ultimately conclude that 'resumption does not help the hearer, or more accurately, the reader' (see also Ferreira and Swets 2005; Asudeh 2011).

The unacceptability of resumptives, compared to gaps, raises the question of why they appear in attested speech (Prince 1990; Jaeger 2006; Bennett 2008). One explanation for their occurrence appeals to the idea that speakers resort to their use only in certain performance conditions (Kroch 1981; Asudeh 2004; Heestand et al. 2011). For instance, Heestand et al. (2011) suggest that 'performance pressures in production could lead to speakers resorting to resumptives as a way of adding more information without breaking the production chain' and thus that resumptives reflect time pressures on speaker fluency. In other words, resumptives are performance-based artifacts. They arise due to either poor planning (Kroch 1981) or to the incremental nature of production which can produce locally licensed, but globally ungrammatical structures (Asudeh 2004, 2011). In the sense that the occasional use of these items follows from local production difficulty and not grammatical principles, these items should not facilitate comprehension processes, or else hinder them.

If we accept the conclusion that resumptives do not help the hearer, we are left with the mystery of why different types of resumptive structures nevertheless lead to differences in acceptability (as in (3) above). One possibility is that the increased acceptability of resumptives in embedded structures is due to the reduced salience of a grammatical violation in longer, complex dependencies. An alternative is that resumptives do in fact facilitate comprehension processes in some conditions.

The idea that resumptives aid comprehension in certain contexts is not without precedent in the functional/typological literature. For instance, Hawkins (1994) suggests resumptives aid in dependency processing because these explicit elements serve to identify the syntactic position of the dependent argument (as opposed to empty categories). Other accounts sketch different mechanisms by which resumptives selectively facilitate processing, but these accounts share the common prediction that resumptives should be favored in difficult-to-process contexts (Ariel 1999; Alexopoulou and Keller 2007; Givón 1973; Keenan and Comrie 1977). An accompanying prediction of some of these accounts is that resumptives should be dispreferred where processing a linguistic dependency is easy or trivial. That is, a competing preference for economy in language penalizes overinformative expressions (see the literature on referential form choice, e.g. Ariel 1990, 1999, 2001; Almor 1999; Gundel et al. 1993). On this view, dependency processing is subject to two independent, but potentially conflicting constraints: (1) the preference for explicit features which support identification, retrieval, and integration of the dislocated element and (2) the preference for economy of referential forms.

Existing empirical data do not allow us to definitively rule in favor or against the hypothesis that resumptives can help the hearer. Experimental investigations into the role of resumptives in language comprehension have so far come entirely from acceptability judgments. Unfortunately, these one-dimensional measurements have a limited capability in reflecting processing differences (see Sprouse 2008). Although it is commonly accepted that processing difficulty influences acceptability judgments (Chomsky and Miller 1963; Miller and Chomsky 1963; Gibson 1991), the precise nature of this relationship remains largely unexplored (Staum Casasanto et al. 2010). For instance, Staum Casasanto and Sag (2008) find that repetition of *that* in sentences like (4) facilitates processing at the subsequent subject NP, although it yields lower acceptability judgments than a minimally different sentence without the repeated *that*:

(4) I truly wish that if something like that were to happen that my children would do something like that for me.

Given the lack of a clear relationship between processing difficulty and acceptability, our goal in the current paper is to examine the effects of resumptive pronouns on online sentence processing and on acceptability judgments for the same items. By looking at the moment-by-moment processing of sentences with and without resumptives, we can form more direct conclusions about the effect of resumption on language comprehension.

In this paper, we report the results from two experimental studies which test whether both the acceptability and processing difficulty caused by resumptive pronouns changes with the relative difficulty of local sentence processing contexts. Experiment I considers how resumption affects acceptability judgments for sentences with differing processing complexity. Experiment II takes the same materials and looks at whether resumption facilitates reading times in a self-paced, moving window reading experiment.

1 Experiment I: Acceptability judgments

1.1 Methodology

For the acceptability experiment in Experiment I, we used the thermometer judgment (TJ) methodology described by Featherston (2008) (see also Bard et al. 1996 and Sorace and Keller 2005 for the related methodology of Magnitude Estimation). In the TJ task, participants judge items relative to two reference sentences. One of these references is quite good and the other quite bad, and we follow Featherston (2008) in assigning these sentences the arbitrary values 20 and 30. In our study, we used the following reference sentences.

(5) a. The way that the project was approaching to the deadline everyone wondered. = 20
b. The architect told his assistant to bring the new plans to the foreman's office. = 30

Sentences were presented word-by-word at a fixed rate of presentation in the center of the screen (250 ms + 33.33 ms * the number of characters in the word), so that longer words remained visible for longer. We used word-by-word presentation over full sentence presentation to prevent participants from excessive introspection about the test sentences, and we used auto-paced presentation rather than self-paced presentation so that there would be no differences in how long each participant studied a given stimulus. After judging each item, participants also answered a comprehension question for each item to ensure reading.

Judgments were transformed into z-scores for each subject on the basis of their judgments for all experimental items, including fillers. After this, we excluded data points with z-scores more than 2.5 standard deviations from the subject's mean to further normalize the data and remove the skewing effects of extreme outliers.

We used linear mixed-effects models (LMEMs) to analyze the effect of experimental factors. All predictors/fixed effect variables were sum coded (which reduces effects of collinearity, as compared to treatment coding). As LMEMs with random effect correlation parameters do not yield p-values, we provide coefficient estimates, standard errors, and t-values (Baayen 2008; Baayen et al. 2008; Pinheiro and Bates 2000). As noted by Baayen et al. (2008), significance at the .05 level can be conservatively estimated for fixed effects coefficients with t-values that have an absolute value greater than 2.

1.2 Materials & Participants

The experimental materials in the experiments described here involve two manipulations: dependency length (long vs. short) and resumption (pronoun vs. gap), as in the following sample item:

(6) a. Mary confirmed that there was a prisoner who the prison officials had acknowledged that the guard helped ___ to make a daring escape.
  b. Mary confirmed that there was a prisoner who the prison officials had acknowledged that the guard helped him to make a daring escape.
  c. The prison officials had acknowledged that there was a prisoner that the guard helped ___ to make a daring escape.
  d. The prison officials had acknowledged that there was a prisoner that the guard helped him to make a daring escape.

In the long conditions, the filler-phrase (*a prisoner*) was always separated from its selecting lexical head by two clause boundaries—a relative clause and a complement clause. In the short conditions, only a single relative clause boundary intervened between the filler and its head. Longer dependency length should lead to higher levels of processing difficulty compared to the sentences with shorter dependencies. Several different sentence processing accounts uniformly predict these longer dependencies should engender more difficulty than the shorter dependencies, although the details differ for the proposed mechanisms involved (Gibson 1998, 2000; Gordon et al. 2002, 2001; Grodner and Gibson 2005; Kluender and Kutas 1993). Of importance here is merely the consensus view that the longer dependencies should burden processing more than the shorter dependencies.

In all long conditions, the gender of the sentence-initial proper name contrasted with the gender of the resumptive pronoun. Furthermore, in all conditions, there were no other singular referents in the sentence besides the target (the clefted indefinite) and the clause-mate subject noun phrase (*the guard* in (6d)).

Presentation of the items was pseudo-randomized by the experimental software DMDX (Forster and Forster 2003). Each participant saw

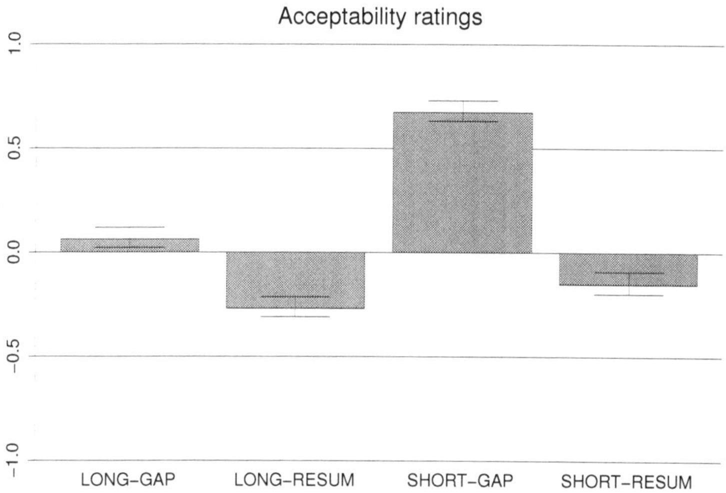

FIGURE 1 Mean acceptability z-scores for Experiment 1

one and only one condition from each of the 24 experimental items. These were accompanied by 72 fillers.

In Experiment 1, we used the maximal random effect structure in the linear mixed effects model: in addition to random subject and item intercepts, the random effect structure included by-subject and by-item random slopes for dependency length, resumption, and their interaction. Outlier removal affected .006% of the data (4 out of 672 data points).

28 individuals from Stanford University—all of whom identified as native English speakers—participated in this study for $14/hr.

1.3 Results

As Figure 1 shows, both manipulations had significant effects on acceptability. Sentences with longer dependencies received significantly lower acceptability judgments than those with short dependencies. In addition, items containing a resumptive pronoun were judged far worse than sentences with gaps.

However, the results also reveal a highly significant interaction between dependency length and resumption. As noted above, resumptive pronouns lead to lower acceptability in both LONG and SHORT conditions; indeed, the mean ratings for the two conditions with resumptives are statistically indistinguishable. Comparing the difference between

	Coffecients	Standard Error	t-value
DEPENDENCY LENGTH	0.001	0.024	0.03
RESUMPTION	−0.068	0.018	−3.85
DEPENDENCY LENGTH × RESUMPTION	0.089	0.041	2.21
SPILLOVER	0.153	0.025	6.17

TABLE 1 Fixed effects summary for averaged residual log reading times at two words after gap or resumptive pronoun.

the gapped and resumptive versions at each dependency length, though, we see that the acceptability penalty is far smaller in the context of a long dependency (see Figure 1). That is, the difference between the means for the SHORT-GAP and SHORT-RESUM conditions is roughly 2.5 times greater than the difference between the LONG-GAP and LONG-RESUM conditions. This is unlikely to be the result of a floor effect, as the experimental fillers in this study also included a set of twelve sentences with jumbled word orders (e.g. *Iran has gun-control strict laws that bar private citizens carrying from firearms*), which received substantially lower mean judgments ($\mu = -0.63$, SE = 0.05) than the items in the LONG-RESUMP condition ($\mu = -0.27$, SE = 0.05).

1.4 Discussion

Resumptive pronouns do not make sentences sound better than those with gaps, even in difficult-to-process contexts. However, the interaction shows that resumptives are less egregious in difficult-to-process contexts. If resumptives had a uniform effect on judgments across sentence contexts, then the LONG-RESUMP condition should have a significantly lower mean acceptability score. These findings replicate past results that resumptives never lead to more acceptable structures than gaps, but that increased embedding depth can reduce the penalty for resumptives (Alexopoulou and Keller 2007; Heestand et al. 2011).

This pattern of results also echoes the findings of Staum Casasanto and Sag (2008) regarding the acceptability of sentences with multiple *that*s, as in (7):

(7) I truly wish that if something like that were to happen that my children would do something like that for me.

They observed that sentences with multiple-*that*s were always judged to be more unacceptable than their counterpart sentences with a single *that*; however, the unacceptability was modulated by the distance between the two thats. In particular, the acceptability difference for sentences with and without multiple *thats* was significantly smaller when the distance between the two *that*s was greater. To explain these findings, Staum Casasanto & Sag entertain several hypotheses: (1) the presence of multiple *that*s is more noticeable when they are close together or (2) a second *that* may have more functional utility the greater the distance from the initial *that* due to activation decay.

The question at hand, therefore, is why resumptives become more acceptable with embedding. Following the logic in Staum Casasanto & Sag (2008), if resumptive pronouns constitute an ungrammatical means for completing a long-distance dependency in English, then the salience of this violation may be reduced by increasing the distance between the filler-phrase and the pronoun. Alternatively, the resumptive pronoun may have some functional utility in long dependency contexts that it lacks in shorter dependency contexts. In Experiment II we consider these alternative hypotheses by looking at how resumptives are processed during on-line sentence comprehension.

2 Experiment II: Self-paced reading

One explanation for the reduced penalty for resumptives under embedding is that the ungrammaticality of the RPs becomes less salient in these environments. On this hypothesis, reading times should be faster after resumptives at the tail of long dependencies compared to short ones, but never faster than after gaps. Alternatively, RPs might possess functional utility in sentence contexts that impose substantial processing difficulty. In contexts without such difficulty, this functional utility may be absent or counteracted by principles of economy.

These two hypotheses make different predictions about how resumptive pronouns should affect online sentence processing. On the hypothesis that the grammaticality violation simply becomes less salient with embedding, resumptive pronouns are not predicted to make processing any faster than gaps in any context. That is, resumptives pronouns do not have a facilitatory role on this hypothesis. The violation of constraints on dependency formation is simply less conspicuous. But if resumptives prove to actually elicit faster reading times than gaps in certain contexts, this argues for a facilitating role of resumptives.

2.1 Methodology

We used the self-paced, moving window display paradigm in this experiment (Just et al. 1982). At the beginning of each item, participants see a row of dashes, separated by spaces, that represent the words in the sentence. By pressing a predefined key, the first word in the sentence appears, replacing the dashes. Each subsequent key-press uncovers the next word in the sentence and reverts the previous word to dashes. Longer reading times are interpreted as indicators of greater processing difficulty. Participants answered a comprehension question about each sentence and received feedback if they answered incorrectly. Materials were presented and randomized with the reading time software LINGER v. 2.94, developed by Doug Rohde (available at http://tedlab.mit.edu/~dr/Linger/).

Reading times were analyzed with LMEMs, using the lme4 package in R (version 2.12.1). Prior to statistical analysis, raw reading times (greater than 2500 ms or less than 100 ms) were removed from each data set. In addition, data from subjects with overall question-answer accuracies below 67% or more than 2.5 standard deviations from the sample mean were entirely excluded.

Subsequently, raw reading times were logged to normalize the data. Following this, the log reading times for all stimuli (fillers included) were regressed against a number of predictors known to affect reading times in self-paced reading tasks: word length, log list position, and material type, e.g. filler vs. critical item (Ferreira and Clifton 1986; Hofmeister 2011). The residuals of this model – residual log reading times – serve as the dependent variable in the model we report. In essence, these residual reading times reflect the variation in reading times that remains after eliminating the estimated effects of word length, list position, and material type. Once these residual log reading times were calculated, we removed data from all stimuli where the participant answered the comprehension question incorrectly. Finally, reading times more than 2.5 standard deviations from the mean at each word region were eliminated, affecting 2.74% of the total dataset.

In Experiment 2, we take the critical region for analysis to consist of the two words following the resumptive or gap. The reading time model for Experiment 2 also included a fixed effect factor that models the relationship between reading times at word region $n-1$ and n—that is, spillover effects from the preceding word regions (either the pronoun in conditions with a resumptive, or the verb in gapped conditions) on reading times at the critical region (Sanford and Garrod 1981). Prior to analysis, we centered the factors of dependency length and resumption at the critical region. As in Experiment 1, we used a random effect structure with random intercepts for participants and items, and by-participant and by-item random slopes for dependency length, resumption, and their interaction.

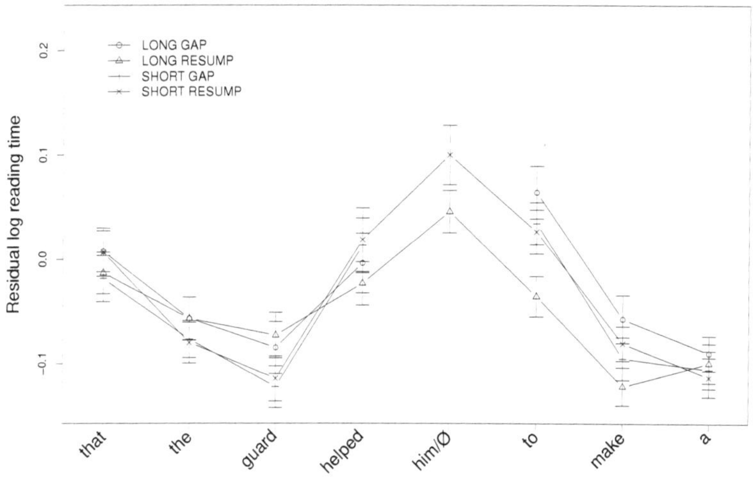

FIGURE 2 Mean residual log reading times by region in Experiment 2; error bars show ± one standard error

2.2 Materials & Participants

The materials for this experiment were identical to those in Experiment I. 72 filler items accompanied the 24 critical items. For analyzing the reading time results, we take the critical region to include the two words after either the pronoun or the gap.

28 University of California-San Diego undergraduates participated in this study for course credit.

2.3 Results

According to the reading time results, resumption significantly speeds up the reading rate in the critical region (see Table 2). The faster average reading times for resumptive conditions overall, however, is driven exclusively by the LONG-RESUMP condition, as shown in Figure 2: reading times in the LONG-RESUMP condition were the fastest overall. Moreover, while gap processing slows down with deeper embedding, processing after a resumptive speeds up with deeper embedding. This accounts for the significant interaction of dependency length and resumption, and the lack of a main effect of dependency length. Unsurprisingly, reading time differences at the previous word region also account for a significant amount of variation. As the positive coefficient indicates, longer reading times at the previous word region tend

	Coffecients	Standard Error	t-value
DEPENDENCY LENGTH	0.001	0.024	0.03
RESUMPTION	−0.068	0.018	−3.85
DEPENDENCY LENGTH × RESUMPTION	0.089	0.041	2.21
SPILLOVER	0.153	0.025	6.17

TABLE 2 Fixed effects summary for averaged residual log reading times at two words after gap or resumptive pronoun.

to make reading times at the next word region longer.

In short, the effect of resumption on processing depends on the length of the dependency. Resumptives in hard-to-process contexts lead to more efficient processing as compared to resumptives in easy-to-process contexts. In contrast, processing times after gaps increases with distance between the filler and gap. Crucially, the reading time results also clearly show that the resumptive pronoun facilitates processing compared to a gap in high difficulty contexts.

2.4 Discussion

In confirmation of the facilitation hypothesis of resumptives, the reading time data show that a resumptive at the tail of a relatively difficult dependency improves processing speed, compared to a gap. These results are unexpected if increasing the distance between a filler-phrase and a resumptive simply makes a grammatical violation less noticeable. In other words, the evidence argues for a facilitating role of resumptive pronouns in certain sentence contexts. While resumptives have some processing advantages compared to gaps in high difficulty contexts, there is no evidence of such an advantage in less difficult contexts.

3 General Discussion

The acceptability results from Experiment 1 indicate a significant interaction between dependency length and resumption: the penalty for resumptives is reduced in hard-to-process contexts. To explain these results, we explored how the relevant items are processed in a self-paced reading study and found a facilitatory role for resumptives in these same hard-to-process contexts, whereas resumptives in easier-to-process contexts had no facilitatory effects. Put together, these results suggest that the cause of the decreased acceptability penalty for resumptives reflects the facilitated processing at or immediately after the retrieval site. That is, resumptive pronouns are preferable (in terms of processing difficulty) in hard-to-process contexts, as opposed to relatively easy-to-process contexts.

Following the logic of Staum Casasanto & Sag (2008), where they find a similar pattern of reading times results, the data from Experiment 2 demonstrate that not only are reading times after a resumptive in a long dependency faster compared to a short one, but also faster as compared to a gap in a long dependency. This argues against the hypothesis that the advantage for the resumptive in the long dependency context is due to reduced saliency of the grammatical violation. In other words, such a hypothesis fails to predict the processing advantage for the resumptive in the hard-to-process context, compared to a gap.

Assuming that differential processing difficulty is one source of variation in judgments of linguistic acceptability, the observed processing difference potentially lies behind the differing penalties of resumption in acceptability judgment tasks. Nevertheless, resumptives are judged worse than gaps in difficult-to-process contexts, meaning that processing difficulty by itself fails to accurately predict acceptability patterns. If we make the assumption, however, that resumptive pronouns are ungrammatical in English, then the cause of the pattern of acceptability judgments becomes evident: (i) long dependencies are harder to process than shorter dependencies, accounting for the acceptability difference in 'gapped' sentences; (ii) resumptives in English incur an acceptability penalty, regardless of context; (iii) resumptive pronouns aid in processing linguistic dependencies, compared to gaps; and (iv) a general constraint on reference processing requires referential forms in the sense of Ariel (1990, 1999, 2001) to be as economical as possible, while ensuring successful communication.

With respect to (iv), processing efficiency may be at a sufficiently high level in a short, easy-to-process dependency context, such that any functional support the pronoun provides amounts to overkill. Such a hypothesis is well-supported not only by pragmatic principles such as Grice's 1975 Principle of Quantity, but also psycholinguistic research that points to processing penalties for overly specific referential forms (Almor 1999, 2004). Ariel (1990, 1999, 2001) argues in this regard that referential descriptions that are non-specific, such as pronouns and gaps, are preferentially used in contexts when the corresponding mental referent is highly salient or accessible. Thus, in long dependency contexts, where processing challenges can be substantial, the overall accessibility or retrievability of the dislocated constituent may be lessened (e.g. this can be realized in terms of lowered activation levels).

Up until now, we have not identified a precise mechanism that explains why resumptives facilitate comprehension. In fact, a number of different pragmatic, typological, and cognitive accounts lay out arguments to motivate such a conclusion. While the details of these accounts differ, they uniformly support the idea that resumptives should facilitate processing at the tail of long-distance dependencies. In the functionalist literature, for instance, Keenan and Comrie (1977) speculate that resumptives aid in the identification of an extraction site (see also Givón 1973; Givón 1975). More recently, Hawkins (1994, 1999) similarly argues that resumptive pronouns facilitate processing because an empty category does not need to be inferred from its environment, but rather, is expressed formally in the surface structure. On this view, the resumptive pronoun functions to explicitly identify the dislocated element's role in the structure, making it 'as clear as it can possibly be'.

In addition to this identification-based theory, the difference between gaps and pronouns can also be viewed in terms of principles of referential form choice (Almor and Nair 2007). From this perspective, the information content of a referring expression is interpreted as a measure of cognitive accessibility, i.e. how cognitively salient a mental representation is and thus how hard it will be to restore from memory. Wherever an antecedent is difficult to retrieve from memory, more information is needed to aid that retrieval process (Ariel 1990, 2001). Referential content thus acts as instructions to the comprehender for resolving a reference. Just as complex instructions for a simple task will be considered infelicitous (e.g. 'lift one of your hands, move it away from your body toward the wine bottle, grasp the wine bottle, and then move the grasped object until it is close enough for me to reach easily' as a request to pass the wine), so too will complex referring forms be infelicitous for easily restorable referents.

As pointed out by Ariel (1990), the distance between references to the same referent predicts the 'accessibility-marking' of anaphoric forms: greater distance between references lowers overall accessibility, thereby necessitating the use of more informative, weighty expressions to ensure successful reference. Where retrieval costs are minimal, excessive information is perceived as marked, because information is assumed to have a pragmatic purpose. In brief, the pressure for successful communication and reference competes with the requirement to be as economical as possible. Ariel (1999) argues that accessibility marking is visible not only at the discourse level, determining the degree of specificity of referents across sentences, but also intersententially, governing the distribution of resumptives and gaps: less accessible antecedents trigger less attenuated anaphoric forms (resumptives). As with the case of the multiple *thats*, a resumptive may serve to re-activate features of the dislocated phrase, making retrieval of the appropriate representation easier.

A third hypothesis for the processing advantage of resumptive pronouns concerns differential structural complexity (e.g. Hawkins 2004; Alexopoulou and Keller 2007; Alexopoulou 2010). Accounts along these lines presume that resumptive pronouns and gaps initiate two distinct types of syntactic resolution (see also Asudeh 2004, 2011, 2012 for theoretical arguments for distinguishing resumptive dependencies from gap dependencies). These structures have some similar and some different processing costs. Alexopoulou & Keller (2007) suggest that, whether a gap or a resumptive ultimately appears at the end of a dependency, processing expectations are set up for a gap upon encountering a filler-phrase, i.e. by default, the parser assumes a filler-gap dependency up until the point of the resumptive. Appealing to ideas expressed by Gibson (1998, 2000), they argue that storing these expectations incurs a cost that does not vary with the nature of the material at the end of the dependency. In other words, processing dependencies with resumptives is not cost-free.

However, when the parser encounters a resumptive pronoun rather than a gap, it initiates a 'backward search' through the preceding discourse for an appropriate discourse antecedent. In other words, resumptives trigger processing akin to standard intrasentential anaphor-antecedent dependencies. Hawkins (2004) similarly proposes that a resumptive pronominal causes the parser to abandon all lexical co-occurrence dependencies registered between the filler and the predicate. Restoring a filler-phrase in the presence of a gap, on the other hand, requires a 'cyclic resolution of the dependency'. This post-gap resolution process, they claim, is sensitive to distance in terms of syntactic units, á la Gibson (1998, 2000). Critically, their account requires the assumption that anaphor-antecedent dependencies lack these 'backward' locality costs, and that not all resumptives trigger these anaphoric dependencies. That is, to explain why resumptives are worse in *wh*-questions like 'Who$_i$ will we fire him$_i$?' compared to 'Who$_i$ does Mary think that we will fire him$_i$?', AK assume that 'these structures are speciÞed for movement (AGREE/MOVE) which yields a phonologically empty element in situ.'[1]

[1] In general, accounts that pose different syntactic analyses for resumptive and gapped structures do not clarify why resumptives are not consistently preferable to gaps in embedded contexts, since the former arguably do not incur locality costs. Secondly, as noted above, the categorical distinction between resumptives under

A fourth way of explaining the selective facilitation of resumptives relates to predictability theories of referential form choice (Arnold 1998, 2010; Tily and Piantadosi 2009). Probabilistic approaches to referential form choice in discourse assume that the referential form chosen (e.g. definite NP vs. pronoun) is dependent on how probable the mention of that referent is in context. Language users employ longer forms where the referent is less predictable (Tily and Piantadosi 2009). This also has advantages for the listener, because it provides more instructions for reference resolution where comprehender expectations are low. On this view, comprehension processing should be easier for gaps over resumptives where the extraction site is highly predictable, while resumptives should be easier where it is less predictable.

Yet another hypothesis, previously unexplored in the literature, is that resumptive pronouns provide an additional region to complete processing related to the preceding lexical head, including retrieval and integration. Behavioral and electrophysiological studies show that processing difficulty at retrieval points in embedded or structural complex contexts spills over onto subsequent word regions (see, for instance, Hofmeister 2011; Vasishth and Lewis 2006). Hence, a reader or listener may have to struggle to complete processing related to a previous word, while simultaneously perceiving, categorizing, and integrating the next several words. Given sufficient difficulty, this overlap may lead to superadditive processing difficulty or a temporary processing breakdown. An informationally-light or even redundant lexical item in between regions would provide a buffer between them, allowing for more time to process the first region before the second is reached.

However one might interpret the functional role of resumptives, there seems to be clear theoretical support for the idea that resumptives facilitate comprehension. The results from the above reading time study add novel empirical data by showing that resumptives are not merely the byproduct of production pressures. When comprehension pressure is high, resumptive pronouns make reading easier than gaps; when comprehension pressure is low, resumptives present more information than is necessary for successful and efficient comprehension and thus have no beneficial effects on comprehension.

The current body of evidence, therefore, contradicts the claim that 'resumption does not help the hearer' (Heestand et al. 2011). It seems

embedding and those in simple wh-questions is ad hoc and without explanation. Third, the available evidence does not support the view that anaphoric dependencies are not subject to locality costs. Sanford and Garrod (1981), for instance, show that processing an anaphoric expression becomes more difficulty as the distance to its antecedent increases.

reasonable to suppose that resumptive pronouns may have simultaneous advantages for both comprehension and production. While production pressures may sometimes drive production choices rather than the needs of the listener, this does not rule out the possibility that those production choices nevertheless result in a mutual advantage for the listener (see e.g. Arnold 2008; Brown and Dell 1987; Gennari and MacDonald 2009). Our claim that resumptive pronouns sometimes facilitate comprehension, however, does not exclude the possibility that incremental language production gives rise to unique demands that favor the use of resumptives (see Asudeh 2004, 2011, 2012).

Although our results suggest some parallel effects of resumption on comprehension and production, there also remain some unexplained contrasts. As noted by Heestand et al. (2011), resumptive pronouns tend to be produced most in English in the subject position of an embedded or relative clause. But this is also the context where it is judged most ungrammatical. It has also been shown in corpus studies that resumptives are more frequent for subjects in unembedded contexts than in embedded contexts (Jaeger 2006; Bennett 2008). It would be surprising if the contexts in which they occur most frequently in production are those in which they facilitate comprehension the least. It is an open question, therefore, whether the same cognitive mechanisms and discourse factors that promote the use of resumptives in production are those which cause resumptives to facilitate comprehension in contexts of high processing difficulty.

3.1 Grammar & Processing

To account for the pattern of acceptability found with resumptives and gaps, we claimed that resumptive pronouns live a double life in English. They aid dependency processing in difficult-to-process contexts, but they also incur a structural constraint violation. The basis for this interpretation is that faster processing times for resumptives compared to gaps do not correspond to higher judgments of acceptability. The picture that emerges, therefore, is one where structural constraints and processing-based constraints can be in conflict with one another.

Looking within and across languages, such a combination of features is perhaps surprising. Syntactic constraints and typological implicational patterns often align with processing constraints: dispreferred or unacceptable structures frequently accompany high processing or learning difficulty, and vice versa (Bever 1975, 2009; Hawkins 1994, 1999, 2004; Jaeger and Tily 2010). Far less commonly noted are cases where the two are in conflict with another, although there are some attested cases where ungrammatical sentences are easier to read than minimally different, grammatical ones (Vasishth et al. 2008). Besides the previously mentioned cases of multiple *thats* (Staum Casasanto and Sag 2008), Gibson and Thomas (1999) illustrate that acceptability judgments for doubly center-embedded constructions lacking a required verb are as acceptable as those with all three:

(8) The ancient manuscript that the graduate student who the new card catalog had confused a great deal (was studying in the library) was missing a page.

Gibson and Thomas (1999) convincingly argue that these unexpected results can be explained by appealing to the idea that the ungrammatical variant is actually easier to process, due to the forgetting of prior content.

Heestand et al. (2011) also report evidence that hints at facilitating effects of resumptive pronouns on comprehension. They found that acceptability judgments were faster for resumptives than for gaps. 'In cases where RP judgments were faster than judgments for sentences with illicit gaps, the gaps seem to be less helpful to the parser, despite being just as unambiguously ungrammatical'. To the extent these results replicate, they suggest that 'we can conclude that the extra information available in RPs is useful in parsing difficult dependencies, making its unacceptability all the more puzzling.'

The puzzle they allude to is the very same conflict between grammatical and processing constraints that we have argued for here. Nothing theoretically precludes the possibility that syntactic constraints penalize a particular structure or word order, while this same structure simultaneously poses functional advantages for the listener in certain sentential contexts. How such a competition between grammatical constraints and processing advantages arises is, of course, an unanswered question. On the assumption that language-specific grammatical constraints can emerge diachronically through frequency of use (Bybee 1998; Haspelmath 2008; Krug 1998), the mismatch could ultimately be traceable to frequency distributions of *speaker-oriented* production choices. An important part of the puzzle will therefore be to determine under what conditions resumptives are preferred in production, and whether or not, as we discussed above, production preferences mirror comprehension preferences in this domain.

4 Conclusion

In keeping with prior research, our studies here show that while resumptives never make a sentence more acceptable than a minimally different 'gapped' sentence, resumptive pronouns are nevertheless considerably less 'intrusive' in hard-to-process sentence contexts. The limitation of previous studies in interpreting these effects relates to the lack of measurements of comprehension difficulty. The reading time evidence here, though, offers an explanation of the acceptability pattern based on processing difficulty. Namely, the reduced penalty for resumptives in embedded contexts, compared to resumptives in non-embedded contexts, aligns with reduced processing difficulty. Indeed, processing is faster after resumptive pronouns compared to gaps in embedded positions. On the straightforward assumption that processing difficulty feeds into acceptability judgments, this facilitation accounts for the reduced penalty. The persistence of unacceptability in sentences with resumptives follows from the assumption that structural constraints rule out resumptives in English, despite the processing facilitation. Such an account may be relatively anomalous, given the usual correspondence between structural and processing constraints, but it is not without precedent. Most importantly, our findings corroborate the general prediction of numerous treatises on resumption which claim that resumptive pronouns can not only compensate for production pressures, but also can ease comprehension difficulty.

References

Alexopoulou, Theodora. 2010. Truly intrusive: resumptive pronominals in questions and relative clauses. *Lingua* 120:485–505.

Alexopoulou, Theodora and Frank Keller. 2007. Locality, cyclicity and resumption: At the interface between the grammar and the human sentence processor. *Language* 83:110–160.

Almor, Amit. 1999. Noun-phrase anaphora and focus: The informational load hypothesis. *Psychological Review* 106(4):748–765.

Almor, Amit. 2004. A computational investigation of reference in production and comprehension. In J. Trueswell and M. Tanenhaus, eds., *Approaches to Studying World-Situated Language Use: Bridging the Language-as-Product and Language-as-Action Traditions*, pages 285–301. Cambridge, MA: MIT Press.

Almor, Amit and Veena Nair. 2007. The form of referential expressions in discourse. *Language and Linguistics Compass* 1(1):84–99.

Ariel, Mira. 1990. *Accessing Noun-Phrase Antecedents*. London: Routledge.

Ariel, Mira. 1999. Cognitive universals and linguistic conventions: The case of resumptive pronouns. *Studies in Language* 23:217–269.

Ariel, Mira. 2001. Accessibility theory: An overview. In T. Sanders, J. Schilperoord, and W. Spooren, eds., *Text Representation: Linguistic and Psycholinguistic Aspects*. Amsterdam: John Benjamins.

Arnold, Jennifer E. 1998. *Reference Form and Discourse Patterns*. Ph.D. thesis, Stanford University.

Arnold, Jennifer E. 2008. Reference production: Production-internal and Addressee-oriented processes. *Language and Cognitive Processes* 23(4):495–527.

Arnold, Jennifer E. 2010. How speakers refer: The role of accessibility. *Language and Linguistics Compass* 4(4):187–203.

Asudeh, Ash. 2004. *Resumption as resource management.* Ph.D. thesis, Stanford University.

Asudeh, Ash. 2011. Local grammaticality in syntactic production. In E. M. Bender and J. E. Arnold, eds., *Language from a Cognitive Perspective: Grammar, Usage, and Processing. Studies in Honor of Thomas Wasow.* Stanford, CA: CSLI Publications.

Asudeh, Ash. 2012. *The Logic of Pronominal Resumption.* Oxford: Oxford University Press.

Baayen, R. Harald. 2008. *Analyzing Linguistic Data: A Practical Introduction to Statistics.* Cambridge, UK: Cambridge University Press.

Baayen, R. Harald, Douglas J. Davidson, and Douglas M. Bates. 2008. Mixed-effects modeling with crossed random effects for subjects and items. *Journal of Memory and Language* 59:390–412.

Bard, Ellen G., Dan Robertson, and Antonella Sorace. 1996. Magnitude Estimation of Linguistic Acceptability. *Language* 72(1):32–68.

Bennett, Ryan. 2008. English resumptive pronouns and the highest subject restriction: A corpus study. Paper presented at the Trilateral Linguistics Weekend (TREND), UC Santa Cruz.

Bever, Thomas. 1975. Functionalist explanations presuppose independently motived theories of behavior. In R. Grossman, L. J. San, and T. J. Vance, eds., *Papers from the Parasession on Functionalism*, pages 580–635. Chicago: Chicago Linguistics Society.

Bever, Thomas. 2009. Remarks on the individual basis for linguistic structures. In M. Piattelli-Palmarini, J. Uriagereka, and P. Salaburu, eds., *Of Minds and Language: A Dialogue with Noam Chomsky in the Basque Country*, pages 279–295. Oxford: Oxford University Press.

Brown, Paula M. and Gary S. Dell. 1987. Adapting production to comprehension: The explicit mention of instruments. *Cognitive Psychology* 19:441–472.

Bybee, Joan. 1998. A functionalist approach to grammar and its evolution. *Evolution of Communication* 2:249–278.

Chomsky, Noam and George Miller. 1963. Introduction to the formal analysis of natural languages. In R. Luce, R. Bush, and E. Galanter, eds., *Handbook of Mathematical Psychology*, pages 269–321. New York: Wiley.

Erteschik-Shir, Nomi. 1992. Resumptive pronouns in islands. In H. Goodluck and M. Rochemont, eds., *Island Constraints: Theory, Acquisition and Processing*, pages 89–108. Dordrecht: Kluwer.

Featherston, Sam. 2008. Thermometer judgments as linguistic evidence. In M. Claudia and A. Rothe, eds., *Was ist linguistische Evidenz?*. Aachen: Shaker Verlag.

Ferreira, Fernanda and Chuck Clifton. 1986. The independence of syntactic processing. *Journal of Memory and Language* 25(3):348–368.

Ferreira, Fernanda and Benjamin Swets. 2005. The production and comprehension of resumptive pronouns in relative clause "island" contexts. In A. Cutler, ed., *Twenty-first Century Psycholinguistics: Four Cornerstones*, pages 263–278. Mahway, NJ: Lawrence Erlbaum Associates.

Forster, Kenneth I. and Jonathan C. Forster. 2003. DMDX: A windows display program with millisecond accuracy. *Behavioral Research Methods, Instruments and Computers* 35:116–124.

Gennari, Silvia P. P. and Maryellen C. MacDonald. 2009. Linking production and comprehension processes: The case of relative clauses. *Cognition* 111:1–23.

Gibson, Edward. 1991. *A Computational Theory of Human Linguistic Processing: Memory Limitations and Processing Breakdown*. Ph.D. thesis, Carnegie Mellon University, Pittsburgh.

Gibson, Edward. 1998. Linguistic complexity: Locality of syntactic dependencies. *Cognition* 68(1):1–76.

Gibson, Edward. 2000. The dependency locality theory: A distance-based theory of linguistic complexity. In A. Marantz, Y. Miyashita, and W. O'Neil, eds., *Image, Language, Brain*, pages 95–126. Cambridge: MIT Press.

Gibson, Edward and J. Thomas. 1999. Memory limitations and structural forgetting: The perception of complex ungrammatical sentences as grammatical. *Language and Cognitive Processes* 14(3):225–248.

Givón, Talmy. 1973. The time-axis phenomenon. *Language* pages 890–925.

Givón, Talmy. 1975. On the role of perceptual clause in Hebrew relativization. *Afroasiatic Linguistics* 2(8):1–17.

Gordon, Peter, Randall Hendrick, and Marcus Johnson. 2001. Memory interference during language processing. *Journal of Experimental Psychology: Learning, Memory, and Cognition* 27(6):1411–23.

Gordon, Peter, Randall Hendrick, and William H. Levine. 2002. Memory-load interference in syntactic processing. *Psychological Science* 13:425–430.

Grice, H. Paul. 1975. Logic and conversation. In P. Cole and J. Morgan, eds., *Syntax and semantics: Vol. 3. Speech acts*. New York: Academic Press.

Grodner, Daniel and Edward Gibson. 2005. Consequences of the serial nature of linguistic input for sentential complexity. *Cognitive Science* 29:261–290.

Gundel, Jeanette, Nancy Hedberg, and Ron Zacharski. 1993. Cognitive Status and the Form of Referring Expressions in Discourse. *Language* 69(2):274–307.

Haegeman, Lilliane. 1994. *Introduction to Government and Binding Theory*. Oxford: Blackwell Publishing.

Haspelmath, Martin. 2008. Frequency vs. iconicity in explaining grammatical asymmetries. *Cognitive Linguistics* 19(1):1–33.

Hawkins, John A. 1994. *A Performance Theory of Order and Constituency*. Cambridge: Cambridge University Press.

Hawkins, John A. 1999. Processing complexity and filler-gap dependencies across grammars. *Language* 75:244–285.

Hawkins, John A. 2004. *Efficiency and complexity in grammars*. Cambridge: Oxford University Press.

Heestand, Dustin, Ming Xiang, and Maria Polinsky. 2011. Resumption still does not rescue islands. *Linguistic Inquiry* 42(1):138–152.

Hofmeister, Philip. 2011. Representational complexity and memory retrieval in language comprehension. *Language and Cognitive Processes* 26:376–405.

Jaeger, T. Florian. 2006. *Redundancy and Syntactic Reduction in Spontaneous Speech*. Ph.D. thesis, Stanford University.

Jaeger, T. Florian and Hal Tily. 2010. On language 'utility': Processing complexity and communicative efficiency'. *WIRE: Cognitive Science* .

Just, Marcel, Patricia A. Carpenter, and J.D. Woolley. 1982. Paradigms and processes in reading comprehension. *Journal of Experimental Psychology: General* 111(2):228–238.

Keenan, Edward L. and Bernard Comrie. 1977. Noun phrase accessibility and universal grammar. *Linguistic inquiry* 8(1):63–99.

Kluender, Robert and Marta Kutas. 1993. Subjacency as a processing phenomenon. *Language and Cognitive Processes* 8(4):573–633.

Kroch, Anthony S. 1981. On the role of resumptive pronouns in amnestying island constraint violations. In *Proceedings of the Annual Meeting of the Chicago Linguistics Society*, pages 125–135. Chicago Linguistics Society, Chicago.

Krug, Manfred. 1998. String frequency: a cognitive motivating factor in coalescence, language processing and linguistic change. *Journal of English Linguistics* 26:286–320.

McCloskey, James. 2002. Resumption, successive cyclicity, and the locality of operations. In S. D. Epstein and T. D. Seely, eds., *Derivation and Explanation in the Minimalist Program*, pages 184–226. Oxford: Blackwell.

Miller, George A. and Noam Chomsky. 1963. Finitary models of language users. In R. D. Luce, R. R. Bush, and E. Galanter, eds., *Handbook of Mathematical Psychology*, vol. 2, pages 419–492. New York: Wiley.

Pinheiro, Jose C. and Douglas M. Bates. 2000. *Mixed-effects Models in S and S-PLUS*. New York: Springer.

Prince, Ellen. 1990. Syntax and discourse: A look at resumptive pronouns. In *Proceedings of the 16th Annual Meeting of the Berkeley Linguistics Society*, pages 482–497.

Ross, John R. 1967. *Constraints on Variables in Syntax*. Ph.D. thesis, MIT, Cambridge, MA. Published in 1986 as *Infinite Syntax!* by Ablex, Norwood, N. J.

Sanford, Anthony J. and Simon C. Garrod. 1981. *Understanding Written Language*. Chichester, England: Wiley.

Sells, Peter. 1984. Syntax and semantics of resumptive pronouns. *Linguistic Review* 4(3):261–267.

Sells, Peter. 1987. Binding resumptive pronouns. *Linguistics and Philosophy* 10(3):261–298.

Sharvit, Yael. 1999. Resumptive pronouns in relative clauses. *Natural Language and Linguistic Theory* 17(3):587–612.

Sorace, Antonella and Frank Keller. 2005. Gradience in linguistic data. *Lingua* 115(11):1497–1524.

Sprouse, Jon. 2008. The differential sensitivity of acceptability judgments to processing effects. *Linguistic Inquiry* 39(4):686–694.

Staum Casasanto, Laura, Philip Hofmeister, and Ivan A. Sag. 2010. Understanding acceptability judgments: Distinguishing the effects of grammar and processing on acceptability judgments. In S. Ohlsson and R. Catrambone, eds., *Proceedings of the 32nd Annual Conference of the Cognitive Science Society*, pages 224–229. Austin, TX: Cognitive Science Society.

Staum Casasanto, L. and Ivan A. Sag. 2008. The advantage of the ungrammatical. In B. Love, K. McRae, and V. M. Sloutsky, eds., *Proceedings of the 30th Annual Meeting of the Cognitive Science Society*. Austin, TX.

Tily, Harry and Steve Piantadosi. 2009. Refer efficiently: Use less informative expressions for more predictable meanings. In *Proceedings of the Workshop on Production of Referring Expressions, CogSci 2009*.

Vasishth, Shravan, Sven Brüssow, Richard L. Lewis, and Heiner Drenhaus. 2008. Processing polarity: How the ungrammatical intrudes on the grammatical. *Cognitive Science* 32(4):685–712.

Vasishth, Shravan and Richard Lewis. 2006. Argument-head distance and processing complexity: Explaining both locality and anti-locality effects. *Language* 82(3):767–794.

3

Digging Deeper: Experimental Methods in Syntactic Research

PHILIP HOFMEISTER

> I dislike reliance on intuition as much as anyone . . . We should substitute rigorous criteria just as soon as possible, instead of clinging to intuitions. (Chomsky 1962)

> In linguistics, it seems to me that sharpening of the data by more objective tests is a matter of small importance for the problems at hand. One who disagrees with this estimate of the present situation in linguistics can justify his belief in the current importance of more objective operational tests by showing how they can lead to new and deeper understanding of linguistic structure. Perhaps the day will come when the kinds of data that we can now obtain in abundance will be insufficient to resolve deeper questions concerning the structure of language. (Chomsky 1965)

Since these pronouncements were made, many language researchers have heeded their spirit by replacing intuitions with more rigorous forms of data collection. Particularly with the increased ease and cheapness of collecting data from human participants, searching massive language corpora, and applying ready-made statistical solutions, the past 10 years have witnessed a sea change with respect to how syntacticians obtain and use data. Tools such as Mechanical Turk, featured in the following article by Joanna Nykiel, enable researchers to acquire ratings from large numbers of participants — sometimes even in the hundreds — without evaporating their yearly research budget in one fell swoop.

Ivan has been responsible for fostering and collaborating with a generation of researchers at Stanford, including myself, who took Chom-

The Core and the Periphery.
Philip Hofmeister and Elisabeth Norcliffe (eds.).

sky's words seriously in the sense that we thought that the need to adopt rigorous methods for judgment collection was not so much an indictment of previous methods but a means to construct a deeper, more nuanced understanding of syntactic data. For example, grammatical theories that rely on stark contrasts between what's grammatical and what's ungrammatical often overlook intermediate data points or consider such data 'peripheral'. One thing Ivan imparted to us all was that such peripheral data may be of just as much importance, if not more, than the data points which are extreme and obvious.

He also imparted the idea that a syntactician who claims that acceptability differences between members of a minimal pair reflect grammatical principles should have also minimized any other differences. It was Ivan's suggestion that at least some classic, entrenched datasets were suspect in this regard. A graduate seminar in 2004 on *wh*-movement taught by Ivan, in particular, dealt heavily with the case of Superiority and the eponymous Superiority violations (which Ivan dubbed SuVs), as seen in the examples below:

(1) Who used what?

(2) What did who use?

On standard transformational accounts, movement constraints prohibited one *wh*-phrase from 'hopping' over another and thus ruled out examples like (1). But several observations emerged in Ivan's seminar: first, examples like (2) could be made substantially better as noted elsewhere (Karttunen 1977; Bolinger 1978; Pesetsky 1987, 2000); second, even the purportedly most odious type of example, as in (2), were not difficult to find in corpora and edited documents online. At the same time, the literature on the topic was a virtual zoo of diacritics, including #, ?, ??, and $*$. This led our group to try and pin down what the relevant data were. In doing so, it became clear that there were some robust patterns with respect to SuVs: a *which*-N phrase in either the subject or object position bumped acceptability ratings higher, and the most acceptable configuration involved two *which*-N phrases, as opposed to bare *wh*-items. This additivity of effects, interestingly, did not seem to follow from any proposed grammatical principles, but was easily explicable in terms of combining processing factors.

These initial observations sparked an exciting and productive research atmosphere, where we sought to substantiate or de-substantiate, as it were, various entrenched datasets. Soon, we widened the net to reconsider other movement constraints, particularly the class of movement constraints known as syntactic island constraints. These configurational constraints are particularly noteworthy because they are a poster child for Universal Grammar: they are attested across many languages, children receive no instruction to avoid violating them, and they were, in some sense, arbitrary, i.e. other complex syntactic environments that give rise to severe unacceptability are not saddled with the same distinction.

As Ivan, Neal Snider, and myself soon discovered, these island constructions were also rife with features that gave rise to processing difficulty. Besides the long-distance dependencies that necessarily occur, standard examples in the literature often co-occur with embedded clauses, odd pragmatic import, possibilities for garden-pathing, and syntactic features that give rise to similarity-based interference. Each one of these on its own might be considered a minor inconvenience, but when multiple such factors combine, they conspire to drastically reduce the acceptability of islands. The magnitude of the difference is evident in the following two examples, both of which violate the so-called Wh-Island Constraint:

(3) What did John wonder whether Mary bought?

(4) Adoption is something you should consider whether you are willing to commit to.

Most readers will find the first example atrocious, yet read (4) in an appropriate context without thinking twice. The latter example avoids the decontextualized question in (3), uses a single referring expression, *you*, in between the filler, *Adoption*, and the subcategorizing verb, has a plausible meaning, and requires little to no context to understand why someone might say or write such a thing. This kind of data, as well as reading time data showing that island-violating sentences could be simultaneously made substantially easier to process and more acceptable, caused us to question the necessity of many kinds of islands constraints entirely.

One of the offshoots of this enterprise was my own dissertation where I investigated how properties of filler-phrases affected dependency processing in English (Hofmeister 2007). Directly building off my collaboration with Ivan, I found that the effects of *wh*-complexity (how many syntactic and semantic features contained in *wh*-expression) were not specific to island contexts or any other purportedly ungrammatical environment. In fact, it wasn't even something specific to *wh*-phrases. Even in perfectly grammatical, relatively simple syntactic environments, the reading time data suggested that dependencies are easier to process as the syntactic and/or semantic complexity of the filler increases (up to some unknown limit).

(5) a. It was a communist that members of the club banned from ever entering the premises.
b. It was an alleged communist that members of the club banned from ever entering the premises.
c. It was an alleged, Venezuelan communist that members of the club banned from ever entering the premises.

At the word 'banned' in the above examples, reading times were increasingly faster as the complexity of the indefinite, clefted NP increased. As these facilitatory effects of filler complexity emerged only (and not before) putative retrieval sites in long-distance dependencies, it was evident that these were essentially retrieval effects. In turn, the effects observable in island contexts appeared to be independent of any peculiarities of islands themselves.

Joanna's chapter represents yet another grandchild of Ivan's ideas, as she has explored how patterns of acceptability in sluicing constructions depend on interactions involving the complexity of correlates and remnants. This is exactly the sort of work that encapsulates the general ethos that Ivan has championed: syntactic effects potentially represent the interaction of multiple linguistic factors. In short, Ivan, more than any other linguist I know, embraces the view that the constellation of linguistic phenomena we observe reflect the interaction of principles of language along multiple dimensions.

References

Bolinger, Dwight. 1978. Asking more than one thing at a time. In H. Hiz, ed., *Questions*, pages 107–150. Dordrecht: D. Reidel.

Chomsky, Noam. 1962. The logical basis of linguistic theory. In M. Halle, ed., *Preprints of the Papers for the Ninth International Congress of Linguists, August 27–31, 1962*, pages 509–574.

Chomsky, Noam. 1965. *Aspects of the Theory of Syntax*. Cambridge, MA: MIT Press.

Hofmeister, Philip. 2007. *Representational Complexity and Memory Retrieval in Language Comprehension*. Ph.D. thesis, Stanford University, Stanford, CA.

Karttunen, Lauri. 1977. Syntax and semantics of questions. *Linguistics & Philosophy* 1:3–44.

Pesetsky, David. 1987. *Wh*-in-situ: movement and unselective binding. In E. Reuland and A. ter Meulen, eds., *The Representation of (In)Definiteness*, pages 98–129. Cambridge: MIT Press.

Pesetsky, David. 2000. *Phrasal Movement and its Kin*. Cambridge: MIT Press.

8

Wh-phrases in Sluicing: An Interaction of the Remnant and the Antecedent

JOANNA NYKIEL

1 Introduction

A much-discussed finding in the sentence processing literature is the difference in acceptability produced by using two different types of *wh*-phrases in English multiple *wh*-questions. Multiple *wh*-questions are known to obey the Superiority Condition, as stated in (1) (Chomsky 1973).

(1) No rule can involve X, Y in the structure:

$$\ldots X \ldots [_{\alpha} \ldots \quad Z \ldots \ -WYV \ \ldots]$$

where the rule applies ambiguously to Z and Y and Z is superior to [m-commands] Y.

This condition is violated in (2), but not in (3), if the interrogative pronouns are bare *wh*-phrases.

(2) *What does who carry?

(3) Who carries what?

However, *which*-NP phrases used in place of bare *wh*-phrases improve the acceptability of (2), as shown in (4) (Karttunen 1977; Maling and Zaenen 1982; Culicover and Wilkins 1984; Pesetsky 1987, 2000).

The Core and the Periphery.
Philip Hofmeister and Elisabeth Norcliffe (eds.).

(4) Which brand does which store carry?

As a way of capturing this pattern, Pesetsky (1987, 2000) proposes that *which*-NP phrases are D(iscourse)-linked phrases, and that this property allows them to escape the Superiority Condition. *Wh*-phrases are interpreted as D-linked if their referents belong in a set that either has been previously mentioned in the discourse, and hence, consists of entities familiar to the speaker and hearer, or a set that is salient in the speaker and hearer's mind. The property of D-linking is thus mediated by the discourse context.

The same two types of *wh*-phrases (*which*-NP phrases vs bare *wh*-phrases) are also used in the elliptical construction sluicing, which is the focus of this paper, but before discussing this, I walk the reader through the relevant issues addressed in connection with *wh*-interrogatives.

An alternative explanation for the ability of *which*-NP phrases to escape the Superiority Condition is offered in Hofmeister 2007, 2011, Hofmeister and Sag 2010, Hofmeister et al. 2007, and Hofmeister et al. 2013. Given that *wh*-phrases and their retrieval sites are separated from each other by some distance, the retrieval process operates over strings of phrases such that *wh*-phrases are first processed and then re-accessed at the retrieval sites. In this context, the advantage associated with *which*-NP phrases is attributed to their linguistic complexity. That is, *which*-NP phrases encode more unique semantic and syntactic features than do bare *wh*-phrases, which makes them more complex than bare *wh*-phrases. The more complex a *wh*-phrase is, the easier it is to retrieve from memory, because it has a strong and accessible mental representation. Hence, given multiple candidates for retrieval present in the type of question discussed here, *which*-NP phrases facilitate retrieval by bearing distinct features. This proposal is based on the idea that the ease of retrieving a phrase is a function of the distinctness of that phrase with respect to other candidates for retrieval (Criss and McClelland 2006; Ericsson and Kintsch 1995; Nairne 1990, 2001, 2006). A phrase with distinct semantic and syntactic features is less likely to be confused with other candidates, while a less distinct phrase is vulnerable to interference from other candidates.

Also known from the memory retrieval literature is an advantage associated with representations that have been processed at a deeper level. A deep level of processing of a phrase involves 'semantic or cognitive analysis', which ensures a strong and long-lasting representation for that phrase (Craik and Lockhart 1972). A similar argument is voiced by Anderson et al. (2001), Lewis and Vasishth (2005), Vasishth and Lewis (2006), and Hofmeister et al. (2007). Mental representations that are subject to extensive syntactic and semantic processing receive an activation boost, such that they remain salient and accessible for future retrieval. Hofmeister et al. (2007) argue in particular that *which*-NP phrases require a greater level of processing than do bare *wh*-phrases, which leads to their accessibility in terms of retrieval.

Overall, the processing alternative to Pesetsky's (1987, 2000) proposal points to variables involved in memory retrieval in accounting for the behavior of *wh*-phrases. Those *wh*-phrases that alleviate violations of the Superiority Condition do so because they are easier to retrieve from memory. However, Frazier and Clifton (2011) argue that this approach is insufficient to fully explain the behavior of *which*-NP phrases. In support of their argument, Frazier and Clifton present acceptability judgment data, where *which*-NP phrases served as sluicing remnants and were rated significantly better than bare *wh*-phrases serving as sluicing remnants in the control condition.

Sluicing is a construction where a *wh*-phrase (a remnant) is left stranded and has an overt correlate in the antecedent (Ross 1969). An interpretation for the remnant is retrieved based on the surrounding context. In contrast to *wh*-questions, sluicing does not require comprehenders to access representations created for *wh*-phrases in past language processing, because *wh*-phrases are processed in situ. Sample experimental items used by Frazier and Clifton are given in (5)–(6). The two kinds of *wh*-phrases were paired with the same NP correlate (*a new vehicle*), and hence, only the *wh*-phrases varied in the items.

(5) Britney likes this guy who destroyed a new vehicle, but she didn't reveal what.

(6) Britney likes this guy who destroyed a new vehicle, but she didn't reveal which vehicle.[1]

Frazier and Clifton point out that higher ratings for *which*-NP phrases are inconsistent with the processing account to the extent that *wh*-phrases are not dislocated under sluicing, and hence, are not retrieved from memory after intervening material has been processed. Therefore, it seems plausible that *which*-NP phrases are not merely easier to process, but 'may immediately receive a discourse representation in addition to their syntactic representation' (Frazier and Clifton 2011, 46). That is, as soon as a *which*-NP phrase is processed, it becomes associated with a discourse referent. Being represented this way allows

[1] The remnant here is a *which*-NP phrase with the overt head noun (*vehicle*), but Frazier and Clifton (2011) also tested remnants whose head nouns were replaced with the pronoun *one*, and found an unreliable difference between the two types of *wh*-remnants.

which-NP phrases to remain active longer than bare *wh*-phrases, which receive only syntactic representations. This proposal builds directly on Pesetsky's distinction between D-linked and non-D-linked *wh*-phrases.

In this paper, I offer experimental evidence that what sluicing shows us about *wh*-phrases cannot be interpreted as relating to these phrases alone, but rather as relating to an interaction of *wh*-phrases with their antecedents. *Wh*-phrases themselves are not targets of the retrieval process, but their function is instead to provide retrieval cues for the antecedents. On this assumption, the syntactic and semantic properties of *wh*-phrases are likely to be mediated by the properties of the antecedents. That is, the specificity of the cues provided by *wh*-phrases should depend on how much linguistic information is required to point to the correct antecedent. The notion of linguistic complexity proposed in Hofmeister (2009, 2011) leads us to expect that *which*-NP phrases and bare *wh*-phrases differ in the specificity of semantic and syntactic information that they encode. Intuition suggests that this difference is exploited in sluicing as a means of varying the amount of retrieval cues at the ellipsis site, without offering any insight, at least not unambiguously so, into the role played by *which*-NP phrases (as opposed to bare *wh*-phrases) in isolation from their antecedents.

The paper is organized as follows. The next section overviews memory operations involved in the retrieval of linguistic material, and in particular, in the retrieval of antecedents for sluicing remnants. §3 reports data from an experimental study of speakers' preferences for two types of sluicing remnants, given particular antecedents. §4 first explores how the findings fit in with research on sentence processing and on complexity-based effects present in retrieval of linguistic signs from memory. §5 concludes.

2 A direct-access mechanism

Language processing often requires that dependencies among various nonadjacent constituents be established as discourse evolves. To establish such dependencies comprehenders must re-access items they have previously processed. Crucial to this process is the manner in which such items are re-accessed, which can be either a sequential search (backward or forward) through memory representations or a direct-access mechanism that locates the target without a search. The latter mechanism is argued to be employed in the resolution of sluicing and Verb Phrase Ellipsis (*Kelly had a wardrobe malfunction, and Kate did too*) (Martin and McElree 2008, 2009, 2011), and filler-gap dependencies, such as clefts (*It was a wardrobe malfunction that Kelly had*)

(McElree 2000; McElree et al. 2003).

The direct-access mechanism is understood as having the property that constituents, whether dislocated phrases or ellipsis remnants, to be integrated into the evolving discourse provide retrieval cues to memory representations that must be re-accessed for the integration to succeed. Retrieval cues in turn point to memory representations needed in this process, and hence, provide direct access to them (McElree 2000, 2006; Van Dyke and McElree 2006; Martin and McElree 2008). McElree (2006) notes that this manner of accessing previously processed items in memory generalizes well beyond the resolution of elliptical constructions and filler-gap dependencies and to retrieval of representations form both short- and long-term memories.

If retrieval of items from memory proceeds this way, it should exhibit interference effects. That is, cues provided at retrieval can become less diagnostic of the target if several items sharing properties similar to the cues have been processed in between the target and the retrieval site. This may have the consequence that it is impossible to reliably discriminate the target from the other items, a phenomenon called cue-overload (Anderson and Neely 1996; Watkins and Watkins 1975, 1976). Indeed, Van Dyke et al. (2006) found that this is the case in sentence processing. In particular, they demonstrate that interference effects occur at exactly the point that previously stored representations are retrieved from memory.

The nature of interference effects is such that the likelihood of retrieving a representation stored in memory is affected by the degree of similarity between the target representation and the retrieval cues for it in context. That is, the proportion of features that the retrieval cues share with the target is assessed relative to the proportion of features that the retrieval cues share with possible non-target representations (Gillund and Shiffrin 1984; Nairne 1990, 2001, 2006). A match between the retrieval cues and the target does not increase the probability that the target will be retrieved, if other candidates for retrieval also exhibit similarity to the retrieval cues.

However, a target representation sharing linguistic features with retrieval cues for it is associated with some advantages, whether or not interference effects are present. Almor (1999), for example, points out that the capacity of working memory is such that the increasing distance between an anaphor and its antecedent leads to a decay of the mental representation of the antecedent. This decay has the consequence that more features are required to be shared between the anaphor and the antecedent for successful resolution. At the same time that overlapping features help overcome the difficulty of recovering the antecedent, there is a processing cost associated with processing a maximally explicit anaphor. This is because working memory resources must be channeled into simultaneously maintaining representations for all relevant referents, processing the anaphor in question, and recovering its antecedent, a task that places a burden on the capacity of working memory (Almor 1999). Hence, maximal overlap between an anaphor and its antecedent is not always beneficial from the processing perspective.

The relationship between an anaphor (an NP anaphor, but not a *wh*-remnant) and antecedent is given a formal characterization in terms of informational load by Almor (1999). Simply put, if a single antecedent is paired with two different anaphors, the anaphor that is more general (that is, has a less specific semantic representation, and hence is less complex in the sense of Hofmeister 2007, 2011) with respect to the antecedent produces a less informationally loaded anaphor-antecedent pair.[2] To illustrate, consider an example from Almor (1999). Pairing the antecedent *a robin* with the anaphor *the bird* produces a less informationally loaded pair than the same antecedent and the anaphor *the crippled robin.* Note that *the bird* has a less specific semantic representation with respect to the antecedent than *the crippled robin.* If a repetitive anaphor (*the robin*) was used with this antecedent, it would produce a more informationally loaded pair (due to the anaphor's level of specificity) than *a robin* and *the bird*, but a less informationally loaded one than *a robin* and *the crippled robin.* Based on these types of semantic relationship, Almor (1999) argues that in general the less informationally loaded an anaphor-antecedent pair is, the easier it is to process it. Anaphor-antecedent pairs with high informational load are associated with a high processing cost that may be alleviated if the antecedent is not focused, and hence hard to recover.[3]

The research on interference effects and informational load makes predictions about the behavior of *wh*-phrases in sluicing that are not borne out by the results of Frazier and Clifton's (2011) study. In sluicing, retrieval cues are provided by *wh*-phrases, and target representations that must be retrieved based on these cues are the correlates of *wh*-phrases (hosted by the antecedents). The remnant and the target

[2] This reasoning is based on the semantic distance between the anaphor and antecedent as affected by the level of specificity of each. For more information, see Almor (1999).

[3] Almor (1999) discusses the processing of anaphor-antecedent pairs as an interaction of informational load, discourse focus of the antecedent, and whether or not anaphors add new information. Since sluicing remnants do not normally add new information, I do not address this factor in this paper. I do, however, address the discourse focus of correlates for sluicing remnants.

candidate for retrieval in (6), repeated here for convenience as (7a), share phonological, syntactic, and semantic features. On the phonological level, the noun *vehicle* appears in both the *which*-NP remnant and the correlate NP. Both the remnant and the correlate overlap in terms of syntactic category (NP), and both exhibit the semantic features [–animate] and [–abstract]. Finally, the correlate presupposes the existence of a set of new vehicles rather than an individual or singleton set, and the remnant picks out an element from that set.

Note that another potential candidate for retrieval in (7a) is the larger NP *this guy who destroyed a new vehicle*. The match between the remnant *which vehicle* and the correlate *a new vehicle*, compared to the match between *what* and *a new vehicle* (see 7b), is expected to exert a beneficial effect on the probability of retrieving the correlate: the correlate should be protected from interference from the other candidate, the larger NP.

(7) a. Britney likes this guy who destroyed a new vehicle, but she didn't reveal which vehicle.
   b. Britney likes this guy who destroyed a new vehicle, but she didn't reveal what.

The bare *wh*-phrase (*what*) in (7b) only carries animacy information as a means to discriminate the correlate from the distractor, without overlapping with the correlate in terms of phonology or syntactic category. It is easy to see that the correlate in (7b) would not be protected from interference effects if it shared more features with the distractor. Consider (8), where *this car park set* and *a new vehicle* are both inanimate, and hence, the retrieval cues provided by the remnant *what* would have little ability to correctly pick out the target phrase.

(8) Britney likes this car park set that has a new vehicle, but she didn't reveal what.

It is an environment of this kind that should cause speakers to prefer *which*-NP remnants (which overlap with the correlate in terms of more features) over bare *wh*-remnants.

Frazier and Jr. 2011 did not control for the number of candidates for retrieval in their experimental items (see their Appendix). In eight out of sixteen items, only the target phrase was an adequate candidate for retrieval, the other candidates being proper names serving as subjects NPs, and hence, not fully consistent with a sluicing interpretation. In the remaining items, at least one other NP besides the subject appeared in the antecedent clause. Further, for all items except two, the target phrase appeared as the rightmost NP in the antecedent clause.

This position imparts to the target phrase the status of a focused constituent and makes it quite likely to be selected as the correlate (Carlson et al. 2009). The rightmost constituents in the clause are the default location of informational focus in English. Carlson et al. (2009) show that English speakers have a strong tendency to select the syntactically lowest NP in the clause as the correlate for a sluicing remnant. If this is so, then the correlates occurring late in the clause in Frazier and Clifton's (2011) data do not appear to be subject to much interference from non-target phrases. Nor should they require that many retrieval cues be provided by the remnants on Almor's (1999) analysis (Recall that focused antecedents are not paired with explicit anaphors). The significant preference for (7a) over (7b) is thus unexpected.

This preference is even more unexpected, given Almor's (1999) characterization of the relationships between anaphors and antecedents. The remnant *what* in (7b), by only encoding animacy information, has a less specific semantic representation with respect to the correlate than does the remnant *which vehicle* in (7a), which should make the former correlate-remnant pair less informationally loaded, and hence, more preferred.

I suggest that Frazier and Clifton's (2011) data reflect a conventionalized preference for sluicing remnants to maximally overlap with their correlates, a pattern much unlike that found in NP anaphors discussed by Almor (1999). That is, remnants tend to have semantic representations that are exactly as specific as those of their correlates. As a means to quantify overlap, I make reference to the linguistic complexity of a phrase, and hence, following Hofmeister (2007, 2011), to the linguistic features encoded by it. Degrees of overlap between a remnant and its correlate can then be measured in terms of how many features encoded by the correlate are matched by the features encoded by the remnant.

It is possible to manipulate the complexity of correlates for sluicing remnants, because either indefinite pronouns or NPs may serve as correlates. On Hofmeister's (2009, 2010) definition of complexity, indefinite pronouns are less complex than NPs in that they only encode animacy information. Differences in complexity produce four possible configurations in which sluicing remnants may appear. These are shown in (9)–(12).

(9) Britney likes this guy who destroyed a new vehicle, but she didn't reveal which vehicle.

(10) Britney likes this guy who destroyed a new vehicle, but she didn't reveal what.

(11) Britney likes this guy who destroyed something, but she didn't reveal what.

(12) Britney likes this guy who destroyed something, but she didn't reveal which vehicle.

Examples (9) and (11) instantiate maximal overlap, such that the correlates delineate sets of entities, more specific in (9) than in (11), which the remnants point to by providing retrieval cues that match all the properties of these sets that can be matched. The correlate and remnant in (9) are equally complex: all the phonological, syntactic, and semantic features expressed by the correlate are also marked on the remnant. The correlate and remnant in (11) are also equally complex, though they share fewer features overall (only animacy and syntactic category). Note that it is impossible for the remnant in (11) to share phonological features with the correlate.

Examples (10) and (12) instantiate partial overlap. The remnant in (10) is less specific and less complex than its correlate. That is, it provides fewer cues than are licensed by the correlate (only the animacy feature is shared between them). In example (12), the reverse is the case: the remnant is more specific and more complex than the correlate (and again, only the animacy feature is shared).

It appears that for the partially overlapping cases, (12) is less natural than (10) despite the fact that a *which*-NP remnant is used in (10). This pattern falls out straightforwardly from Almor's (1999) analysis of NP anaphors. The *which*-NP remnant in (12) is more specific than its correlate, and hence the informational load of this pair is the highest of all four pairs shown in (9)–(12). This is unjustified, given that the correlate appears clause-finally in the antecedent, bearing informational focus.

Given that Almor's (1999) analysis of NP anaphors does not predict the pattern observed in Frazier and Clifton's (2011) study, and so seems inconsistent with the behavior of sluicing, one might suggest that a *which*-NP phrase is not licensed in (12) for another reason. This is because no specific set of familiar entities is provided by the antecedent. However, there is experimental evidence that an appropriate discourse context (recall the definition of D-linking) is not required for *which*-NP phrases to be rated better than bare *wh*-phrases. For example, Fedorenko and Gibson (Forthcoming) report higher acceptability ratings for multiple interrogatives with *which*-NP phrases with or without an appropriate context (see Frazier and Clifton 2011 for some discussion). It is thus unclear that the absence of an appropriate context in (12) necessarily results in a failure to compute a coherent representation for the sluicing remnant.

While accepting Almor's analysis, we might consider another dimension of the unnaturalness of (12). The remnant provides retrieval cues that are too specific, reducing the overlap between it and the correlate, and doing so in a context where the accessibility of the correlate is already lower than the accessibility of an NP correlate would be. The research of Hofmeister (2009, 2011) leads us to expect that the properties of the correlate itself influence the ease of retrieving it. More linguistically complex correlates should receive mental representations that remain accessible in memory longer than representations created for less complex correlates. This should have the effect that even if few retrieval cues are provided for a complex correlate, it can still be adequately retrieved. Less complex correlates, however, should be harder to retrieve in the event that few retrieval cues are provided by remnants.

Reduced overlap between the remnant and correlate is also observed in (10): the remnant provides less specific retrieval cues than are licensed by the correlate, which is, however, a complex and accessible phrase. Thus examples (10) and (12) differ in terms of the complexity of the correlates, suggesting that the degradation of (12) is at least partly attributable to the low complexity of the correlate. The apparent degradation of (12) might be linked to the difficulty of retrieving the correlate due to both its low accessibility in memory and the high informational load of this correlate-remnant pair.

The present paper addresses two questions related to the view that a direct access mechanism is involved in the resolution of sluicing. The first question is whether maximal overlap between correlate and remnant (sentences like (9) and (11)) is better than partial overlap (sentences like (10) and (12)) regardless of the type of *wh*-phrase used and even if interference effects are unlikely. Frazier and Clifton's (2011) results suggest that maximal overlap might indeed be the preferred option in sluicing. Second, the paper asks if sentences like (10) are preferred over sentences like (12). These questions are taken up in the experiment presented in the next section.

3 Experiment

The experiment explored to what extent the use of *wh*-phrases as sluicing remnants is sensitive to two types of phrases serving as correlates, given a direct-access mechanism. I varied the complexity of sluicing remnants and their correlates as a means to investigate whether maximally overlapping features are the preferred pattern even if the correlates are protected from interference from potential distractors. Toward this end, I used antecedent clauses with only one NP other than the subject. This NP always appeared clause-finally, which made it a salient candidate for retrieval at the ellipsis site (as predicted by Carlson et al. 2009). This design permitted a direct insight into whether *which*-NP phrases serve as better sluicing remnants than bare *wh*-phrases independently of the complexity of the correlates, which is a prediction of Frazier and Clifton's (2011) proposal.

The experimental data were collected via Amazon's Mechanical Turk, a marketplace interface allowing workers to perform various tasks in return for payment. This method of collecting data is quicker and less expensive than more traditional methods, such as acceptability judgments collected in a laboratory setting, and its results are comparable to those collected in a laboratory setting (Munro et al. 2010; Cable and Harris 2011; Gibson et al. 2011; Sprouse 2011).

As a means of minimizing the risk that non-native speakers of English took part in the experiment, I followed two procedures. I set a requirement that all participants have US IP addresses. Before completing the experiment participants were asked to answer two comprehension questions about sentences containing appositives, taken from Harris and Potts (2009).[4] Incorrect answers to one or both of these questions, which non-native speakers find difficult to interpret, led to exclusion of that participant's data.

3.1 Participants

120 self reported native speakers of English participated in the experiment.

3.2 Materials and procedures

The materials for this experiment consisted of 12 items, which were pairs of antecedent clauses, each with two possible continuations hosting *wh*-remnants. I followed a 2 × 2 design, crossing Type of correlate with Type of *wh*-remnant. A sample experimental item is shown in (13). The full set of materials is found in Appendix 1.

(13) a. Nick got attacked by a customer, but
A1: he couldn't tell who.
B1: he couldn't tell which customer.

b. Nick got attacked by someone, but
A2: he couldn't tell which customer.
B2: he couldn't tell who.

[4]This strategy was employed by Cable and Harris (2011) in their study conducted via Amazon's Mechanical Turk in order to guard against participants falsely reporting English as their first language.

The B-continuations represent maximal overlap between the correlate and remnant, and the A-continuations represent partial overlap.

Participants were asked to provide judgments of naturalness about the experimental items in a 100-split task (see Bresnan and Ford 2010). They were asked to consider two continuations of a clause and assign to both a number of points that reflected their assessment of how natural the continuations were, given the context. All points summed to 100, but any combination was allowed, for example, 21 and 79, or 60 and 40. I then recoded these points as the proportion of time that either type of *wh*-remnant was preferred over the other. Scores higher than 50 were coded as expressing a preference for the given continuation; scores of 50 and less were coded as expressing no preference for the continuation.

Each participant saw no more than two antecedent clauses (from two different items, selected randomly), one with a pronominal correlate and the other with an NP one, followed by two continuations. These clauses were interspersed with 15 fillers from an unrelated experiment.

Twelve tasks were uploaded on Amazon's Mechanical Turk in total, corresponding to the 12 experimental items. All participants who completed more than one task were removed from the dataset. Also removed from the dataset were participants whose total time spent on an item exceeded 2.5 standard deviations of the mean. This resulted in the loss of 3% of the data. The remaining data are shown in Fig. 1. The proportion of time that the two types of remnants were preferred is shown here as the function of the correlate used in the antecedent clause.

The data were analyzed by fitting mixed-effects linear regression models to them, with participants and items as random effects (see Baayen 2008). The type of correlate and the type of *wh*-phrase were entered as fixed effects in the model.

3.3 Results

The main effect of Type of *wh*-remnant was observed. *Which*-NP phrases were preferred significantly less often than bare *wh*-phrases across both types of correlate ($t = -17.74$; $p < .00001$). This main effect entered into a significant interaction with Type of correlate such that *which*-NP phrases were preferred more often than bare *wh*-phrases if NPs served as correlates ($t = 15.03$; $p < .00001$). Additional analysis revealed that in contrast to NP correlates, pronominal correlates caused *which*-NP phrases to be preferred significantly less often than bare *wh*-phrases ($t = -29.07$; $p < .00001$).

To further probe the nature of these effects, I conducted pairwise comparisons. Bare *wh*-phrases were preferred 94.2% of the time when paired with pronominal correlates and only 36.7 % of the time when paired with NP correlates, a difference that was significant ($t = 9.18$; $p < .0001$). Another significant difference was produced by *which*-NP phrases being preferred 54.2% of the time if they had NP correlates and 5.8% of the time if they had pronominal correlates ($t = 8.08$; $p < .0001$). The proportion of time that *which*-NP phrases with pronominal correlates were preferred also differed significantly from the proportion of time that bare *wh*-phrases with NP correlates were preferred ($t = 5.33$; $p < .0001$).

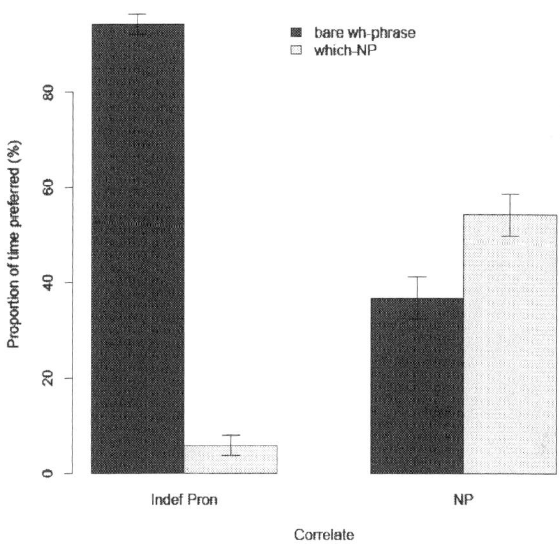

FIGURE 1 Average preference by correlate type (indefinite pronoun vs. NP) and remnant complexity

These results support the assumption that maximal overlap in terms of linguistic features between a remnant and correlate is better than partial overlap across both types of *wh*-phrases. Hence, this preference is not driven by the presence of *which*-NP phrases, and cannot be accounted for by Frazier and Clifton's (2011) proposal. Further, the results align with the intuition articulated in §2 that among the two configurations representing partial overlap, bare *wh*-phrases are better remnants when paired with NP correlates than are *which*-NP phrases when paired with pronominal correlates. This finding is consistent with Almor's (1999) account of NP anaphors. However, the overall degradation of partial overlap with respect to maximal overlap calls for another explanation than Almor's.

4 General discussion

The results of the experiment provide clear answers to the question of whether a sluicing remnant enters into an interaction with its correlate. The nature of this interaction is such that the degree of match between the phonological, syntactic, and semantic features of the remnant and the features of the correlate affects speakers' preferences regarding the remnant. Specifically, a finding to be gleaned from the current data is that remnants with properties matching those of their correlates are preferred regardless of the type of *wh*-phrase used.

This finding is of theoretical interest as the number of possible distractors is held constant across the conditions in the current experiment, making interference effects an unlikely explanation. Recall that all correlates were the final NPs in their clauses (and the only NPs other than the subjects), and hence, salient candidates for retrieval. In trying to account for this finding, it is instructive to take another look at Frazier and Clifton's (2011) proposal.

The key point in the proposal is that *which*-NP phrases are better sluicing remnants than bare *wh*-phrases simply by virtue of receiving both a syntactic representation and an immediate discourse representation.[5] However, it seems incorrect to assume that bare *wh*-phrases always differ from *which*-NP phrases in terms of how they are represented. Romero (1998, 47) argues that a bare *wh*-remnant inherits its semantic content from the correlate in contexts like that illustrated in example (14), which corresponds to (10).

(14) I know she talked to some students, but I don't know who.

[5] Frazier and Clifton (2011: 43) consider in passing the possibility that *which*-NP phrases provide more specific retrieval cues than bare *wh*-phrases, suggesting that the retrieval of the correlate is easier with the former. They tested this possibility by replacing the head nouns in *which*-NP phrases with the pronoun *one*. This manipulation reduced the number of retrieval cues provided by the remnants. The manipulation did not lead to any significant differences in the results, which Frazier and Clifton took to mean that the advantage associated with *which*-NP phrases is not merely due to the quality of the retrieval cues they provide. This result is surprising because interference effects seem unlikely in these data, and because the pronoun one reduces the overlap between the remnant and an NP correlate to syntactic and semantic features. Hence, a *which one* remnant should be preferred as producing the less informationally loaded pair than a *which*-NP remnant and an NP correlate. I leave this issue open in this paper, although it is possible that the surprising result was due to Frazier and Clifton's (2011) failure to fully control for interference effects.

Since the correlate is a set of students, the remnant *who* can only be interpreted as also referring to a set of students, and not to an individual or a set of people in general, which would be its usual semantic content. On this view, the semantic content of *who* consists of the same set of individuals as the semantic content of a *which*-NP remnant (e.g. *which students*), which means that both remnants receive the same representations.

One plausible difference between a bare *wh*-remnant and a *which*-NP remnant in a context like (14) is that the former inherits semantic content rather than receive it by default, which incurs a processing cost. The current data strongly suggest that this cost outweighs the advantage associated with the low informational load of anaphors that are less complex than the antecedents with which they are paired. The data also indicate that inheriting semantic content from the correlate is a more costly operation than processing a remnant whose complexity maximally overlaps with the complexity of the correlate. Based on this evidence, I propose that the bias toward maximal overlap in this case (pairing an NP correlate and a *which*-NP remnant) is a conventionalized performance preference (in the sense of Hawkins 2004) shaped by the difficulty of processing the two types of *wh*-remnants, given an NP antecedent. Although maximal overlap is not necessary for retrieving a focused NP correlate, the alternative remnant – a bare *wh*-phrase – requires that additional working memory resources be spent on providing it with the correct semantic content. This preference should be observed cross-linguistically if the relevant types of *wh*-phrases are available in sluicing.

Also conventionalized is the preference for the other type of maximal overlap. Speakers strongly prefer pronominal correlates paired with bare *wh*-remnants as opposed to *which*-NP remnants. This preference aligns well with Almor's conclusion that processing an anaphor whose complexity is greater than the complexity of its antecedent is costly due to the high informational load of the pair. Almor shows that processing an anaphor whose complexity maximally overlaps with that of the antecedent is less costly, and the results of the current experiment provide further empirical support for this position. Notice also that given pronominal correlates, maximal overlap is the least costly option, because a *wh*-remnant whose complexity is lower than the complexity of an indefinite pronoun is unavailable in English.

Turning to the question of whether one type of partial overlap is better than the other, we find strong evidence for a one-way direction of partial overlap. The preferred pattern is for bare *wh*-phrases to serve as remnants for NP correlates but not for *which*-NP phrases to serve as remnants for pronominal correlates. This pattern is as expected on Almor's analysis, but it may also be attributed to the fact that an NP correlate has a more accessible mental representation in working memory than an indefinite pronoun. The job of retrieving an NP correlate could then be easier despite the cost of processing a bare *wh*-remnant.

Of particular interest here is the finding that *which*-NP phrases lack any inherent properties that would make them better sluicing remnants than bare *wh*-phrases in absolute terms. Both types of phrases exhibit variable behavior relative to the type of correlate that they serve to retrieve. Their linguistic features fall short of accounting for this behavior unless they are considered together with the features of the correlates. This behavior clearly differs from the behavior of *wh*-phrases in interrogative clauses, which are themselves targets for retrieval.

As we have seen, *wh*-remnants also differ from NP anaphors. While NP anaphors show a bias toward anaphor-antecedent pairs with low informational load, *wh*-remnants favor maximally overlapping pairs. The least informationally loaded pairs representing partial overlap (NP correlates and bare *wh*-remnants) are dispreferred compared to pairs with higher informational load representing maximal overlap (NP correlates and *which*-NP remnants). This contrast is attributable to the features of *wh*-phrases in context, but not to independent differences in their syntactic and discourse representations.

Additional work is needed to explore the cost of processing pairs of correlates and remnants that differ in the number of overlapping features. The current results lead one to expect that an eye movement study of sluicing, for example, should reveal that maximal overlap in features is read faster than partial overlap. There should also be an observable difference reflecting the contrast between a *which*-NP remnant paired with a pronominal correlate and a bare *wh*-remnant paired with an NP correlate.

5 Conclusion

I have offered experimental data as evidence that sluicing remnants enter into an interaction with their correlates. This interaction manifested itself as differential preferences for particular remnants relative to the complexity of their correlates. A remnant and its correlate can overlap maximally or partially in terms of phonological, syntactic, and semantic features. Maximal overlap involves either an NP correlate and a *which*-NP remnant or an indefinite pronoun correlate and a bare *wh*-remnant. Partial overlap involves either an indefinite pronoun correlate and a *which*-NP remnant or an NP correlate with a bare *wh*-remnant.

The data revealed a bias toward maximal overlap over partial overlap, and this bias did not depend on the type of *wh*-remnant (*which*-NP phrase vs bare *wh*-phrase). As for partial overlap, NP correlates paired with bare *wh*-remnants were preferred over indefinite pronoun correlates paired with *which*-NP remnants. I have attributed these patterns to the function of *wh*-remnants as retrieval cues for their correlates and to the semantic content of *wh*-remnants in context.

6 Appendix: Experimental materials

1. Jani's driveway was blocked with something, but
   A: I don't know which boulder. B: I don't know what.

   Jani's driveway was blocked with a boulder, but
   A: I don't know which boulder. B: I don't know what.
2. Kelly is moving in with someone, but
   A: she didn't say who. B: she didn't say which friend.

   Kelly is moving in with a friend, but
   A: she didn't say who. B: she didn't say which friend.
3. Danny has heard from someone, but
   A: we don't know who. B: we don't know which reporter.

   Danny has heard from a reporter, but
   A: we don't know who. B: we don't know which reporter.
4. The little girl was singing for someone, but
   A: she didn't say which aliens. B: she didn't say who.

   The little girl was singing for some aliens, but
   A: she didn't say which aliens. B: she didn't say who.
5. These people are suffering from something, but
   A: it's hard to say which chemicals. B: it's hard to say what.

   These people are suffering from some chemicals, but
   A: it's hard to say which chemicals. B: it's hard to say what.
6. Fred needs to be protected against somebody, but
   A: he won't say who. B: A: he won't say which criminals.

   Fred needs to be protected against some criminals, but
   A: he won't say who. B: he won't say which criminals.
7. Jon is recuperating from something, but
   A: I don't know what. B: I don't know which pills.

   Jon is recuperating from some pills, but
   A: I don't know what. B: A: I don't know which pills.
8. Paula Abdul was replaced by someone, but
   A: I don't know which musician. B: I don't know who.

Paula Abdul was replaced by a musician, but
A: I don't know which musician. B: I don't know who.

9. Nina sympathized with someone, but
A: she didn't say who. B: she didn't say which victim.

Nina sympathized with a victim, but
A: she didn't say who. B: she didn't say which victim.

10. Brady was proud of something, but
A: he didn't say which photoshoot. B: he didn't say what.

Brady was proud of a photoshoot, but
A: he didn't say which photoshoot. B: he didn't say what.

11. Jake hit on someone, but
A: he didn't say which waitress. B: he didn't say who.

Jake hit on a waitress, but
A: he didn't say which waitress. B: he didn't say who.

12. Nick got attacked by a customer, but
A: he couldn't tell who. B: he couldn't tell which customer.

Nick got attacked by someone, but
A: he couldn't tell which customer. B: he couldn't tell who.

References

Almor, Amit. 1999. Noun-phrase anaphora and focus: The informational load hypothesis. *Psychological Review* 106(4):748–765.

Anderson, John R., Raluca Budiu, and Lynne Reder. 2001. A theory of sentence memory as part of a general theory of memory. *Journal of Memory and Language* 45:337–367.

Anderson, Michael C. and James H. Neely. 1996. Interference and inhibition in memory retrieval. In E. Bjork and R. Bjork, eds., *Handbook of Perception and Memory*, pages 237–313. San Diego, CA: Academic Press.

Baayen, R. Harald. 2008. *Analyzing Linguistic Data: A Practical Introduction to Statistics*. Cambridge, UK: Cambridge University Press.

Bresnan, Joan and Marilyn Ford. 2010. Predicting syntax: Processing dative constructions in American and Australian varieties of English. *Language* 86(1):168–213.

Cable, Seth and Jesse A. Harris. 2011. On the grammatical status of PP-pied-piping in English: Results from sentence-rating experiments. In J. A. Harris and M. Grant, eds., *University of Massachusetts Occasional Papers in Linguistics*, vol. 38. Amherst, MA.

Carlson, Katy, Michael Walsh Dickey, Lyn Frazier, and Charles Clifton, Jr. 2009. Information structure expectations in sentence comprehension. *The Quarterly Journal of Experimental Psychology* 62(1):114–139.

Chomsky, Noam. 1973. Conditions on transformations. In S. Anderson and P. Kiparsky, eds., *A Festschrift for Morris Halle*, pages 232–86. New York: Holt, Reinhart & Winston.

Craik, Fergus I.M. and Robert S. Lockhart. 1972. Levels of processing: A framework for memory research. *Journal of verbal learning and verbal behavior* 11(6):671–684.

Criss, Amy H. and James L. McClelland. 2006. Differentiating the differentiation models: A comparison of the retrieving effectively from memory model (REM) and the subjective likelihood model (SLiM). *Journal of Memory and Language* 55(4):447–460.

Culicover, Peter W. and Wendy K. Wilkins. 1984. *Locality in Linguistic Theory*. San Diego: Academic Press.

Ericsson, K. Anders and Walter Kintsch. 1995. Long-term working memory. *Psychological Review* 102(2):211–244.

Frazier, Lyn and Charles Clifton, Jr. 2011. D-linking and memory retrieval: The annoying case of sluicing. In J. A. Harris and M. Grant, eds., *University of Massachusetts Occasional Papers in Linguistics*, vol. 38, pages 37–52. Amherst, MA.

Gibson, Edward, Steve Piantadosi, and Kristina Fedorenko. 2011. Using Mechanical Turk to obtain and analyze English acceptability judgments. *Language and Linguistics Compass* 5(8):509–524.

Gillund, Gary and Richard M. Shiffrin. 1984. A retrieval model for both recognition and recall. *Psychological Review; Psychological Review* 91(1):1–67.

Hawkins, John A. 2004. *Efficiency and Complexity in Grammars*. Cambridge: Oxford University Press.

Hofmeister, Philip. 2007. *Representational Complexity and Memory Retrieval in Language Comprehension*. Ph.D. thesis, Stanford University, Stanford, CA.

Hofmeister, Philip. 2011. Representational complexity and memory retrieval in language comprehension. *Language and Cognitive Processes* 26:376–405.

Hofmeister, Philip, T. Florian Jaeger, Inbal Arnon, Ivan A. Sag, and Neal Snider. 2013. The source ambiguity problem: Distinguishing the effects of grammar and processing on acceptability judgments. *Language and Cognitive Processes* 28(1):48–87.

Hofmeister, Philip, T. Florian Jaeger, Ivan A. Sag, Inbal Arnon, and Neal Snider. 2007. Locality and accessibility in *wh*-questions. In S. Featherston and W. Sternefeld, eds., *Roots: Linguistics in Search of its Evidential Base*, pages 185–206. Berlin: Mouton de Gruyter.

Hofmeister, Philip and Ivan A. Sag. 2010. Cognitive constraints and island effects. *Language* 86:366–415.

Karttunen, Lauri. 1977. Syntax and semantics of questions. *Linguistics & Philosophy* 1:3–44.

Lewis, Richard and Shravan Vasishth. 2005. An activation-based model of sentence processing as skilled memory retrieval. *Cognitive Science* 29:1–45.

Maling, Joan and Annie Zaenen. 1982. A phrase structure account of Scandinavian extraction phenomena. In P. Jacobson and G. Pullum, eds., *The Nature of Syntactic Representation*, pages 229–282. Dordrecht: Reidel.

Martin, Andrea E. and Brian McElree. 2008. A content-addressable pointer mechanism underlies comprehension of verb-phrase ellipsis. *Journal of Memory and Language* 58(3):879–906.

Martin, Andrea E. and Brian McElree. 2009. Memory operations that support language comprehension: Evidence from verb-phrase ellipsis. *Journal of Experimental Psychology: Learning, Memory, and Cognition* 35(5):1231.

Martin, Andrea E. and Brian McElree. 2011. Direct-access retrieval during sentence comprehension: Evidence from sluicing. *Journal of Memory and Language* 64(4):327–343.

McElree, Brian. 2000. Sentence comprehension is mediated by content-addressable memory structures. *Journal of Psycholinguistic Research* 29(2):111–123.

McElree, Brian. 2006. Accessing recent antecedents. In B. H. Ross, ed., *The Psychology of Learning and Motivation, Vol. 46*. San Diego, CA: Academic Press.

McElree, Brian, Stefani Foraker, and Lisbeth Dyer. 2003. Memory structures that subserve sentence comprehension. *Journal of Memory and Language* 48(1):67–91.

Munro, Robert, Steven Bethard, Vicky Tzuyin Lai, Victor Kuperman, Robin Melnick, Christopher Potts, Tyler Schnoebelen, and Harry Tily. 2010. Crowdsourcing and language studies: The new generation of linguistic data. In *NAACL 2010 Workshop on Creating Speech and Language Data with Mechanical Turk*. NAACL.

Nairne, James S. 1990. A feature model of immediate memory. *Memory & Cognition* 18(3):251–269.

Nairne, James S. 2001. A functional analysis of primary memory. In H. Roediger, J. S. Nairne, and A. Suprenant, eds., *The Nature of Remembering: Essays in Honor of Robert G. Crowder*, pages 282–296. Washington, D.C.: American Psychological Association.

Nairne, James S. 2006. Modeling distinctiveness: Implications for general memory theory. In *Distinctiveness and Memory*, pages 27–46. New York: Oxford University Press.

Pesetsky, David. 1987. *Wh*-in-situ: movement and unselective binding. In E. Reuland and A. ter Meulen, eds., *The Representation of (In)Definiteness*, pages 98–129. Cambridge: MIT Press.

Pesetsky, David. 2000. *Phrasal Movement and its Kin*. Cambridge: MIT Press.

Romero, Maribel. 1998. *Focus and Reconstruction Effects in Wh-phrases*. Ph.D. thesis, University of Massachusetts Amherst.

Ross, John R. 1969. Guess who? In R. Binnick, A. Davison, G. Green, and J. Morgan, eds., *Papers from the 5th Regional Meeting of the Chicago Linguistics Society*, pages 252–286. Chicago Linguistics Society, Chicago.

Sprouse, Jon. 2011. A validation of Amazon Mechanical Turk for the collection of acceptability judgments in linguistic theory. *Behavior Research Methods* 43:155–167.

Van Dyke, Julie and Brian McElree. 2006. Retrieval interference in sentence comprehension. *Journal of Memory and Language* 55:157–166.

Vasishth, Shravan and Richard Lewis. 2006. Argument-head distance and processing complexity: Explaining both locality and anti-locality effects. *Language* 82(3):767–794.

Watkins, Michael J. and Olga C. Watkins. 1976. Cue-overload theory and the method of interpolated attributes. *Bulletin of the Psychonomic Society* 7:289–291.

Watkins, Olga C. and Michael J. Watkins. 1975. Buildup of proactive inhibition as a cue-overload effect. *Journal of Experimental Psychology: Human Learning and Memory* 1(4):442–452.

Index